Archaeological Surveying and Mapping

The definitive practical guide to surveying for archaeologists in the twenty-first century.

The geometrical principles and techniques involved in surveying are often considered prohibitively complex by fieldworkers.

In this book, Phil Howard unravels the basic principles involved in surveying and shows how they can be used by archaeologists to log the results of their fieldwork. User's guides to methods and instruments of surveying provide clear and comprehensive instructions to enable archaeologists to represent their own fieldwork confidently and independently.

- Provides beginner's instructions to software used in computerised surveying, including IntelliCAD 2000, Terrain Tools, Christine GIS and Global Mapper.
- Introduces the archaeologist to a range of surveying instruments such as GPS, electronic distance measures, theodolites and magnetic compasses.
- Uses low-cost software.
- Includes detailed case studies from the UK, Europe and the US.

This textbook is an essential read for any field archaeologists who are in need of an introduction to surveying, or simply wish to update their techniques.

Phil Howard's background in archaeological fieldwork extends over 30 years. He is currently employed at Durham University, where he specialises in surveying, geophysical prospection, geographic information systems and archaeological computing.

Archaeological Surveying and Mapping

Recording and depicting the landscape

Phil Howard

Routledge
Taylor & Francis Group

LONDON AND NEW YORK

First published 2007
by Routledge
2 Park Square, Milton Park, Abingdon, Oxon, OX14 4RN

Simultaneously published in the USA and Canada
by Routledge
270 Madison Avenue, New York, NY 10016

*Routledge is an imprint of the Taylor and Francis Group,
an informa business*

© 2007 Phil Howard

Typeset in Sabon by
RefineCatch Limited, Bungay, Suffolk
Printed and bound in Great Britain by
TJ International Ltd, Padstow, Cornwall

British Library Cataloguing in Publication Data
A catalogue record for this book is available from the British Library

Library of Congress Cataloging in Publication Data
Howard, Phil.
   Archaeological surveying and mapping: recording and depicting the
landscape / Phil Howard.
      p. cm.
   Includes index.
   1. Archaeological surveying—Handbooks, manuals, etc.
2. Cartography—Handbooks, manuals, etc.   3. Archaeology—Field work—
Handbooks, manuals, etc.   I. Title.
   CC76.3.H68 2006
   930.1072—dc22
   2006017954

ISBN10: 0–415–30662–0 (hbk)
ISBN10: 0–415–30663–9 (pbk)
ISBN10: 0–203–41751–8 (ebk)

ISBN13: 978–0–415–30662–1 (hbk)
ISBN13: 978–0–415–30663–8 (pbk)
ISBN13: 978–0–203–41751–5 (ebk)

Contents

List of illustrations

Chapter 1

The science and profession of surveying

The science of surveying, and the status of the surveyor, have been differently perceived at different times. In the ancient world (Lewis, 2001) the aspects of surveying, engineering, astronomy and astrology were closely linked, and the practitioners of these sciences were of high status – some achieved a renown which has come down to the present day, such as Hero of Alexandria and Archimedes. Closer to our own time, when surveying as we know it was beginning to take shape, a good grasp of surveying was seen as essential to the gentleman, landowner and soldier. Peacham (1634, p.77) offered this summary of the uses of geometry:

> But in briefe the use you shall have of Geometry, will be in survaying your lands, affoording your opinion in building anew, or translating; making your milles aswell for grinding of corne as throwing foorth water from your lower grounds, bringing water farre off for sundry uses; Seeing the measure of Timber, stone and the like (wherein Gentlemen many times are egregiously abused and cheated by such as they trust) . . . you cannot without Geometry fortifie your selfe, take the advantage of hill or levell, . . . order your Battallia . . . [or] plant your Ordnance.

In the famous work *Pantometria*, often quoted, though mistakenly I think, as the origin of the word 'theodolite', Digges (1571) had already said

> . . . neither is there any liberall or free minde . . . that will not take great delight and pleasure to see how by Arte a man may measure the distances of places remote and farre a sunder, approaching nighe none of them, and that as well, yea and farre more exactly than if with Corde or pole he should paynfully passe them over.

His work has many illustrations of surveying practices which are designed to facilitate the conduct of war (in assessing the height of fortifications, for example), and these have as marginal items cannon breathing rather languid-looking plumes of smoke, and men setting out lines and angles using halberds as markers. In recent years (Ronan, 1991) it has even been suggested that Leonard Digges and his son Thomas may have invented a reflecting telescope a century before Isaac Newton, but that this invention was kept secret by the government because of its potential value in identifying enemy ships at sea. (This suggestion was thought sufficiently interesting to appear in the *Daily Telegraph* on 31 October 1991, and even made its way into *Hansard*, the daily record of the UK Parliament, though for the purpose of making a political point rather than as a matter of scientific importance.) Many surveying instruments (as well as other kinds) which survive from this period (see, for example the Online Register of Scientific Instruments, http://www.isin.org or the Museum of the History of Science, Oxford, http://www.mhs.ox.ac.uk) seem from their rich decoration to have been display items for the wealthy who wished to be associated with this branch of science.

As surveying became a more common activity, first for the landowner and later for the state, the task of carrying out the work no doubt fell more often on humbler folk (as it probably always did), and as the carrying-out of a survey was often regarded as the precursor to something worse the status and favour of these workers suffered accordingly. Partridge and Beale (1984), Barrère and Leland (1889), and Grose (1785, quoting 'Ray 1678') all give a slang name for the surveyor's chain as 'the devil's guts', 'So called by farmers, who do not like that their land should be measured by their landlords' (Grose, op. cit.) Usill (1900) indicates that the surveyor is often regarded as a trespasser, and this is made even more starkly evident in a leading article in *The Times* (Wednesday 5 September 1855), discussing the early railway surveyors:

> . . . what of those young gentlemen who were transformed for the nonce into civil engineers, in full employment at five guineas a day, and travelling expenses paid? Lads who scarcely knew the difference between a theodolite and a gridiron were disseminated through the country, to the sore discomfiture of the country gentlemen, in whose nostrils they stank even as poachers.

So, contempt from farmer and squire was the lot of the surveyor, though Debenham (1955, preface to the first edition of 1936) notes that for the public the profession has an air of mystery: '. . . involving, it is thought, the use of strange and expensive instruments, acquaintance with the higher mathematics, and a high degree of perfection with the pen'. Some at least of his predecessors seem to have been of the same opinion; quoting Usill again:

> . . . it may be proper to mention the previous knowledge which a surveyor ought to possess, and to notice the instruments which he is to employ in his operations. As a surveyor has perpetual occasion for calculation, it is necessary that he be familiar with the first four rules of Arithmetic, and the rule of Proportion, both in Whole Numbers and in Fractions, especially Decimals, with the nature of Logarithms and the use of Logarithmic Tables, and with at least Algebraic Notation. As it is his business to investigate and measure lines and angles, and to describe them on paper, he should be well acquainted with the elements of Geometry and Trigonometry, and with the application of these principles to the mensuration of Heights, Distances, and Surfaces. In particular, he should be familiar with the best practical methods of solving the ordinary geometric problems, and should be expert in drawing lines and describing figures. He should be acquainted with the principles and practice of Levelling; he should know something of the principles and practice of Optics and Magnetism, and he should possess at least a smattering of the arts of drawing and Painting.

Debenham goes on to say, however, that 'awe is partly due to the fact that the surveyor is hardly ever seen', and that if one should be sighted 'the disappointment in what he is doing will generally be intense, since he has . . . practically none of the paraphernalia which is normally associated with the occult art of topographic surveying'. Greed (1991), while making valid points about the difficulties faced by women seeking to make their way in a predominantly male profession, displays some prejudices of her own in making a distinction between the 'professional' work of the surveyor (quantity surveying, estate management issues, etc.) and the merely 'technical' business of making the accurate measurements on which the rest of the work is based. At one point she even refers to 'obscure technical trivia . . . *which only technicians are meant to know* in order to do their job' [my italics].

So from being fêted elite members of society, practitioners of surveying have descended through the social ranks of the gentry to the hated status of interlopers, perhaps rising a little to stabilise as at least the possessors of some knowledge, if only of an obscure nature, and which no one else would want.

My own experience of being identified as a surveyor has been variable. I have been assumed by members of the public, who didn't know that I was an archaeologist, to be doing work in advance of something they regarded as undesirable: a new road, new houses, and so on. Among other archaeologists I have occasionally encountered the feeling that what I was doing was rather a waste of time; once I was told that 'a theodolite is more trouble than it's worth'. This isn't just my experience, either. Alcock (1980) offers the opinion that 'the making of plans to an appropriate level of accuracy is the central discipline of field archaeology. But it is a discipline which is often sadly neglected by practising field workers.' Hogg (1980) is even more clear on the subject:

> Field Archaeology and Excavation are the foundations upon which the whole structure of archaeological knowledge is built, and of the various techniques which make up these methods of investigation surveying is probably the most important. The need for *accurate* plans is surely self-evident . . . Nevertheless, of these techniques surveying is also the most neglected. There is an illusion that it is difficult, and as a result works which are otherwise excellent describe idiosyncratic methods which are both unduly laborious and potentially inaccurate.

This last sentence is the most telling. There is a widespread impression that surveying is difficult, and often quite sensible people cause themselves more trouble by trying to avoid it. The caution is perhaps understandable. Standard textbooks on surveying still include many pages of geometrical formulae and explanations which can appear confusing. Some time ago I came across a very short work which emphasises this point: 'Fundamental trigonometry and geometry for topographic science: a summary of trigonometric formulae and proofs' (Gordon, 1993). The title of this (very useful) work encapsulates the difficulties faced by many people when coming to grips with the more sophisticated aspects of surveying; almost every word is calculated to strike fear into the heart – 'fundamental', 'trigonometry', 'formulae and proofs'. I am one of the very many for whom school experience of mathematics beyond simple arithmetic involved bewilderment, boredom, and occasional humiliation. It was only when archaeology led me into regions where the application of this kind of science was necessary that it really started to make sense, and I was fortunate to have good teachers when I needed them. I hope in turn to encourage some others.

A lot of things have changed since I started surveying; the advent of powerful and affordable computers ought to have made a difference, but there remain problems. One is the old danger of 'a little learning'. Bettess (1992) makes the point that the use of electronic technology enables those with limited mathematical knowledge to extend the range of their surveying, while Bowden (1999) cautions against assuming that the ability to push buttons makes a surveyor. It should be possible to avoid the worst of this difficulty, but a greater one is that of getting access to the necessary software. The standard packages for surveying, CAD (computer-aided drafting) and GIS (geographic information systems) are all priced well into four figures, and their purchase causes problems even for some small companies, let alone individuals or groups such as local archaeological societies. I hope to be able to show in the succeeding pages that there are indeed suitable kinds of software available at low prices and in some cases even free, which enable those who are interested to extend their surveying ability to a remarkable extent.

Of course, not everyone agrees that the use of electronic methods of data collection and representation are necessarily a good thing. Two recent publications (Bowden 1999, English Heritage, 2002) have emphasised the continuing use of simple traditional techniques of surveying, and in particular the plane table (described in more detail later), a device which allows drawings to be created in the field. I wouldn't personally reject the use of any technique, provided that it is applied properly and the producers of a survey make it quite clear exactly what they have done, but Bowden (op. cit., p.60) presents a series of arguments for traditional methods of surveying and drawing actually being superior to electronic ones. The points he makes are these:

- An experienced team can work 'at least as fast' with traditional methods as with electronic ones.

    This is arguably true.
- 'The end product is superior' because the traditional techniques 'entail a close observation of the ground', and 'allow the fieldworker to treat … features as complete entities rather than as series of lines to be chased … [it] forces the archaeologist to look at them properly in a way which electronic survey does not'.

    I don't accept that this is really true. Certainly I have come across examples of poor surveys carried out with electronic instruments, but they were done by people who weren't good surveyors. You can be a bad surveyor with traditional techniques as well, and a good one with electronic ones.
- Drawing in the field instantly identifies errors.

    There is something to be said for this, but this benefit is now available from a variety of electronic devices which have graphical screens to display the survey data as they are collected. Producing the drawing in the field has a down side as well. While the photographs in Bowden's book (and the English Heritage pamphlet) show plane table surveys taking place in good weather, Wright (1982) makes very clear his own experience of plane-tabling in less favourable conditions, whether too wet, too cold, too hot, too windy or otherwise disagreeable (as when beset by insects).
- Electronic systems are prone to breakdown.

    Again, I don't really accept this. We all remember the occasions when any device breaks down, rather than all the other times when it doesn't, but my own experience of electronic surveying equipment is that it isn't particularly liable to fail (though proper care and maintenance is called for).

- Disadvantages of digital drawings are that 'they are usually aesthetically challenged', and that 'digital media are not archivally stable'.

   The first depends; electronic drawings can look good, but they need skill and care, as do manual ones. Electronic methods don't do away with the need for skill, but how many people have the time or native ability to learn to draw hachures (for example) so that they look good? There are few more ugly additions to a survey drawing than badly drawn hachures, repeated many, many times. Hachures produced by computers may be more mechanical-looking, but I would rather see that than bad manual ones. We may be talking about the difference between an ideal and something fully acceptable that most people can achieve.

   The second point is true: digital media aren't 'archivally stable'. We are moving into an era in which many kinds of material which were formerly stored in the form of paper are being replaced by digital archives. My own experience of university libraries is that electronic versions of texts, particularly current issues of periodicals, are becoming more and more common; this isn't without its own problems, but the ever-increasing demands for physical space can't be met. Stability in this world means something different, not the longevity of a particular piece of paper or plastic film, but the management of live data sets. (Condron *et al.*, 1999; see also the Archaeology Data Service web site, http://ads.ahds.ac.uk/.)

Traditional methods of surveying will continue to be of use for a long time, particularly in fields like archaeology where a lot of work is carried out with low levels of funding, but this doesn't mean that traditional methods of *drawing* have to be used as well. Not only are computer methods more easily capable than the average person of producing acceptable results, but you don't also need the space for a drawing office in a house which already has a computer. Perhaps I should give my own list of reasons *for* 'going digital' (not necessarily in order of importance):

- It's easy to copy results; one hard copy has almost no intrinsic value, unlike manually produced drawings which may have taken hours or days to generate. Files containing maps and other drawings can be duplicated and disseminated freely.
- Many different representations of a set of data can be made from one file – multiple scales and combinations of map features are possible. It gives a better result to create a new drawing at a different scale rather than to enlarge or reduce hard copy (for example, you can reduce the scale of drawn features while keeping the text the same size). There is, of course, always a *maximum* scale at which data can be plotted, but that's true of traditional methods as well.
- Drawing quality doesn't depend on individual skill.
- Much more accurate plotting is possible, and this can exploit the accuracy of field instruments. (There is little point using a theodolite to measure angles to twenty seconds of arc and then plotting them with a protractor which can't define an angle smaller than half a degree.)
- The digital drawing can itself be used as a dynamic environment in which to carry out further work. When some features have been surveyed, perhaps using

sophisticated instruments, they can become the 'control' for other detail features, e.g. by making 90° offsets from a wall. This can be done manually, but it's much easier and more accurate in an electronic drawing.

- Through organisations like the Archaeology Data Service, large complex data sets can be stored safely and accessed easily by a dispersed community of users.
- Surveys can be georeferenced (given co-ordinates in a real-world system) and combined with other data – from an archaeological point of view one of the most important 'other' data types is the oblique aerial photograph, which can be rectified and incorporated into digital vector maps in a way which isn't possible using manual methods. You can then pinpoint features on the photograph, obtain their grid co-ordinates, and use a satellite navigation unit (GPS) to find them on the ground for further investigation, perhaps by fieldwalking or geophysics.
- If traditional techniques have been used in the field, spreadsheet programs make it easy to perform repetitive calculations (with much lower probability of making mistakes), and results can be copied and pasted directly into electronic drawings, automatically creating features.

A note on software packages

At various points in this book examples will be given of the use of particular software packages. None of these is being endorsed as superior to any other, but they represent those which the author has found satisfactory for the specific purpose and which are available at very modest cost or free. Other software may exist which is as good or better, though often at a much higher cost.

Two packages need to be mentioned specifically. One is the CAD software IntelliCAD (http://cadopia.com). This is the only serious rival I have been able to find to the 'industry standard' AutoCAD. IntelliCAD is available in several versions, some of which cost several hundred dollars (US), although still much cheaper than AutoCAD. In keeping with the philosophy of this book, I have used a version from 2001 (which was still available in 2004 from the Product Archive on the web site) which cost approximately $200. In some respects this version is limited, especially in the absence of solid modelling, but it is still a very comprehensive package and will perform very well in surveying applications.

The other is a spreadsheet package. I have tried in many places to show how a spreadsheet can be used to take a lot of the labour (not to say pain) out of the calculations which ought to make a surveyor's life easier. Most PC computers are bought with a set of software including 'office' applications, one of which will be a spreadsheet. I have looked at a number of these, and while all can be used for surveying purposes, not all of them have all the functions which are desirable. The one I have used, therefore, is the spreadsheet which is part of OpenOffice (http://www.openoffice.org). This is designed to emulate the Microsoft Office spreadsheet Excel, and uses the same commands, as well as reading and writing Microsoft format files. OpenOffice is available as a free download from the web site.

Chapter 2

The aims of an archaeological survey

The Royal Commission on the Historical Monuments of England (RCHME, 1999, p.1), describes the aims of recording archaeological features in this way:

> A record of an archaeological feature is a mixture of description and interpretation, providing information about the monument's form, construction, function, condition and on how it has been affected by subsequent developments and later use.

The aim of this book is to equip the reader with tools to enable the recording of the form of a wide range of archaeological features, and to create visualisations of the landscape in which they exist. The question of interpretation is beyond the scope of the work, but its absence is not intended as an indication that the author is unaware of its importance. It should be clearly in the mind of any archaeological surveyor, however, that recording and description of a monument are quite separate from interpretation; that the former are intended as an accurate (within the limits set for the survey) statement of the current form of the archaeological structures, while the latter may change (and quite properly so) in the light of developments in the wider study of sites of similar kinds. An accurate record of form is necessary as part of the basis of a satisfactory interpretation, but there may be occasions when a record has to be made of a structure which is difficult or impossible to interpret. I am aware that some people will disagree with this, but interpretations of certain kinds of archaeological monument, particularly, perhaps, earthwork enclosures, are often so tentative as to be of little use, and even to have the potential to be misleading.

The RCHME volume sets out a series of guiding principles for surveys, many of which are concerned with documentary research and the written report, but those relevant to the measurement of features in the field are:

- A record should aim to be accurate.
- The level of record (see below) and its limitations, should be clear.
- The report and supporting material must be clear and concise.
- The sources used must be cited in full.
- The report and supporting material should be produced using media which can be copied easily and are archivally stable.
- A security copy of the report and supporting material should be made as soon

as possible (it's also suggested that hard copies should be made of data held in digital form).

- The fieldwork project isn't complete until all the necessary records have been entered in the appropriate database and archive, and adequate time must be set aside for this.

It would be hard to find anything to disagree with in these guidelines, though the first point will bear some more examination. The survey should aim to be accurate, but *how* accurate? Every book ever written on surveying contains the same piece of good advice about the accuracy with which measurements need to be made in the field, e.g. Bettess, 1992, p.3: 'There is no point in taking the time and trouble to measure something to exceptional accuracy if it is impossible to plot the work to a corresponding degree of accuracy.' The example Bettess gives is that it would be entirely futile to measure the width of a wall to the nearest millimetre if the scale of the final plot is to be 1:100, since it would be impossible to plot a distance of one hundredth of a millimetre. This of course relates to manual plotting, where not only the skill of the plotter but the physical dimensions of the pencil or pen point give an absolute limit to the smallest distance which can be drawn. When working digitally, no drafting skill as such is required, and since no physical instruments are involved it is possible to plot extremely small distances, and of course to reproduce the survey drawing at any scale at all, so that a wall measured to the nearest millimetre could indeed be accurately plotted. The considerations on field accuracy become slightly different. It is *possible* to measure the wall to the nearest millimetre, but is it *desirable*? It will certainly take much longer to do this than to measure to the nearest centimetre, and most walls likely to be encountered in archaeological survey work will vary in width from place to place by much more than a centimetre, never mind a millimetre. There are two things to be decided *in advance* of the survey: How much detail needs to be recorded in order to conform to the design of the survey? What is the *maximum intended scale of use* of the survey product? Although a digital drawing can be presented at any scale, there is of course no such thing as absolute accuracy in measurement, so the scale at which the drawing is intended to be used is the factor which governs the appropriate accuracy of measurement, and this is related to the purpose for which the survey is designed. Both pieces of information (intended scale of use and design purpose) are what are known as 'metadata' – a term used in the archiving of information. This is not the place for a detailed discussion of the importance of metadata (which may be found in the web pages of the Archaeology Data Service, http://ads.ahds.ac.uk) but anyone creating a digital model of survey information should ensure that these two pieces of metadata are clearly stated and reproduced every time the information is copied, so that any subsequent user of the survey will be able to judge whether the work is suitable for *their* own purpose or not.

The fifth point in the RCHME guidelines also needs some consideration. 'The report and supporting material should be produced using media which can be copied easily and are archivally stable.' The increasing use of digital recording methods and data storage makes copying the data very easy. The issue of archival stability has already been mentioned, and the term is open to different interpretations. Much of the work done by the RCHME has had at its core their excellent hand-drawn plans, and a good deal is known about the long-term survival of the materials used to produce these (as well as what I suppose will soon be regarded – if they aren't already – as 'traditional' photographic materials), but the field of digital data management is still extremely fluid, and it seems destined to remain that way. 'Stability' for digital material will obviously have to mean something else, as made clear by the publications of the Archaeology Data Service and other data services. The physical stability of storage media seems to be relatively unimportant compared with the built-in obsolescence of the hardware needed to read the media. Punch-cards are probably as archivally stable as any other sort of paper, but where could a digital data record stored on punch-cards be read today (perhaps in a museum somewhere)? Eight-inch and 5.25-inch floppy disks have come and gone, as have various kinds of magnetic tape, and many computer manufacturers think the 3.5-inch disk should go the same way. CDs are still with us, but for how long? A stable digital archive is going to have to be 'live', and this involves maintenance. The RCHME suggestion that digital data should also be stored in hard copy is one with which I feel a good deal of sympathy, but there are problems here, too. What exactly do we mean by 'hard copy'? One meaning, obviously, is a printed copy of a plan, but there are uncertainties over the long-term stability of the ink used in ink-jet printers (not at all the same as traditional ink used in pens) and the ability of laser-printer toner to remain attached to paper. A published version of a plan, printed in multiple copies in books which are distributed to numerous locations, is probably much 'safer', but this isn't what happens to all plans by any means, and what it is appropriate to publish may be quite different from the 'original' versions. A survey conducted using digital recording, or one in which locations are recorded in the form of numbers, could be preserved as lists of co-ordinates and attributes, and this might be a solution in some cases, though the very sophistication of some survey methods may undermine this as well. I recently conducted a very brief (45 minutes) topographic survey of a small earthwork enclosure using centimetre-accuracy GPS equipment which generated 1,248 three-dimensional points. As a text file this modest data set fills 43 pages, and that only consists of point number, easting, northing and orthometric elevation (it could have included the time of each observation, latitude, longitude, ellipsoid height and an estimate of co-ordinate quality, which would have made the file about twice as long). As a digital file this information fills 106Kb of storage space – a trivial amount.

The RCHME document gives specifications for the scale of drawing appropriate to each of its recording levels, but also points out that the overall extent of the archaeological site and the use which will be made of the survey are factors of importance. At their smallest scale and lowest level of recording they have 'a locating symbol on a map or a delineated area showing the approximate extent of the site'. This level of recording requires archaeological knowledge but little application of surveying skill, and yet it can bring its own problems. Many archaeological field workers will have annotated Ordnance Survey maps to show the locations of sites, but if the record is to be used by others the question of copyright arises. It isn't permissible to copy OS maps without licence, except for very restricted purposes, and even if the site location is determined by measurement from features mapped by the OS then copyright is claimed over the positional information in the survey, and this may limit the extent to which the surveyor is free to disseminate their own work. This applies to any OS product, whether digital or hard copy (see the Archaeology Data Service *GIS Guide to Good Practice*, http://ads.ahds.ac.uk/project/goodguides/gis/). The best solution is to use a GPS instrument to obtain co-ordinates which are *equivalent* to those of the Ordnance Survey, but which are not copyright. (The issue is rather complicated, but it is the OS *products* which are copyright, not the mathematical transformation which is used to turn GPS latitude and longitude into grid co-ordinates.) GPS-derived locations can be used by those who hold OS digital data to overlay the archaeological survey information without placing any restrictions on the surveyor.

The situation regarding national map data sets varies from country to country. In the United States, for example, data from the United States Geological Survey may be obtained for the cost of delivery only, and some types (in the SDTS and TIGER formats) may be downloaded free of charge from web sites, while the UK Ordnance Survey is established as a profit-making business. In some other countries map data are held to be politically or militarily sensitive, and may not be readily obtainable at all. The existence of GPS has made a great deal of difference to the way in which field surveyors can operate, and the inception of the European Union's Galileo project, designed to create a wholly civilian satellite navigation system is an indication of the perceived importance of the continuation and enhancement of this kind of facility.

Beyond the lowest level of recording, the scales of drawing required are given as 1:2500 and 1:1250 (which correspond to scales of OS mapping). Working in a digital environment the surveyor is much less bound by the idea of finished drawing scales, because digital data may be plotted at a range of scales, varying line thicknesses and symbol sizes, with little additional effort (though not *no* additional effort, as each scale of plotting needs to be designed to communicate effectively, but much less than producing another complete drawing by hand). The survey must be designed, however, to suit the *maximum* intended scale of plotting, and this governs the amount of effort which needs to be put into fieldwork. Whatever the intended maximum scale of reproduction, a complex site may require some areas to be surveyed for plotting at larger scales anyway. The aims of the survey, and methods employed, must always be made clear.

In the case of earthworks it is also recommended that profiles are drawn at a scale of something like 1:250. Many modern surveys will also produce terrain models based on large numbers of spot-height measurements, and these should give a clear idea of the shape of banks and ditches, especially when three-dimensional displays and artificial illumination are employed, but capturing sufficient detail in the form of spot-heights may not be practical in terms of time if total-stations or survey-grade GPS are not available, and the measurement of specific profiles may still be useful in these cases. It is commonplace when displaying terrain models to exaggerate the vertical axis in order to show small variations in elevation; the RCHME discourages this for drawn profiles, and for good reasons, but in modelled surfaces it may be useful to use careful exaggeration, as long as un-modified views are included as well.

The surveyor working digitally also has to consider the different ways in which their data may need to be used. The RCHME document refers for the most part to *drawings*, and the scales at which they should be made. This is natural, as most of their work up to the time of that publication had been produced in that way. However, a body of digital data is more often referred to as a *model* (whether it is two- or three-dimensional), and a drawing is one view of the model, generated for one purpose. The model is much more flexible than any set of drawings, but to manipulate it the user has to have access to the appropriate software, and the expertise to use it. This won't be true of everyone who needs or wants to use the survey results, and even if they have, they won't always have the time to become sufficiently familiar with a model to be able to understand it properly. One product of the survey, therefore, must be a series of images, designed by the surveyor, which can be experienced in the same way as hard-copy drawings, even if they aren't actually printed out by the end users. All software packages of the kind considered here have facilities for saving images in popular formats (jpg, tiff, bmp, etc.), and the ones which can be considered to be 'CAD' or 'GIS' will also have the ability to produce publication-quality page images, including not only the graphics representing the survey data but also scales, legends, titles, etc. With the more sophisticated graphical representations such as illuminated terrain models it is often the case that image files viewed on computer screens are far more satisfactory than any printouts made with the sort of equipment available in most offices or homes.

Chapter 3

Basic methods of surveying

In surveying there are two different kinds of quantity which may be measured, distances (or lengths) and angles. When it comes to distances, most people would now expect the metre to be the unit used, and it is. The situation with respect to angles is less clear.

For most of us in the UK there is one way of stating the size of an angle – the degree (symbol °, used for degrees of temperature as well). A complete circle contains 360°, the angles at the corner of a square ('right' angles) contain 90°. Most of the time we hardly stop to think about this arrangement, which really is rather at odds with the 'metric' or 'decimal' way in which we quantify other things, using multiples of ten. No doubt there was even less cause for wonder in the days when 12 inches were equal to one foot, three feet made a yard, and 1,760 yards totalled one mile. There seems little logic in this, but neither is there in the fact that while builders, two of whom are fitting a new window as I write, measure dimensions in millimetres, the sign at the end of the road gives the distance to the next town in miles. The subdivisions of degrees are similarly arcane; one degree is divided into sixty 'minutes' (sometimes called 'minutes of arc' to distinguish them from units of time, and designated by the symbol '), and each minute into sixty 'seconds' (of arc, the symbol being "). This gives the smallest angular unit as $1/3600°$. Angles measured in surveying contexts would be recorded as, for example, $76°23'20''$. If it becomes necessary to refer to an angle whose size is between whole seconds we have to go decimal again, and use tenths of a second. Such precision is, however, only required in the most exacting applications of surveying, and shouldn't trouble the archaeologist.

This strange system has come down to us (as far as we know) ultimately from the Babylonians (Lewis, 2001, pp.40ff.), the earliest record of it dating from the fifth century BC. Our adoption of it is via the classical world, in particular Greece, although they didn't take it up until the second century BC, and then not totally. In the first century BC Posidonius was dividing a circle into 48ths, and as late as the second century AD the astronomer Cleomedes was quoting angles in another Babylonian unit, the dactyl. The name given to this type of measurement, 'sexagesimal', comes from the Latin word for sixty (*sexaginta*). Astronomers were the principal users of angular measurement at that time; land surveyors worked almost entirely on the basis of theories of triangles formulated by Euclid in the third century BC.

All forms of measurement 'made sense' in some way when they were originally devised, but none of them can be considered to be superior in an absolute sense to all others. We may tend to think that there is something 'natural' about measuring angles in degrees, and many of us are unaware that there are two other systems in common use. In many countries on the continent of Europe an arguably more logical system – the 'centesimal' – is preferred. In this, a circle is divided into 400 major parts, each being called a *gon* (Bannister *et al.*, 1998) or a *grad* (Bettess, 1992); a right-angle therefore is 100gon. The gon can be subdivided decimally. Surveyors who find themselves working on the continent must be sure which units are used by their instruments, or unfortunate mistakes can occur; after all, to the unaided eye 23 degrees doesn't seem very different from 23 gon.

Finally, in the SI scheme (Système International d'Unités, the modern metric system) the unit of angular measurement is the *radian*, which is often divided into 1,000 milliradians, or *mil*. (Strictly speaking, this is the unit for *plane angles*, measured in two dimensions, while three-dimensional or solid angles use the *steradian*). Some instruments have graduations in radian measures, and it is common in the case of the prismatic compass, where military practice favours the mil. What may seem unforgivable about the radian is that no whole number of them makes a complete circle, but rather 6.28319 (approximately), a right-angle being 1.5708 radians. One radian is equal to 57.29578°. If degrees seem a little illogical, what is to be made of this? Light may begin to dawn if we work out that 180° is equal to 3.14159 radians (though no-one should feel ashamed if it doesn't), because 3.14159 is an approximate value for a constant fundamental to the geometry of the circle, π (*pi*). The number of radians in a circle is equal to $2 \times \pi$, which is the same as the relationship between the radius of a circle and its circumference, and one radian is the angle made at the centre of a circle by an arc equal in length to the radius of the circle. Logic is restored.

It might be wondered why military usage favours the mil, a subdivision of the radian, over the degree. It is often linked to artillery rangefinding, and the useful simple relationship that an angle of 1 mil subtends a distance of approximately 1 yard at a range of 1000 yards. (In this connection, Huffman (2000) points out that there really should be 6,283 milliradians in a circle, but that the US military simplified things by using a value of 6400, though the Russian army chose 6000.)

Surveyors working in the UK will almost certainly find themselves using instruments which give values for angles in degrees, minutes and seconds, unless they are equipped with a military pattern prismatic compass, which may be graduated in mil. If calculations are being performed with a hand-held calculator it will in most cases be possible to enter angles in sexagesimal form, but they will probably have to be converted to decimal degrees before calculations can be carried out (e.g. 36°30'00'' becomes 36.5°). This function is usually readily available on the calculator. Where it will certainly be necessary to make use of radians is in the use of spreadsheets. Trigonometrical functions in spreadsheets always require angles to be in radians, but there will also be a function to convert degrees into radians. Needless to say, spectacular errors will occur if this step is left out.

The aim in surveying is to take a series of measurements to define an object whose shape and size are initially unknown. These measurements must be taken from a 'control structure', which at its simplest may be a 'baseline' of known length.

The position of an unknown point may be located by the following means:

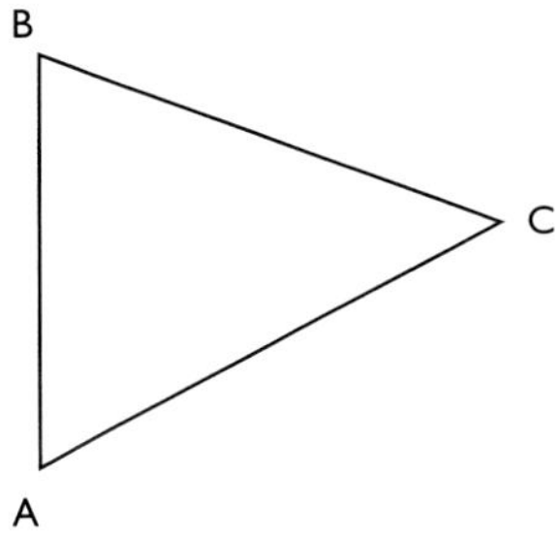

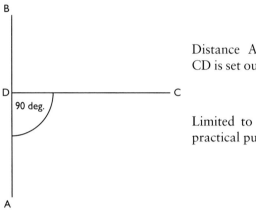

AB is known (the baseline); length AC and BC are measured

Limited to a standard tape length for practical purposes

Figure 3.1 Trilateration.

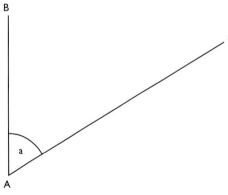

Distance AD along AB is measured; CD is set out at 90° to AB and measured

Limited to a standard tape length for practical purposes

Figure 3.2 Baseline offset measurement.

Angle a and length AC are measured. AB doesn't have to be measured (and B may be very distant from A)

With EDM instruments, range is thousands of metres

Figure 3.3 Bearing and distance measurement.

The method can also be used with a magnetic compass, in which case the bearing is from magnetic north.

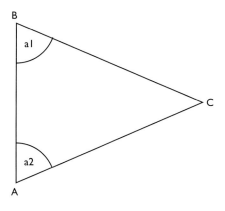

AB must be known, angles a1 and a2 are measured

Range can be thousands of metres, but the distance AB must be proportionate to the distance of C from A and B (no long thin triangles)

Point C can be inaccessible (e.g. the top of a tower)

Figure 3.4 Intersection (triangulation).

Satellite positioning

Any point on the earth's surface can be located by calculations based on broadcast data from satellites. For most purposes the point locations have to be visited, but offset measurement can be made using the methods above. Many instruments allow direct input of offset data and will automatically calculate the co-ordinates of the points.

Surveying instruments

The range of instruments available to the archaeological surveyor is wide, whether measured in terms of their precision of measurement, sophistication of design, ease of use, or financial cost. It is certainly possible to conduct perfectly satisfactory surveys using very simple equipment, though in order to obtain high accuracy it will then be necessary to spend a great deal of time over the survey. Electronic instruments make the survey much easier, and deliver high accuracy for less time spent in the field, though they don't make it any easier to understand the features which are being surveyed, and if their speed of use encourages the surveyor to spend less time than is needed and so produce an inadequate record, then no good purpose is being served. There is no such thing as a bad technique, but any technique can be applied badly.

Linear measurement

Tapes

These made of fibreglass (formerly linen) or steel. The most obvious way of determining a distance is to lay along it a measure of known length, or one calibrated to show various lengths. Historically, a variety of rods and cords were used for this purpose (Lewis, 2001, pp.19ff.), and their successors are still in use. A great virtue of this type of measurement is its simplicity, coupled with the portability and generally low cost of the equipment, but the accompanying disadvantages are not always fully appreciated.

The most commonly used direct measuring devices are tapes (some of them also called 'bands') made of fibreglass or steel, available in lengths from 2m to 100m. The shorter types are usually made of steel, are very compact, and are especially useful in surveys of buildings. The type most often encountered in archaeological practice is the 30m fibreglass tape, a descendant of the 100 foot tape, which was made of linen (another ancient tradition: the Greeks were using flax measuring cords in the second century BC, and there are also references in the Talmud (Lewis op. cit.)).

A word needs to be said about the difference between a steel band and a steel tape, which to the casual observer may look very similar. The difference is essentially one of accuracy, and coupled with this application. The band (or 'drag tape' (Bannister *et al.*, 1998, p.12)) is manufactured to more exacting standards and is designed to be used with a variety of accessories to permit the most accurate measurement. It is typically employed in measuring lines which are greater in length than a single band (30, 50, or 100m), using the procedure which was formerly applied to the chain (see Bannister *et al.*, 1998, and Coles, 1972, the latter describing archaeological use). Each band is marked with the operating tension and temperature for which it is designed. Steel tapes, which come in the same lengths, are designed for less exacting applications, usually for lines which are shorter than the tape length.

Fibreglass tapes are of lower accuracy, and are best used for short measurements, although they can be obtained in lengths up to 100m. A chief advantage of these tapes, especially if they are required in large numbers, is their low cost (£12–15 for a 30m length).

Changes in temperature will result in changes in the length of any tape; the magnitude of such changes is unlikely to be a cause for concern in many archaeological situations where measurements are being made with fibreglass tapes, but if more precise use is being made of steel tapes then corrections for temperature variations have to be made. Bannister *et al.* (1998, p.27) give an example in which a 3mm correction has to be made to the length of a steel tape, given a temperature change of 2°C.

Periodic temperature changes may not be very significant in most archaeological situations, but other variable influences are. Anyone who has ever tried to take a measurement with a tape which isn't laid flat on the ground will be aware of this. Even a light breeze will cause the tape to bow sideways, and however much tension is applied, it can't be made straight. Obviously this effect results in measured lengths seeming to be greater than they really are, and there is really no way to correct this distortion; the only solution is to restrict tape measurements to lengths over which the effect can't be observed. Another unavoidable distortion arises from the fact that any tape not supported along its whole length will sag. Again in the case of high-accuracy steel tapes this factor can be allowed for by the use of a standard tension, or a numerical correction for sag made to each measurement (Bannister *et al.*, 1998), something which is impossible in the case of a fibreglass tape. The latter should be used for measurements where sag is imperceptible, unless the tape can be laid flat on the ground.

When account has been taken of wind and sag factors (and where appropriate temperature), there remains another problem. In the production of a two-dimensional plan, what is needed is a measurement of the horizontal distance between points, whereas in practice the distance between most points is three-dimensional, i.e. a difference in elevation has to be accounted for. Even the most accurate tape measurement between points of different elevation (a 'slope distance') has to be modified in order to produce a horizontal distance. One way to do this, involving no calculation, is to break up a sloping distance into a series of short lengths, over which the tape can be held horizontally without incurring serious errors through sag or wind curvature. Otherwise it will be necessary to measure the angle of slope between the ends of the line, or to determine the difference in elevation, and to apply a numerical correction to the measured length.

The suggested restrictions on the use of fibreglass tapes may seem excessive, but the fact is that something which has the appearance of being simple – the direct measurement of distance – is actually quite difficult to do accurately. Too often, inaccurate measurements will be recorded by people who can see perfectly well with their own eyes that they *are* inaccurate, but either don't know how to avoid the inaccuracy or think that 'it won't be enough to matter'. The difficulty in obtaining measurements of distance of the highest accuracy is so great that for very many years standard surveying practice was to avoid direct distance measurement whenever possible, substituting angular measurement. (Smith, 1970, reports that in 1827 64 workers took 90 days to measure an eight-mile line at Lough Foyle, using 10 ft long 'Colby bars', made of iron and brass in such a way as to compensate for temperature changes. The expense of such a procedure can perhaps be imagined.) Most archaeological applications are less exacting, but this shouldn't allow us to fall into bad habits. 'Simple' methods of distance measurement have to be employed with the same care as more complex ones, and it has to be recognised that their applications are limited.

Chain

The traditional tool, in post-medieval Europe, for distance measurement was the surveyor's chain, originally 66 feet in length, superseded by the 100 foot type, then by metric equivalents in 20 or 30m lengths. The chain was very robust, easy to read in field conditions (tally markers were attached at intervals), and easily repaired, but it has now been replaced by the more accurate steel 'band'. Chains are still available, but they are heavy to carry, require a certain amount of training for proper use, and despite their rugged nature it is possible to bend the links through abuse. Overall they are less satisfactory than tapes.

Short-range laser rangefinder (such as the Leica 'Disto' range)

These portable distance meters are designed to be held in the hand (although they can usually be mounted on a photographic tripod), and are very simple to use. Typically they have a range of up to 200 metres, depending on the surface texture of the target, and are accurate to a few millimetres. They are very suitable for measuring buildings, both inside and out, and can usually be made to stand upright on a floor to measure to ceilings. Some types have integral data-loggers, and/or can interface with computers. Prices start at around £200. Their relatively short range makes them less useful for field surveys.

Long-range laser rangefinder

These are less accurate (usually ± 1m) but can measure distances of upwards of 1000m, depending on the target (its size and reflectivity). Experiments by the author suggest that while a road sign gives a good reflection at a distance in the region of 1000m, many other targets, even the sides of substantial buildings, need to be no more than about 750m away, although this still gives these instruments a very useful reach. Some apparently promising targets may not yield measurements even at lower ranges, and other problems can occur. When measuring to targets through trees, for example, or when lines of sight pass close to the ground surface in the presence of long grass, measured distances may be shorter than they should be, presumably because of reflection from the surface of leaves, etc. In these circumstances it would be a good idea to take a number of measurements so as to establish repeatability. The sophistication of these instruments varies considerably, as does price. A simple instrument may cost £500, while Leica and Bosch produce models which incorporate electronic compasses and clinometers (for measuring slope), and have the capability to connect directly to GPS equipment, and these are priced in the region of £3000.

Optical distance measurement

Also called 'tacheometric' methods (the word tacheometry coming from Greek, and meaning 'rapid measurement'). These methods were devised by surveyors to avoid the problems associated with direct distance measurement. The method most commonly encountered is also sometimes called 'stadia tacheometry', and is itself a technique with a considerable history, having apparently been independently invented by a Dane, a Scot, and an Englishman, all of whom were working in the second half of the eighteenth century. It requires a theodolite (or a level if absolutely necessary, though this is really an inappropriate use of the instrument) and a standard levelling staff. The view through the eyepiece of the theodolite includes a *graticule* of lines, one vertical (sometimes two parallel vertical lines) and three horizontal. One horizontal line bisects the vertical and extends across the field of view; the other two are much shorter and are placed equidistantly above and below the centre line. The two short horizontal lines are the *stadia lines*, and the position of these lines against the staff is recorded, the lower value then being subtracted from the upper to give the *intercept distance*. This distance, multiplied by 100, gives the distance of the staff from the instrument.

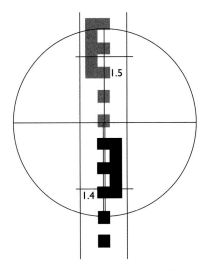

In this example, the stadia readings (to the nearest centimetre) are 1.41m and 1.52m, so the intercept distance is 1.52 – 1.42 = 0.11m, and the distance to the staff is 0.11 × 100 = 11m

Figure 3.5 Details of levelling staff used in tacheometry.

The application of trigonometrical formulae allows the slope distance to be converted to a horizontal one, and for the difference in height between instrument and staff to be determined. The technique is easy to apply, and needs no very specialised equipment, but its accuracy is limited by the accuracy with which the staff can be read, and since the intercept has to be multiplied by 100, every 1mm error in the former leads to 100mm error in the distance. In practice stadia tacheometry should not be used to measure distances of over 100m, or 150m at an absolute maximum.

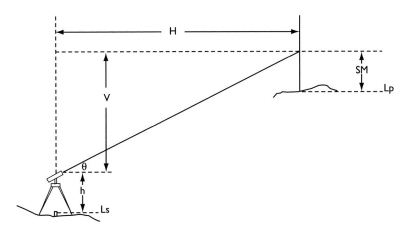

Figure 3.6 Tacheometric measurement.

The above diagram is from Bettess (1992), as are the formulae.

If the intersection points on the staff are designated SH, SM, SL (for higher, middle, and lower), and the angle of the sight line is θ, then

horizontal distance (H) $= 100(SH - SL) \cos^2\theta$
vertical distance (V) $= 100(SH - SL)\cos\theta \sin\theta$
elevation of staff poisition (Lp)$= Ls + h \pm V - SM$

(V is added if the sight is inclined upwards, subtracted otherwise)

Note that the angle of the sight line (θ) isn't the same as the vertical angle reading on the theodolite. The horizontal position may be represented by 0°, 90°, 180° or 270°, and the angle θ is the difference between this angle and that which is actually observed. Another point to note is that $\cos^2\theta$ is the square of the cosine of the angle θ (i.e. take the cosine, then square the result), not the cosine of the square of the angle.

Angular measurement

Optical square

This device is used to establish right-angles, rather than to measure them, but it is useful for creating 90° offsets to baselines, and for setting-out grids. It is a small hand-held device (or can also be mounted on a ranging pole), consisting of two prisms mounted one above the other. To create an offset from a baseline, the user stands on the line, having placed a suitable marker (such as a ranging pole) at one end of the line. Another pole is held by an assistant in a position such that the line from the surveyor to this second pole makes an approximate right-angle with the baseline. Looking through the instrument, the surveyor can now see the bottom half of one pole and the top half of the other, and can direct the assistant to move the second pole until the two halves are co-incident, at which point the offset line is at exactly 90° to the baseline.

Magnetic compass

Traditionally the prismatic type of compass has been used in surveying, and it can still be used effectively for small-scale work (e.g. 1:10,000) and sketch surveys. This type of compass has two folding sighting vanes (some models have instead of one of these a line inscribed on a glass circle which forms part of the instrument's lid) and a prism which folds over the compass card to allow the observer to sight on the target and simultaneously read a bearing. Magnetic bearings accompanied by distance measurements (tape, laser rangefinder, and even pacing) can be used to determine the position of points relative to the observer, and traversing (see Chapter 4) can be carried out using a compass to measure the internal angles.

Prismatic compasses are relatively expensive (about £200 in the UK), but other kinds of compass can also be used to take bearings, although in most cases with less accuracy. The Swedish company Silva produces a wide range of compasses, some of which are suitable for taking bearings. These are equipped with a folding lid lined with a mirror, having a sighting notch at the top and a vertical line engraved the length of the mirror. The compass is held at arm's length, the lid inclined at about 45°, using the sighting notch to locate the target; the compass housing is then rotated until a series of lines engraved on the housing are parallel to the compass needle, this being visible in the mirror, and the bearing can then be read from a scale around the housing (again in the mirror). This sounds rather complex, but it becomes easy with only a little practice. These compasses cost less than £100, and are well-made and durable. They also have the advantage that a device allows the user to make an adjustment to take account of the local magnetic variation, after which bearings will be from true north rather than magnetic north, but they don't permit bearings to be read as precisely as with a prismatic compass.

Another type of magnetic compass which is often encountered is the *lensatic* type. This has a folding lid with a sight vane, and a notch in another vane which also contains a small lens, a combination which again permits the user to sight on a target and read the bearing at the same time. Some examples of this type of compass are very cheap (less than £5 in the UK), but these, unlike the others mentioned above, don't have the compass card in an oil-filled capsule, which means that it takes a long time to settle down, and is generally unsteady (or at least, no more steady than the user's hand). The author has, however, purchased an oil-filled lensatic compass for about £10, which was mechanically robust and quite stable in use. The drawback with these cheaper compasses is that bearings cannot be read with such great precision as is the case with the prismatic or Silva types, but they are certainly much better than nothing, and may still play a useful role when funds are very limited. A type of magnetic compass much favoured in the USA, though not easy to obtain in the UK, is the Brunton 'pocket transit' (http:www.brunton.com). These are again well-made precise instruments of their type, and should serve well in archaeological surveying (the Brunton company produces other types of compass which are also suitable for surveying use).

Theodolite

The pre-eminent instrument for measuring horizontal and vertical angles, and the work-horse of surveying for many decades. Bowden (1999) gives a classification of types:

Class I: used for national triangulation systems and similar work of the highest order of precision, capable of measuring angles to 0.1 seconds of arc. Very expensive, and much more sophisticated than required for surveys of archaeological sites.

Class II: again designed for work of a very high order of precision, measuring angles to one second of arc (and often referred to as 'one-second' theodolites). Justifiable for very large-scale archaeological work, and for tying in to national co-ordinate systems, but not really needed for smaller archaeological projects.

Class III: general purpose instruments, designed for survey and construction work and typically measuring angles to 20 seconds of arc. Very useful for archaeological projects, even relatively large ones.

Class IV: builders, measuring angles to between one and ten *minutes* of arc, robust and cheap, and adequate for most archaeological surveys (a view also expressed by Hogg, 1980, although he didn't really regard theodolites as being necessary for archaeological purposes at all).

These classes are applied to the optical-mechanical type of instrument, but in the almost universal replacement of these by electronic types there has been a general increase in accuracy of measurement, and even modestly priced theodolites will have a precision of 5–7 seconds. The price of theodolites is probably much less in real terms than it was 50 or 100 years ago, given new materials and techniques of manufacture. A new ten-second instrument can be obtained in the UK for about £1,200.

A theodolite can be used for a wide range of surveying purposes, and is particularly useful for locating points accurately by intersection of bearings (avoiding direct distance measurement). It is also useful for tacheometric measurement of distances, which can be effective for plotting earthworks and terrain modelling.

Angle and distance measurement

The theodolite has in recent years been replaced largely by types of instrument which combine the functions of angle and distance measurement in one. The first electronic distance-measurement devices (EDMs) were separate units mounted on top of theodolites, but very quickly these were themselves supplanted by integrated instruments which came to be called by the name of 'total station', as they enabled all necessary measurements to be carried out from a single point. Total stations combine electronic measurement of angles with that of distances (either using infra-red radiation or lasers, the latter especially useful for building surveys, as they can measure without the use of a prismatic reflector), and have digital data-loggers and on-board computers which allow a wide range of surveying functions to be performed. These instruments make surveying extremely rapid, but they need to be used with specialised software packages in order to exploit their power. Total station prices start at about £4,000, though they can be hired by the week for £150 or so. Care needs to be taken that the instrument being purchased is actually suitable for the intended purpose, as some may be designed for very specialised use and not capable of carrying out all surveying tasks. The software packages often cost almost as much to buy as does the instrument, though it may be possible to hire this as well (most such software is protected by either a hardware key – a 'dongle' – or by a software authorisation code, either of which could be returned at the end of the hire period).

The basic instrument needs to be accompanied by not only a tripod but also a range of other accessories – prismatic targets, poles to support them, batteries, chargers, cables, etc., but almost all suppliers will quote a price for a full kit of equipment, depending on the type of work to be undertaken (it is of course up to the purchaser to get this specification right!). One thing which will usually need to be bought separately is a pair of two-way radios to allow communication between the instrument operator and the person holding the target.

Total stations have supplanted very rapidly electronic theodolites for most survey work, as they have far greater functionality and the price differential is not all that wide. It's now ten years since the author asked a representative of a major survey equipment manufacturer what it would cost to buy a new theodolite, to be greeted with a raised eyebrow and the question 'Why would anybody want to buy one of those?' Undoubtedly, theodolites will continue to be used for a good many years yet, by those who still have them, and it may be that some venerable mechanical instruments will still be operating when more recent electronic types have fallen prey to developments in technology which mean that spare components are no longer being manufactured. Barnard (2004) also makes the point that there are situations in which maintaining a supply of charged batteries can be difficult, and without a power supply a total station or electronic theodolite is entirely useless.

Elevation measurement

When surveying with a total station every point can be measured in three dimensions, without any extra work, as long as the operators are careful to measure the height of the instrument above the ground and the height of the prism on the target pole, and to note any change in the height of the target during the survey (which may be necessitated by changes in elevation or obstructions such as bushes or parked cars). Similarly, in tacheometry or intersection work three-dimensional co-ordinates may be obtained directly by calculation, but there may be occasions when other methods of measuring elevation change are needed.

Levels

The level is very familiar to archaeologists from the excavation site, where it is used to measure differences in elevation by taking sightings from a cross-hair in a horizontally-mounted telescope to a graduated staff held on a point of detail. For this purpose it is excellent, but in general the level is unsuited to field survey work, except perhaps as a low-order tacheometer. Like the theodolite, the level graticule is equipped with stadia lines above and below the central horizontal cross-hair, and these can be used as described above to calculate the distance from the instrument to the staff. Since almost all levels are fitted with horizontal circles it is possible to plot the location of detail points by angle and distance. The precision of angular measurement is very low, however, not better (if as good) as a prismatic compass, and since the telescope of the level cannot be pointed up or down significant changes of elevation can easily make it impossible to see the staff. Tacheometric distances are also of limited accuracy, and there is the danger that people involved in the survey may feel that they are doing something more accurate than they really are, since they are 'using an instrument'. Using a level in this way really can't be recommended in anything other than an emergency.

Abney level

Despite its name, this hand-held device is really a clinometer, and is useful in taped measurement for measuring the angle of slope between one end and the other, to allow slope distance to be corrected to horizontal. It can also be used to determine differences of elevation in low-order surveys.

Most Abney levels which can be obtained now are relatively cheap instruments (around £50–70), and while they function perfectly well they aren't built to very high standards and need treating with some care. At least one UK company (Pyser SGI, http:www.pyser-sgi.com) will make Abney levels to order, and these are of very good quality, but they cost in the region of £500.

Hand levels

These are very simple instruments, essentially a tube which is held up to the eye to allow the user to see a view of a spirit-level bubble against an index mark when the tube is horizontal. They can be used in combination with a levelling staff, or even more simply to measure the vertical height of a slope in the way described by Bowden (op. cit., quoting Williams-Freeman, 1915, English Heritage, 2003). The level is held to the eye to establish the horizontal line, and a distinctive tussock of grass, stone, etc. is identified at this level. The user then walks up to this level and repeats the exercise, looking for another distinctive object. After a series of iterations the surveyor reaches the top of the slope, which can now be identified as being as high as the number of 'steps' multiplied by the height of their eye-level, usually with some residual amount which can be measured against a staff, or even a tape held vertically. This certainly isn't a very precise method, but it needs only very lightweight, inexpensive equipment.

Satellite positioning

Usually referred to loosely as 'GPS', this technique has assumed enormous importance in recent years because of its ability to produce very precise and accurate results with great rapidity and using a minimum number of human surveyors. The drawback is that the cost of the equipment needed for the most precise kind of GPS survey is high – in the region of £30,000 in the UK. Even a week's hire will cost £700–800, though a great deal can be accomplished in that time.

High-resolution laser scanning

Laser scanning has been in use for some time in the recording at high resolution of the surface of small objects (up to a few metres across); archaeological examples include carved stone crosses, gravestones and rock-art. This technology has in the last few years been extended and expanded so that it can now be used to record much larger surfaces at a very high resolution. The scanner is set up on a tripod in the same way as a theodolite or total station, and can be set to automatically record the 3-dimensional position of a series of points to define the surface of the object under consideration. Buildings have been the most common subjects of this type of survey, which can be applied to ground surfaces as well. The instrument can be sited tens or even hundreds of metres from the target, and can scan points with an accuracy of a few millimetres, only a few millimetres apart. The resulting 'point cloud' is so dense that when viewed on a computer screen, even without further processing to create surfaces between the points, details of the target surface are clearly visible. The requirement for staff in this kind of survey is low (one or two) and the speed of recording is very rapid, so that for example a complex building façade can be recorded in an hour or so.

   At the time of writing archaeological applications of this technology are only beginning, for as ever technical sophistication comes at a high financial cost, in this case in the region of £100,000, but no doubt this situation will begin to change.

Photographic methods

The potential of photography to enhance surveys carried out by other means has been recognised for many years. Wright (1982), Wright and Dahl (1995) and Atkinson (1946) describe the use of photographic prints in plane table surveys as a means of capturing detail rapidly in situations where it may be undesirable to occupy a survey station for an extended period, and a number of manufacturers produced 'photo-theodolites' to enable the production of precisely oriented photographs which could be used to locate detail points by intersection. More complex is the technique of photogrammetry, which uses very specialised equipment to produce stereophotographs from which precise measurements can be made, the end product being a digital CAD model (Swallow *et al.*, 2004). In addition to these techniques, which plot points and lines, whole photographs can be modified to produce images in which distortions caused by camera tilt and lens characteristics (rectified photographs) or by the three-dimensional nature of the subject (orthophotographs) are removed.

Photographs taken with 'ordinary' cameras can also be used for surveying purposes. Scanned prints or digital photographs can be imported into CAD drawings of two-dimensional plans and used to plot intersection lines, and even three-dimensional models can be generated through the use of special software packages such as PhotoModeler (http://photomodeler.com).

Plane table

This surveying method has to be mentioned, partly because of its long history and great contribution to surveying in general and archaeological surveying in particular, and because it still has passionate advocates (English Heritage, 2003). The method is simple in its conception, though very effective, and involves no mathematics of any kind, though as in all surveying care and precision in its use is vital. The basic idea is that a drawing board is mounted on a tripod, centred over a survey station at one end of a baseline and levelled. The baseline will itself be drawn to scale on a sheet of drawing film which is attached to the board. A sight rule ('alidade') is laid along the drawn baseline, then the whole board is rotated so that the alidade points along the baseline to the station at the other end, and the board is clamped in position. A point of detail is then identified, the alidade is rotated to point towards it (making sure that it still runs through the point marking the location of the table), and a ray is drawn on the film, marking the direction of the detail point from the current station. This is repeated for as many other points as desired. The table is then moved to the other end of the baseline, oriented on the first station, and the exercise is repeated, creating pairs of intersecting rays marking the locations of the detail points. The alidade has to be no more than a straight edge of metal, wood or plastic with sights at either end, but various improvements can be made on the basic model. Telescopic alidades make it easier to sight on the detail points, and these can be equipped for tacheometry, so that distance measurements can be made and elevations calculated. Some types have even been fitted with EDM devices.

There is no doubt that excellent results can be obtained by the use of the plane table, but for every enthusiast there may be found a detractor. Hogg (1980, p.251) qualifies as one of the latter ('The plane table has a respectable ancestry . . . but it has serious disadvantages . . . I would most strongly advise against its use'), and so does Digges (1571):

> Onely I meane to give a breefe Note of one kinde of plaine Instrument for the ignorant and ruder sort not inconvenient. Insteade of the Horizontall Circle use onely a plaine Table or boarde: whereon a large Sheete of Partchment or Paper may be fastened. And thereupon in a fayre daye to strike out all the Angles of Position, even as they finde them in the Field without making Computation of the Grades and Scruples.

Apart from personal preference, there are some drawbacks which seem to me to rule it out of contention as a serious technique for the twenty-first century. The first of these is hinted at by Digges: 'in a fayre day . . .'. A drawing on a board in the open air must be vulnerable, and while all the photographs in the recent works by Bowden and English Heritage show surveys taking place in fair weather, common sense tells us that these conditions don't always obtain, and other writers (e.g. Wright, 1982) refer to the sometimes extreme difficulties of using a plane table in wet, windy or hot weather (with sweat dripping onto the drawing). One of the strengths of the plane table method is that the survey appears before your eyes, making errors or omissions easy to detect, and therefore correct, but this can also be a weakness, in that the drawing is the only record there is (even if heights and distances have been calculated, the angles aren't), and it is difficult to integrate this survey record with other sources of information which, increasingly, come in digital form.

Finally, and perhaps most tellingly, as far as manufacturers are concerned, time has finally run out for the plane table, and the necessary pieces of equipment, particularly alidades, are almost impossible to obtain outside the second-hand market. In 2003 the Japanese company Sokkia had one model of telescopic alidade in its catalogue, but by 2004 this had disappeared, and even the most basic type is no longer to be found. It seems that in order to take up plane tabling the new surveyor will have to be a do-it-yourself enthusiast as well.

Chapter 4

Control surveying

In classical surveying practice, there are two parts to every survey, the *control* survey and the *detail* survey. The 'control' is a network of points marked on the ground at which instruments may be positioned, or between which baselines may be set out, so that the 'detail', the unknown points in which we are interested, may be located. It may be necessary to locate the whole survey within some existing frame of reference (the Ordnance Survey grid, or another national grid framework, traditional latitude and longitude, or one of the recently developed co-ordinate systems such as WGS84 or ETRS89), but in other cases a 'divorced' survey (English Heritage, 2002, Bowden, 1999) may be entirely adequate, in which case the surveyor supplies an arbitrary co-ordinate system, although probably one in which grid north is approximately the same as true north or magnetic north to avoid confusion when others are using the results of the survey.

In the simplest type of survey, often regarded as a reconnaissance survey, a prismatic compass may be used to give angular measurements, and if the site is not too large and the ground not too undulating the 'control network' could conceivably consist of just one single point, detail being located by magnetic bearings and distances measured in a way which is appropriate to the type of survey (taping, laser rangefinder or pacing). If a taped survey is contemplated, or one using a theodolite or total station, there must be at least two control points; in the taped survey there has to be at least one baseline from which other distances can be measured, and with instruments which measure angles there must be a reference point to give an orientation to the survey. In a divorced survey it would be convenient to set out a second point which was approximately north, east, south or west of the first station, and to set the horizontal angle on the instrument to read 0°, 90°, 180° or 270° when pointed towards it. The compass automatically gives angles relative to magnetic north, but the horizontal circle on a total station has no natural orientation. It used to be possible to obtain a device called a 'trough compass' to fit onto a theodolite, which could be used to establish the direction of magnetic north and give an orientation to the survey, but these are no longer encountered. (The name derived from the fact that the compass needle was contained in a long narrow capsule, rather than a round one, and the device was only capable of giving readings a few degrees either side of north.)

A baseline with two stations may suffice for surveys of many kinds of archaeological site, especially those which consist of low-relief earthworks, and more particularly when electronic distance measurement is being used, as this gives the instrument a very long reach and large amounts of detail may be surveyed from one station. The baseline should be constructed so that it covers something like the diameter of the site, or its longest dimension if it extends much further one way than it does in others, and this may call for a variation on the practice of making it run east–west or north–south. It would be unsatisfactory (English Heritage, 2002) to have a baseline 50m long if the site extended over a diameter of 150m; the control should encompass as much as possible of the site.

For larger sites, those with upstanding remains, or where the terrain is more variable, it will be necessary to have more than two stations just to be able to take measurements to all the detail, but there are other reasons for having at least three stations in any survey, although in my experience many archaeologists are either unaware of them or think them unimportant. Every measurement that can be made is subject to error; this word doesn't refer to 'human error' (referred to by some writers as 'mistakes' or 'blunders'), which may consist of misreading an instrument or recording the reading incorrectly, and it applies just as much to measurements which are automatically recorded. Errors may be divided into 'systematic errors', which may be caused by an instrument which is out of adjustment for example, and 'random errors', which arise from many causes but are related to limitations in the instruments themselves and in the observers. Bannister *et al.* (1998, p.7, and Chapter 8) note that random errors have the following characteristics:

- Small errors are more common than large ones.
- Positive and negative errors are equally likely.
- Very large errors seldom occur.

They recommend some general strategies to minimise the effects of random errors:

- Cover the survey area in the simplest possible framework of high-quality measurements, and carry out the rest of the work *within* [my italics] this framework (this is often described as 'working from the whole to the part').
- Follow procedures which are likely to minimise systematic errors and discover mistakes at once.
- Make additional ('redundant') measurements so that data can be checked (such as measuring all three angles in a triangle, rather than deducing the size of one of them).
- Many quantities are observed several times; this both detects mistakes and makes it possible to use averages to improve precision.

It seems strange to many people that it is impossible to measure the true value of any quantity. If you use a precise instrument, they argue, it must give the right answer. But 'right' can't mean 'absolutely accurate'. All measurements give approximations of a true value; a precise instrument gives better approximations, but if you measure the same quantity several times with the same precise instrument you will get several different results, and it isn't possible to pick one and say that it is right while the others are slightly wrong. The implication of this is that if you set up an instrument at one point, then measure the angle and distance to another, there is an amount of uncertainty as to where the second point is. If the measurement is made with a total station this uncertainty will be small (a few millimetres), but if a magnetic bearing is taken with a compass and a distance measured with a tape, the bearing will only be accurate to a degree or so, and the distance to within a few centimetres (depending on the distance and other factors such as how the tape is being used). The problem is that there isn't any way to find out exactly how much error there is in total, though it can be reduced by measuring more than once and using an average.

Even using multiple measurement doesn't allow us to find out how much error there is, and over the years surveyors have developed a number of ways of getting an idea of the total amount of error in the measurements of a control survey by setting out the control points using shapes which have certain geometric properties which are *known*, and with which the measured quantities are compared. The simplest example is the triangle. If three points are set out in a triangle, and the angles at each corner measured and added up, they *should* total 180°; if the angles are measured to the nearest degree using a magnetic compass it may be that they *do*, but an instrument measuring angles to a few seconds of arc will probably produce a sum of angles which is either a bit more or a bit less (what surveyors call a 'misclosure'). This amount represents the total error in the measurement of the angles, but it doesn't tell you how much error there is on each angle; all that can be done is to assume that the errors are equal, and to distribute the total amount between all of them. If the angles add up to 179°59'10", the total error is 50"; dividing this by three gives 17" (actually 16.67", but fractions of seconds are only ever used in the most precise kinds of surveying), and this amount is added to each of the measured angles. If the sum is greater than 180° the residual amount will of course be subtracted. This procedure doesn't *eliminate* the error, it just distributes it in the only way possible. A point to consider is just how much total error it is reasonable to distribute in this way. If a mistake has been made in recording one angle, say it has been recorded as 54°30'20" instead of 45°30'20", the total error will be several degrees, which is far too much if the angles are measured with a theodolite. In such a case the only solution would be to re-measure the angles, but what is an 'acceptable' error? It must depend on the type of instrument being used. In the case of a small prismatic compass, which may only be graduated in whole degrees, it can't be possible to read the angles to better than about half a degree, so it will be quite likely that the total error will be something like 1½°, and it would be reasonable to distribute this. (On the other hand, as noted above, with low-precision instruments it may be that there is no apparent error.) In the case of more precise instruments, guidance may be taken from Bannister *et al.* (1998, p.205) who suggest total amounts of error which are acceptable in a traverse (see below for a discussion of the traverse). In what they call 'small site surveys' (or 'fourth-order'), which will include the great majority of archaeological surveys, the total amount of angular error which is acceptable is given as $60\sqrt{N}$ seconds, with N being the number of sides in the traverse. In a triangle this gives a figure of about 104 seconds, so if the total error is more than this it would be preferable to check the angles. (In a high-precision survey, what is known as 'first-order', the maximum acceptable error would be about 3½ seconds.)

Triangles have been used as the basis of control surveys for a very long time, and they can be very convenient. Bettess (1992) gives an example of a system of triangles which would be suitable to survey archaeological sites of quite considerable extent, on which this diagram is based.

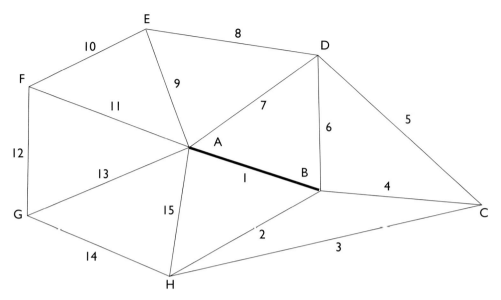

Figure 4.1 A control network of triangles.

It is assumed that a theodolite is available to measure the angles, but that chains or tapes have to be used for distances, so that the former are easier to measure and likely to be more accurate (the typical situation before electronic distance measurement). For this reason, only one distance is measured, the one marked with a heavy line, and this would be one which was easy to measure (e.g. on flat level ground without rough vegetation or other obstructions – supposing this could actually be found!). Notice that most of the triangles are of similar shapes, with angles close to 60° ('well-conditioned' triangles), which are favoured by surveyors although in no survey will it be possible to have *all* the triangles of this preferred shape. The sides are numbered, and the points lettered. At most of the points there will be two angles to measure, but at A there are six, at B four, and at D and H three. When measuring the angles a procedure should be adopted to ensure that they are measured 'independently'. As an example, imagine a theodolite set up at point F. You might suppose that the easiest thing to do would be to point the telescope crosshairs at point E, set the horizontal circle to read zero, then swing the telescope to point A, read the angle, then swing to G and read the angle again. There are two objections to this however. The first is to the setting of the horizontal angle to zero, which in a mechanical theodolite can introduce another source of error, although in a digital instrument it only requires the press of a button, and so shouldn't cause a problem. In any case, the value of the angle can be calculated simply by observing the two angle readings, whatever they happen to be, and subtracting one from the other. More seriously, reading the two angles in this way means that the error on the reading of the first angle will be combined with the error on the second. A better way would be to point at E, observe the angular reading (or set zero), swing to A and read the angle there, and then either set the horizontal reading to zero again or to undo the clamp which holds the circle in place (a mechanical theodolite will have such a device) and move it by a small amount (say 10 or 20 degrees), read this new angle, swing the telescope to point G and read the angle again. In this way each angle will be subject only to its own error.

In very precise work this wouldn't be the end of the story, because the procedure described doesn't take account of any manufacturing defects in the instrument, or wear which may have occurred during the instrument's life. Surveying textbooks will tell you that having observed each angle you should rotate the telescope in the vertical plane through 180°, then through 180° horizontally, so that the index mark on the horizontal circle is now on the other side, and observe the angle again, taking an average of the two values. The two observations are described as 'face left' and 'face right', and these phrases may be encountered when using programs on total stations.

Having measured all the angles, the next step is to adjust them. At points A and B the angles must add up to 360°, so do this first of all. Next, adjust the triangles so that the angles in each add up to 180° (obviously you should use the adjusted value for an angle measured at A or B, not that which was originally measured). Finally, calculate the lengths of the sides which haven't been measured. Many people are put off by calculations, but it is actually easier to calculate all these lengths than laboriously to measure them in the field if this has to be done with tapes, especially if some of them are much longer than can easily be measured in this way. The formula which is used is called the Sine Rule, which is formally described as:

$$a \div \sin A = b \div \sin B = c \div \sin C$$

assuming 'a' to be the length of side a, and side a to be opposite to angle A.

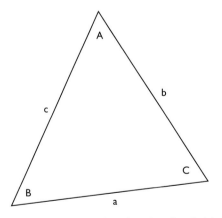

Figure 4.2 Sides and angles of a triangle labelled to illustrate the sine rule.

In the case described here the sides are numbered, so in the case of triangle ABH the equivalent is:

$$\text{side } 2 \div \sin A = \text{side } 1 \div \sin H = \text{side } 15 \div \sin B$$

Side 1 has been measured, and will be given the value 47.42m. The adjusted angles in the triangle are A 80°11'17", B 47°57'41", H 51°51'02". Taking side 2 first,

side 2 ÷ sin 80°11'17" = side 1 ÷ sin 51°51'02"

side 2 ÷ 0.985372393 = 47.42 ÷ 0.786402246

side 2 ÷ 0.985372393 = 60.29992951

side 2 = 60.29992951 × 0.985372393

side 2 = 59.418 (to the nearest millimetre)

Now that we have a value for the length of side 2, side 3 can be calculated in the same way, using the relationships:

Side 2 ÷ sinC = side 3 ÷ sinB = side 4 ÷ sinH

Remembering that in triangle BCH the angles called B and H are different from those in triangle ABH:

B = 146°48'12" C = 16°55'22" H = 16°16'26"

So side 3 can be calculated:

side 3 ÷ sin 146°48'12" = side 2 ÷ sin16°55'22"

side 3 ÷ 0.547514541 = 59.418 ÷ 0.291082549

side 3 ÷ 0.547514541 = 204.1276614

side 3 = 204.1272692 × 0.547514541

side 3 = 111.763

The lengths of all the other sides can then be calculated in the same way, in the order in which they are numbered. Finally side 1, which was actually measured, can be calculated using the length of side 15, and this value, compared with what was measured, gives a check on the accuracy of the whole scheme.

Calculations involving trigonometry are much easier than they were before the days of electronic calculators, and even cheap calculators will normally allow angles to be entered in the form of degrees, minutes and seconds, which makes life even easier, but while the calculations are not difficult for those even a little familiar with algebra, they will still be unwelcome to many, and a spreadsheet can help here, as the formulae only have to be entered once. This extract shows a spreadsheet set up to perform the calculations shown above for side 2, but in order to make this sheet of general use the side of known length is called a, and the angle opposite to it is A, while the unknown side is b, and its opposite angle is B; the grey shaded cells are those which contain the measured values.

	A	B	C		D	E	F		G	H	I
1						angle A				angle B	
2	side a				deg	min	sec		deg	min	sec
3	47.42				51	51	2		80	11	17
4											
5					angles in radians						
6					A	B					
7					0.9	1.4					
8											
9	side b	59.418									
10											

Figure 4.3 A spreadsheet used to calculate the lengths of sides in a triangle.

The degrees, minutes and seconds are entered separately into cells D3–I3, and the length of side a is in A3. Spreadsheets always carry out trigonometrical functions using radians rather than degrees (see Chapter 2), so in cells D7–E7 the angles have been converted; this is only to keep the formulae as simple as possible, and the length of side b could be calculated in one operation. The formulae in the cells are:

D7 = RADIANS(D3 + E3/60 + F3/3600)

E7 = RADIANS(G3 + H3/60 + I3/3600)

These cells work out the decimal value of the degrees, minutes and seconds, then convert the result to radians (using a built-in function of the spreadsheet).

B9 = (A3/SIN(D7))*SIN(E7)

To use the spreadsheet you just enter the length of side a and the values of angles A and B, and when these are complete the length of side b will appear. This removes the need for performing the calculation, pressing the buttons each time with the attendant possibility of making a mistake. It is still possible to make a mistake with the length and angles, of course, and the process of entering these values for each side in the whole network will still be fairly laborious, inevitably so, because the framework is based on a large number of individual triangles which have to be processed separately. As ever, accuracy comes at a price. The system has the virtue of being conceptually simple, but one drawback is the number of calculations which have to be performed, and another is that there is no overall adjustment of the whole network.

Having adjusted and checked the network, there comes the question of plotting it. One option is to draw it at scale using a ruler and protractor, but it will be far more useful to create a rectangular grid to cover the site, and to work out the co-ordinates of each network point within it. Most archaeologists are familiar with co-ordinate grids at a large scale of work on Ordnance Survey maps, or at a small scale on excavation sites, where pegs or other markers have been set out making squares of a size appropriate to the site (5m or 10m for example). In survey work it wouldn't usually be practical to create a physical grid (it would be very time consuming and need far too many pegs) but the surveyor can still work with the concept of a grid, and perhaps set out markers at certain points if these are needed for excavation, geophysical survey or other work. If GPS equipment is available it's very straightforward to give Ordnance Survey co-ordinates to all the survey points, but in the case of a divorced survey the surveyor will define the grid to be used. In the triangular network so far discussed it will be convenient to declare one of the lines to run north–south or east–west; HC seems to be a good candidate, and if this is deemed to be an east–west line, the whole network can be thought of in this way:

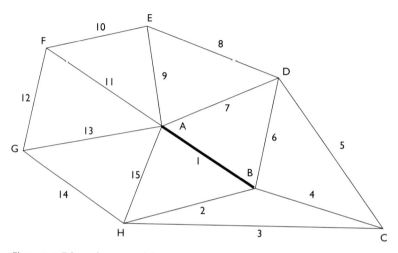

Figure 4.4 Triangular network in a divorced survey, using one side as east–west.

Having given the network an alignment, it becomes necessary to choose some co-ordinate values for one point before those of the other points can be calculated. Since HC is now east–west, it will be convenient to give co-ordinates to point H, and this could be made the origin of the network by making them 0,0. This would mean that some of the other points would be west of the origin and thus have negative x co-ordinates (and in fact some detail points could also be south of it and have negative y co-ordinates). There isn't anything wrong with this, but it does create one more possibility of error, and it's usual to choose co-ordinates for a starting point which are large enough to ensure that all co-ordinates in the survey will be positive; in a network of this size 1000,1000 might be a good choice.

Before proceeding further, it's necessary to consider further the idea of co-ordinates and their relationship to *bearings*.

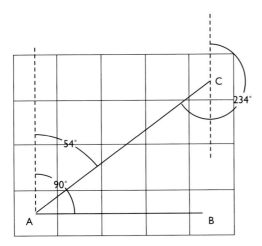

Figure 4.5 Bearings measured in a grid co-ordiante system.

In this diagram the conceptual grid is shown as a series of squares, though these don't have any physical existence. The points A, B and C could be points which do actually exist in a survey network, and AB is a line running east–west. A bearing is the direction of one point when observed from another, defined as an angle measured from grid north in a clockwise direction. In this case the bearing of point B from point A is 90°, while the bearing of C from A is 54°. If you were standing at point C and looking towards A, the bearing would be different, as shown; in fact it would be 234°, a difference of exactly 180°. In most kinds of surveying it isn't easy to measure bearings in the field; angles are measured between points on the ground and bearings are worked out afterwards. The one exception is magnetic compass survey, where bearings are measured directly, but in this case they are magnetic bearings (measured clockwise from the direction of magnetic north) rather than grid bearings.

To come back to the triangulation network, we already have co-ordinates for one point, H, which we have declared to be 1000,1000. Point C is due east of point H (bearing 90°), which means that it has the same x (northing) co-ordinate, 1000, and the difference in y (easting) is the same as the length of the line HC (side 3) which has been calculated as 111.763. The co-ordinates of point C are, therefore, 1000, 1111.763.

Now look at point B. The distance HB (side 2) has been calculated as 59.418, and the angle between HB and HC has been measured as 16°16′26″. The bearing of HC is 90°, and as HB lies between grid north and HC its bearing is 16°16′26″ *less* than 90°, i.e. 90°00′00″ − 16°16′26″ = 73°43′34″. A simple formula allows the calculation of the *difference* in easting and northing between one point and another:

easting HB = HB x (sin BgHB)
northing HB = HB x (cos BgHB)

Here 'easting HB' means 'the difference in easting between H and B' (and similarly for northing), 'HB' means 'the distance between H and B', 'sin BgHB' means 'the sine of the bearing of HB', and 'cos BgHB' means 'the cosine of the bearing HB'. The actual numbers will be:

$$\text{easting HB} = 59.418 \times \text{sine } 73°43'34''$$
$$= 59.418 \times 0.959933099$$
$$= 57.037$$

$$\text{northing HB} = 59.418 \times \text{cosine } 73°43'34''$$
$$= 59.418 \times 0.280229272$$
$$= 16.651$$

Adding these differences to the co-ordinates of point H gives the co-ordinates of B as 1057.037, 1016.651. It's vital to remember that bearings are always measured *clockwise* from north, and that the bearing of a line depends on which end you are looking from.

Now that point B has co-ordinates, it's possible to calculate them for point A. The length BA was measured as 47.42m. Its bearing can be obtained from the bearing of BH and the angle at B between H and A. Notice that this time the bearing is BH, not HB, because we are working from point B. Since the bearing HB was 73°43'34", the bearing BH is 180° more than this, i.e. 253°43'34". (When working out the 'back-bearing', as it's called, you can always add 180° to the bearing from the other end; if the result is more than 360° you just subtract 360° from it.) The angle between BH and BA has been measured as 47°57'41", and because BA is further from north (measured clockwise) than BH, this time the angle is added to the bearing BH, giving

$$253°43'34'' + 47°57'41'' = 301°41'15''$$

The calculations are now:

$$\text{easting BA} = 47.42 \times \text{sine } 301°41'15''$$
$$= 47.42 \times -0.850925729$$
$$= -40.351$$
$$\text{northing BA} = 47.42 \times \text{cosine } 301°41'15''$$
$$= 47.42 \times 0.52528602$$
$$= 24.909$$

Given the co-ordinates of point B as 1057.037, 1016.651, those of point A are

$$1057.037 + (-40.351) = 1016.686$$
$$1016.651 + 24.909 = 1041.560$$

Note that as A is west of B, its easting co-ordinate is smaller, but this is taken account of by the fact that the easting difference comes out as negative, so this is still added to the easting of B.

In this way the co-ordinates of every point in the network can be calculated, and they may very easily be plotted in a CAD system. (If you are really phobic about doing calculations it's also possible to use the CAD software as a sophisticated drawing board to plot the results graphically.)

The system of triangles described here will serve well for a variety of archaeological surveying purposes, but it has one weakness; each triangle is adjusted separately, and there is no overall adjustment of the network. There are many other control networks which may be used, each of which has a more robust method of adjustment. One often found in older books is the *braced quadrilateral* (Olliver and Clendinning, 1978), a figure in which the lengths of the four sides are measured and at each corner angles are measured between the two sides and diagonal line to the opposite corner. This arrangement gives a series of overlapping triangles, and allows the application of a number of equations involving both angles and side lengths to achieve very precise adjustment of the whole figure, though the calculations become quite involved. Another possibility is a polygon with a central point, making a series of triangles arranged radially. A potential problem with both of these is the need for lines of sight from corner to corner or from the centre to a series of other points. This may often be possible in open landscapes, but in rough terrain, or (from an archaeological point of view more important) in towns or in the vicinity of buildings it may be difficult to arrange the necessary lines of sight.

The most flexible control network of all is the *traverse*, and this can be used in any conceivable survey situation. A traverse is a linked series of lines of measured length, where the angles between the lines (or 'legs') are also measured.

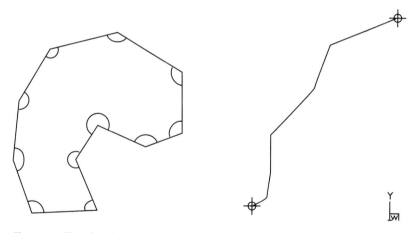

Figure 4.6 Closed and open traverses.

A traverse can have any number of legs, and be of any total length, and it is of extreme usefulness where there are many obstructions to visibility, as when surveying in towns. A traverse may be 'open' (as shown on the right), in which case it can start from any point and go to any point, but while authors do refer to this method (e.g. Bettess, 1992; Bannister *et al.* 1998) there is an inherent danger in that there is no way of determining the amount of error in the traverse, or of doing anything about it. Using high-precision equipment it is likely that errors will be small, but if the traverse extends very far the locations of distant stations will only be approximately known, and there have been cases in archaeological surveys where gross errors caused by the use of open traverses have come to light years after the work has been finished. Bannister *et al.* conclude that open traverses should only be used 'in exceptional circumstances' (op. cit., p.189).

The more usual form is the 'closed' traverse, and in most archaeological work the particular type called the 'closed loop' (shown on the left in the diagram), where the traverse starts and finishes on the same point. (The other closed form is the 'closed line', which starts and ends on points whose co-ordinates have already been precisely determined.) In a closed loop the internal angles should have a total value of

$$(2n - 4) \times 90°$$

with n being the number of legs in the traverse, so that if there are 11 legs the sum of internal angles should be $(22 - 4) \times 90° = 1620°$. The first step in adjustment is to sum the internal angles and distribute the misclosure between them, provided the misclosure isn't too great (for archaeological surveys, as noted above, the acceptable figure would be $60\sqrt{N}$ seconds, which in an 11-leg traverse would be about 200 seconds). Next, as in the example of the triangular network above, the co-ordinates of the points are calculated, starting either with one whose co-ordinates are known, or one to which co-ordinates have been assigned. Having worked out co-ordinates for the last point in the chain, co-ordinates are then calculated for the first point, for which they are already known, and in most cases there will be a small disagreement or misclosure, which can be divided into misclosures in eastings and northings. A number of different methods are available to distribute the total error around the whole traverse, some of them mathematically complex, others not. Any dedicated surveying software package will have a method (or more than one) for adjusting a traverse. If you need to adjust a traverse without access to such software, probably the easiest adjustment method is *Bowditch's*. In this the misclosures in eastings and northings (here called miscE and miscN) are used in these formulae:

1   correction to the easting difference in line AB

$$= miscE \times \frac{AB}{perimeter}$$

(*AB* is the length of the side, *perimeter* the total length of the traverse)

2   correction to the northing difference in line AB

$$= miscN \times \frac{AB}{perimeter}$$

Example

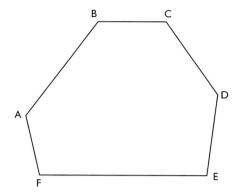

Figure 4.7 Example of a traverse network.

In this six-sided traverse the line FE has been given a bearing of 90°, and the co-ordinates assigned to point F are 1000,1000.

The lengths of the sides are:

AB 100.065m
BC 62.248m
CD 75.630m
DE 69.513m
EF 145.590m
FA 53.527m

The angles measured at the stations are:

A 131°02′01″
B 125°00′15″
C 127°23′55″
D 136°42′20″
E 97°52′30″
F 101°57′15″

The sum of the internal angles is 719°59′58″, but in a six-sided figure like this it should be $(12 - 4)90° = 720°$, giving an angular misclosure of 1′44″ (104″) which is within the acceptable limit (for a six-sided traverse, $60\sqrt{6} = 147″$). The sum of angles is less than it should be, so each angle will be increased by $104 \div 6 = 17″$ (to the nearest second, which will actually leave a residual misclosure of 2″, but this can be ignored). The adjusted angles are:

A 131°02′18″
B 125°00′32″
C 127°24′12″
D 136°42′37″
E 97°52′47″
F 101°57′32″

The bearings of the lines now need to be calculated, and this requires an examination of the diagram.

We have to start with what is known, which is that the line FA has a bearing of 90°. The angle at F is 101°57′32″, and with respect to the line FA this angle goes anti-clockwise, which means that it has to be subtracted from the bearing FA (since bearings increment positively in the clockwise direction). Subtracting 101°57′32″ from 90° gives −11°57′32″, and since bearings are required to be positive 360 is added, to give 348°02′28″. Looking at the diagram it's evident that point A is close to the direction of north when viewed from F, but it's west of north, which means that its bearing will be close to 360° rather than close to zero as it would be if it were east of north. The negative bearing calculated isn't wrong, it just indicates measuring anti-clockwise, and it's conventional to use positive values (it also makes mistakes less likely).

Having started at F we will be working round the traverse in a clockwise direction, so the measured angles will all be subtracted from the bearing of the line which lies to the right of an observer at a station. (If we were going anti-clockwise the angles would be added.) In the case of the next point, A, the bearing of the line joining it to point F has just been calculated, but this was the bearing of the line viewed *from* point F. Looked at from point A, the line which had been running approximately north from F is now obviously running something like south, and its bearing is calculated by adding 180°, to give 168°02′28″. (If the result had been greater than 360° then 360 would have been subtracted from it.)

In writing this, I realise that in successive paragraphs I have described adding 360° to the result of one calculation, and subtracting the same amount from another, and the reasons may not be instantly obvious, though with a little thought they probably would be. The rule is that if a calculation involving bearings results in a number greater than 360, then 360 is subtracted from the result; if the result is a number less than zero, 360 is added.

Coming back to point A, we can subtract the angle of 131°02′18″ from the bearing of 168°02′28″ to give a bearing of 37°00′10″. The same rules can be applied to the other measured angles to produce this list of bearings:

Bearings

FE	90°00′00″
FA	348°02′28″
AB	37°00′10″
BC	91°59′38″
CD	144°35′26″
DE	187°52′49″
EF	270°00′02″

(This last one, the bearing of F from E, should be 270° exactly, since the bearing FE was declared to be 90°; it shows the 2″ misclosure remaining after adjusting the angles, but in this order of survey it's a very small amount. In fact, over the distance of the line EF, 2″ represents an error of less than 1½ millimetres.)

The last bearing is another case in which a negative number results. The bearing ED is 7°52′49″, subtracting 97°52′47″ gives −89°59′58″, and adding 360 makes the true bearing 270°00′02″.

With the bearings, it is now possible to calculate the co-ordinate *differences* between the ends of each line. The difference in easting is calculated by

$$L \times sinBg$$

where L is the length of the line and sinBg is the sine of the bearing, while the difference in northing is

$$L \times cosBg$$

(cosBg being the cosine of the bearing).
   Applying this to the line FA we have

$$53.527 \times \sin 348°02'28'' = 53.527 \times -0.207209792 = -11.091$$
$$53.527 \times \cos 348°02'28'' = 53.527 \times 0.97829653 = 52.365$$

Looking at the diagram it's clear that A is for the most part to the north of F, hence the large northing difference, and slightly to the west, accounting for the smaller (negative) easting difference. The other co-ordinate differences, calculated in the same way, are:

FA   −11.091, 52.365
AB   60.224, 79.913
BC   62.210, −2.166
CD   43.821, −61.641
DE   −9.530, −68.857
EF   −145.590, 0.001

Since this traverse forms a loop, starting back at the point from which it started, the sums of the easting and northing differences should both be zero (since there is no net movement east or north). If we add up the two sets of co-ordinate differences we actually get

Sum of easting differences   0.044m
Sum of northing differences   −0.384m

These are the misclosure values for the traverse, representing the total error in eastings and northings. The easting figure is positive, meaning that the position of F as calculated from E is too far to the east, while the northing figure is negative, indicating that the calculated position of F is too far to the south. Using the Bowditch rule, it's possible to adjust the easting and northing *difference* of each leg of the traverse in proportion to the length of the leg compared with the whole length of the traverse. Adding up all the lengths gives a total of 506.573m, so the adjustment to the co-ordinate differences of the line FA will be:

$$\text{Easting:} \quad 0.044 \times \frac{53.527}{506.573} = 0.005$$

Northing: $-0.384 \times \dfrac{53.527}{506.573} = -0.041$

Both these adjustments have to be subtracted from the co-ordinate difference, though since the northing correction is negative subtracting it will have the effect of *adding* the adjustment amount, while subtracting the positive correction from an easting which itself is negative will result in a bigger negative number. (One of those unforgivable things about numbers is that if you subtract a negative number the result is positive, and subtracting a positive number from a negative one gives a larger negative.) The calculations are:

Easting: $-11.091 - 0.005 = -11.096$
Northing: $52.365 - (-0.041) = 52.406$

The adjustments for the co-ordinate differences, and the adjusted co-ordinate differences themselves, are:

FA	0.005	−0.041	−11.096	52.406
AB	0.009	−0.076	60.216	79.988
BC	0.005	−0.047	62.205	−2.119
CD	0.007	−0.057	43.815	−61.584
DE	0.006	−0.053	−9.537	−68.804
EF	0.013	−0.110	−145.603	0.112

Finally, the adjusted co-ordinate differences are applied to each of the traverse lines, adding the easting and northing differences (whether they are positive or negative) to the co-ordinates of the starting point of the line, and so generating co-ordinates for each of the unknown points in turn (F is the one known point, with declared co-ordinates of 1000, 1000).

line	dE	dN	E start	N start	E end	N end
FA	−11.096	52.406	1000.000	1000.000	988.904	1052.406
AB	60.216	79.988	988.904	1052.406	1049.120	1132.394
BC	62.205	−2.119	1049.120	1132.394	1111.325	1130.276
CD	43.815	−61.584	1111.325	1130.276	1155.139	1068.692
DE	−9.537	−68.804	1155.139	1068.692	1145.603	999.888
EF	−145.603	0.112	1145.603	999.888	1000.000	1000.000

Note that now the co-ordinates of F calculated from E are correct, because the misclosures have been distributed, but it may still seem that there is a problem with the co-ordinates of point E itself. The line FE was given a bearing of 90°, so as F is at 1000.000,1000.000, and FE is 145.590m long, point E should be at 1145.590, 1000.000, yet its calculated position is 1.3cm to the east and 11.2cm to the south.

   The adjustment procedure that has been used (like all of them) has detected errors of measurement and distributed them throughout the traverse, but it hasn't eliminated them, and can't do so. Bannister *et al.* (1998, p.199) note that Bowditch's method of adjustment will result in alterations to the bearings of each line, but that this is tolerable for many types of survey (what they describe as 'the average type of engineering survey') because it is easy to apply, and the alterations to the bearings of the lines 'do not affect the plotting to a noticeable extent'. If we imagine the traverse in this example being plotted at a scale of 1:1000 the error in the northing position of point E will be equivalent to just over one tenth of a millimetre, which is certainly tolerable.

Traverse calculations with a spreadsheet

	A	B	C	D	E	F	G	H	I
1				angle					
2	line	start Bg	deg	min	sec	angle dd	bearing dd		
3	FA	90	101	57	32	101.96	348.04		
4	AB	168.04	131	2	18	131.04	37		
5	BC	217	125	0	32	125.01	91.99		
6	CD	271.99	127	24	12	127.4	144.59		
7	DE	324.59	136	42	37	136.71	187.88		
8	EF	7.88	97	52	47	97.88	270		
9									
10									
11	line	dist	dE	dN					
12	FA	53.53	-11.091	52.365					
13	AB	100.07	60.224	79.913					
14	BC	62.25	62.210	-2.166					
15	CD	75.63	43.821	-61.641					
16	DE	69.51	-9.530	-68.857					
17	EF	145.59	-145.590	0.001					
18									
19	sum of differences:		0.044	-0.384					
20	total traverse length:		506.57						
21									
22									
23	line	adj dE	adj dN	dE	dN	E start	N start	E end	N end
24	FA	0.005	-0.041	-11.096	52.406	1000.000	1000.000	988.904	1052.406
25	AB	0.009	-0.076	60.216	79.988	988.904	1052.406	1049.120	1132.394
26	BC	0.005	-0.047	62.205	-2.119	1049.120	1132.394	1111.325	1130.276
27	CD	0.007	-0.057	43.815	-61.584	1111.325	1130.276	1155.139	1068.692
28	DE	0.006	-0.053	-9.537	-68.804	1155.139	1068.692	1145.603	999.888
29	EF	0.013	-0.110	-145.603	0.112	1145.603	999.888	1000.000	1000.000

Figure 4.8 A spreadsheet used to calculate traverse adjustment.

The process of adjusting a traverse has deliberately been described at some length, partly for clarity, and partly because it involves processes fundamental to surveying: distribution of errors, converting angles to bearings, and calculation of co-ordinates from field measurements of angle and distance. None of the individual steps is very difficult to carry out with the aid of a calculator, but the number of steps is quite large and the whole thing can become tedious. A spreadsheet can be set up to do most of the work, and above is an example of a spreadsheet solution to the example traverse. The numbers should be familiar from reading the preceding pages.

The entries in the unshaded cells are those which are made using the keyboard, while the others are the result of calculation. The adjustment of the angles has already been performed, though that can quite easily be incorporated if desired.

The cells from A3 to A8 contain the line references, and C3–D8 are the measured angles, degrees, minutes and seconds in separate cells as in the triangulation example. Column B has a label 'start Bg'; this refers to the bearing of the line from which the angle is being measured, so on row 3 (line FA) the value of 90 has been entered, this being the bearing of line FE, the only one known at the start. Then comes the angle measured at F, then the same angle converted into degrees and decimals (labelled 'angle dd'. The formula in cell F3 is

$$= C3 + (D3/60) + (E3/3600)$$

and it has been copied into the cells down to F8. Cell G3 has the formula to convert the angle into the bearing of the end of the line viewed from the starting point, which in this case is the bearing of A from F. Because of the need to avoid negative bearings, the formula is slightly complicated:

$$= IF((B3 - F3){<}0,B3 - F3 + 360,B3 - F3)$$

The word IF is one of the spreadsheet's built-in functions, and it indicates that a decision has to be made. If the result of subtracting the number in F3 from the number in B3 is less than zero (which is what '<0' means), the calculation to be performed is B3 − F3 + 360, otherwise it is simply B3 − F3. This calculates the bearing of the first traverse line, and has been copied into the cells down to G8.

The next row relates to the line AB. The first calculation (in B4) is the bearing of the line AF, from which the angle at A is measured. The formula is:

$$= IF((G3 + 180){>}360,G3 + 180 - 360,G3 + 180)$$

Here is another conditional formula, because of the need to avoid bearings greater than 360. If the number in G3 (the bearing calculated for FA) plus 180 is greater than 360, add 180 to the contents of G3 then subtract 360 from the result; otherwise just add 180 to the contents of G3. This formula is copied into the cells down to B8.

In the next block of cells, A12–A14 contain copies of the line references (A12 has the formula = A3, etc.). B12–B17 are the distances entered from the keyboard. Cells C12–C17 contain the values 'dE', meaning the change in eastings between the beginning and end of the line. The formula in C12 is:

$$= B12{*}SIN(RADIANS(G3))$$

which calculates the value of the length of the line multiplied by the sine of the bearing (which is in G3); the bearing is converted to radians first. This formula is copied into cells down to C17. The cells from D12–D17 contain a formula like this:

$$= B12{*}COS(RADIANS(G3))$$

which calculates the northing difference using the length multiplied by the cosine of the bearing.

In cells C19 and D19 the columns of easting and northing differences are added:

$$= SUM(C12:C17) \quad and \quad = SUM(D12:D17)$$

Cell C20 contains =SUM(B12:B17), which calculates the total length of the traverse.

Cells A24–A29 are again copies of the line references. B24–B29 perform the calculation of the adjustment to be applied to the co-ordinate differences; B24 is:

$$= \$C\$19*B12/\$C\$20$$

The $ symbols are needed because the whole series of formulae in these cells must refer to the value in a single cell, so $C$19 means that any formula copied from the original will refer to C19 and not change this into C20, C21 etc. The value in C19 (the total error in eastings) is multiplied by B12 (the length of the line FA) divided by C20 (the total traverse length). Cells C24–C29 similarly calculate the northing adjustment; C24 is:

$$= \$D\$19*B12/\$C\$20$$

Cells D24–E29 now calculate new values for dE and dN, with simple formulae such as = C12–B24 (in D24).

F24 and G24 contain the co-ordinates of the first point, F, and H24 and I24 add the easting and northing differences of the line FA to the co-ordinates of F to generate co-ordinates for point A (= F24 + D24 and = G24 + E24).

Cells F25 and G25 are copies of H24 and I24 (= H24 etc.), and H25–I29 are copies of the formulae in H24–I24.

The traverse is now fully adjusted, and the surveying of detail can begin. Instruments may be placed on the stations to locate detail by measurements of bearing and distance, or by intersection of bearings from two stations. Baselines may be created by joining traverse stations, where this is practicable, for measurements of offsets, or additional points may be measured from the control network to set up new baselines close enough to points of detail for offset measurements to be performed. There is no reason why a mixture of techniques shouldn't be employed on one site, as long as the most accurate methods available are used to create the control; it may even be convenient to set out baselines for offset tape measurements and to have this work proceed while the control network is being created, provided the baselines are secure and don't disappear before they have been properly recorded. It may be inevitable that a small amount of detail is found to lie outside the traverse network (few archaeological sites produce *no* surprises) but if this is more than a very small amount the control should be extended properly (e.g. by constructing a new traverse joining points on the existing one and adjusting this is the usual way).

Compass traversing

The traverse is one of the classic control networks used in high-accuracy work, but there are many times in reconnaissance surveys when there are few mapped landscape features, there is a need to use highly portable equipment and yet produce a map which is reliable within its limits of accuracy. A prismatic compass is often used in such circumstances, perhaps with a tape for distance measurement, both devices being eminently portable. They are also, of course, instruments of low accuracy, and the need to establish procedures for adjustment of surveys in which they are used is at least as pressing as in more precise work, though probably such procedures are less often applied, perhaps in the mistaken belief that 'there isn't any point'. In fact, low-accuracy surveys can be made quite robust by the application of quite simple adjustment techniques, which may not even involve calculation. The following method is provided by Olliver and Clendinning (1978, pp.90–2).

As described earlier, magnetic compasses which are suitable for survey use come in a variety of forms, some capable of being mounted on a tripod, others designed for hand-held use. In archaeological practice the latter are overwhelmingly preferred. Olliver and Clendinning suggest that reading accuracy of a compass is not likely to be better than about ¼°, though in my experience ½° is more realistic, especially with the popular 'military' pattern prismatic compass or one of the other types of sighting compass. This forced limitation of accuracy actually allows the surveyor to save effort elsewhere, since it becomes unnecessary to make very precise distance measurements (Olliver and Clendinning suggest that distance measurements to the nearest metre are appropriate on longer lines, and 10cm on shorter ones). It then also becomes possible to employ further labour-saving measures, such as one of the types of long-distance laser rangefinder; these can measure distances of 500–1000m with an accuracy of about a metre, and are about the same size and weight as a standard 30m fibreglass tape.

The measurement of angles with a compass is more simple than with a theodolite in that the reference direction is already established – the direction of magnetic north – so the bearing of each line in the traverse is given directly and doesn't have to be calculated. This also makes plotting easy in a CAD system, as long as the drawing has been set up so that angles are measured clockwise from north.

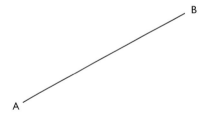

Figure 4.9 The first leg of a compass traverse.

Rather than rely on a single measurement, it's usual to take a bearing of point B (above) from point A, then the 'back bearing' from B to A, and take an average of the two, increasing or decreasing the back bearing by 180°. In the above case, the bearing of B from A has been measured as 59.5°, and the back bearing of A from B as 240°. Subtracting 180 from 240 gives 60, so the bearing AB is taken as

$$(59.5 + 60) \div 2 = 59.75°$$

A difference of up to 1° between the two bearings (called *reciprocal bearings*) may be caused by instrumental and observation errors, and averaging is appropriate. Larger errors should be checked by re-measurement; if they are not found to be a result of a mistake they may be caused by *local attraction*, a phenomenon produced by a strong local magnetic field. Obvious sources are such things as parked vehicles, which are perhaps not so common in areas in which archaeological reconnaissance surveys are being carried out (unless they belong to the surveyors themselves), but they can also be produced by steel fence posts concealed within hedges, or of course by buried objects. If large differences are found between reciprocal bearings, leading to a suspicion of local attraction, it will be better to work with the angles *between* traverse legs, deduced by taking bearings at a station. For example, in the above diagram, if the reciprocal bearings AB and BA had differed not by ½° but 3° it would be reasonable to suspect a local magnetic effect, but it wouldn't be possible to tell if this were affecting point A or point B. In these circumstances it would still be possible to rely on the *difference* in bearings between, say, BA and BC, or AB and AE, which would enable the internal angles to be determined, as they would be in a theodolite traverse, and they could then be adjusted in the same way. A reliable bearing for one leg of the traverse could be obtained between two points with acceptable reciprocal bearings, and bearings for the other legs be calculated using the internal angles.

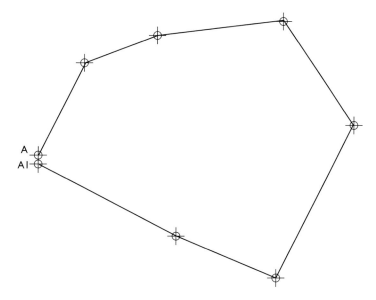

Figure 4.10 Diagram of a compass traverse showing misclosure.

The co-ordinates of the stations can be calculated as for a theodolite traverse, or they could be plotted in a CAD system (an example of direct plotting in CAD is given in the case study on Cockfield Fell). Either way, assuming that the traverse forms a closed loop, when it has been plotted the result is likely to be as above, where the position of 'A1', calculated from the previous point, differs from the position initially given to point A. This amount is the 'misclosure', and an adjustment must be made to remove it – not to eliminate it, which can't be done, but to distribute it in some way so that the error is spread throughout the traverse. In the case of a compass traverse, with its limited accuracy, a simple procedure can be followed, assuming that the amount by which a point needs to be moved is related to its position in the total length of the traverse, and that the direction in which it has to be moved is parallel to the line between A and A1.

The bearing of the line A–A1 can be measured in a CAD system. To determine the amount by which each point has to be moved, divide the cumulative distance along the traverse by the total length, then multiply the result by the total misclosure length.

For example, The first leg is 127m, the total length is 1121m, and the misclosure 15m.

$$127 \div 1121 = 0.113$$
$$15 \times 0.113 = 1.695 = 1.7$$

The second leg is 103m, the cumulative length 230m:

$$230 \div 1121 = 0.205$$
$$15 \times 0.205 = 3.075 = 3.1$$

The values for the bearing and distance can be used to calculate new co-ordinates for each point, or they can be plotted directly.

Magnetic variation

At any point on the Earth's surface the direction of magnetic north differs from true north by a certain amount; the amount varies with both geographic location and time. Users of Ordnance Survey maps in the UK (and of many other national mapping systems) will find information about magnetic variation printed on hardcopy maps. (On a recent Ordnance Survey 1:25,000 Explorer sheet, for example, it states that magnetic north is estimated at 3° 42′ east of grid north for July 2004 with an annual change of approximately 13′ east.)

There are many parts of the world, however, where this information may not be readily available from local maps. It is possible to obtain it from a number of sources, including a web site maintained by Ed Williams: http://williams.best.vwh.net/magvar.html. There is an online calculator, or you can download a stand alone program magi.exe. This is a DOS program, which means that it doesn't need to be installed to be used. Just download it, then find the file with Windows Explorer and double-click on it. This will open a DOS window in which you will see this:

```
Geomagnetic Field and Variation Calculator v1.05
Copyright 2000 E A Williams All rights reserved.
Defaults are:
model IGRF00
date 1/1/0
plus NWW (N latitude, W longitude, W variation are positive)
field no (output mag field components yes/no)

Enter lat lon [alt], type h for help, type q to quit
>
```

The meanings of the Defaults are:

model IGRF00   the geomagnetic model used in the calculations

date 1/1/0   the date, by default 1 January 2000; this can be changed using a command of the form set date **MM/DD/YY**, e.g.

set date 7/13/04 *<enter>*

for 13 July 2004

plus NWW (N latitude, W longitude, W variation are positive)   this tells you how to enter the parameters and how to read the result; enter latitudes north of the Equator as positive, and longitude west of zero as positive, while the magnetic variation will be given as positive if magnetic north is west of true north, and negative if it's east.

field no (output mag field components yes/no)   by default only the magnetic variation east or west of true north will be given; for surveying purposes you don't need the other components of the field which can be output.

Example

Imagine a point with co-ordinates of East 36.4° North 31.2° (E36°24'00", N31°12'00"). You can enter these in either form, but degrees/minutes/seconds have to have colons as the separator (:); using a compass you probably won't be able to read angles to better than half a degree, so the decimal form is probably easiest. You can optionally enter a figure for altitude, but in work of this order of precision there is no need. The following panel shows the result of entering these numbers.

```
Geomagnetic Field and Variation Calculator v1.05
Copyright 2000 E A Williams All rights reserved.
Defaults are:
model IGRF00
date 1/1/0
plus NWW (N latitude, W longitude, W variation are positive)
field no (output mag field components yes/no)


Enter lat lon [alt], type h for help, type q to quit
> 31.2 – 36.4
–3.3
>
```

The latitude is entered first, followed by a space, then the longitude (negative in this case). Just press **enter** and the value of magnetic variation appears on the next line. This is −3.3, i.e. magnetic north is 3.3° east of true north.

When you have finished with the program, type **quit**.

Finding a location within a co-ordinate system

So far in this chapter it has been assumed that we are dealing with 'divorced' surveys, in which a co-ordinate system is created to cover the archaeological site, no attempt being made to connect this to a wider-scale system such as the Ordnance Survey grid or another national mapping scheme. In many cases this is quite satisfactory, but sometimes it is necessary to work with co-ordinates within an exisiting framework. The obvious way to do this today is by means of satellite navigation (GPS), as discussed in Chapter 6, but there may be times when this isn't possible, either because equipment isn't available, or isn't functioning for some reason. There is a classical method of obtaining co-ordinates for an instrument station by making measurements of angles between identifiable objects in the landscape whose co-ordinates are known; this method is known as *resection*.

The logic behind the method is simple in principle.

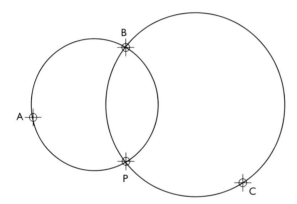

Figure 4.11 The principle of the resection method.

The three known points are A, B, C, and the instrument is at P. Since a circle can be constructed through any three points (unless they are on a straight line), two overlapping circles can be made through ABP and BCP. Since P is somewhere on the circumference of both circles, it has to be at one of the points where they intersect, and one of these is already occupied by B, and since the co-ordinates of all the points except P are known, it must be possible to work out the co-ordinates of the other intersection point, P.

The great drawback to the application of this useful technique is that when set out in a textbook it can look very fearsome. There is no single way of performing a resection, and in the past many surveyors have devised their own. Some methods have been published attached to the name of an individual (such as 'Collins' Point', or 'Bessell's'), while others are just set out as exercises in fundamental geometry (e.g. that of Olliver and Clendinning (1978)). Most of these require a high level of understanding of geometrical principles if they are to be applied, and they certainly take a good deal of time to complete. Hogg (1980) remarks that all the methods are laborious, and offers a semi-graphical method which he describes as 'the least so'; a casual glance at the diagram he gives would be a disincentive to many aspiring surveyors.

Most of the resection methods are not susceptible to being reduced to a formula, but one exception is that which is usually ascribed to Tienstra (Bannister *et al.*, 1998, p.220). J.M. Tienstra was a professor at the Geodetic Institute of the Technical University at Delft in the early twentieth century, and he certainly taught the use of this formula, though Greulich (1999) has pointed out that a very similar formula was published at least as early as 1889 (before Tienstra was born), and it may go back to the work of Möbius in 1827, or even earlier. Nevertheless, Tienstra is the name which has become associated with the method, and that is how it will be referred to.

As in all resection situations, the required data are the co-ordinates of three points which can be seen from the unknown point, and angles measured between them. An ideal situation is shown in the diagram.

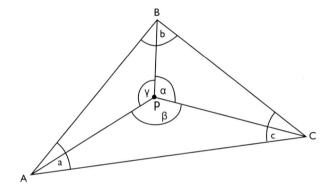

Figure 4.12 Tienstra's method of resection.

Here the unknown location (P) is situated centrally in a well-conditioned triangle made by the three known points (A, B and C). The three angles which have to be measured are labelled α, β and γ, which is the conventional notation in the use of this method. A great advatage of the resection technique is that the known points don't have to be visited, as no distance measurement is involved, so one or more of them may be quite distant from the observer (which can be critical when trying to determine a location in an area of moorland, for example, where there may be few mapped features close by). Naturally, though, it isn't always easy to find three points which are so fortunately distributed. The accuracy with which the observer's location may be determined obviously depends on the precision of the co-ordinates of the known points, and even more on the precision with which the angles are measured. If the known points are fairly distant, errors in their co-ordinates of some metres may have little effect on the calculated position. If digital map data of a suitable scale are available, it may be possible to obtain the co-ordinates to a very high level of precision, or it may be that they have to be scaled from paper maps, in which case all that may be achievable may be co-ordinates to the nearest 10 or 20 metres.

An important thing to note is the way in which the points and angles are named (since these names are used in mathematical formulae it's obviously crucial that the right values are being referred to). The three known points A, B and C must be lettered in clockwise order, as in the diagram. There is, of course, no reason why point A shouldn't be at the top, or on the right, but the order is critical; if A was on the left, as it is, but C was at the top and B to the right (so that the order A, B, C was an anti-clockwise direction) the formula would fail. The angles within the triangle are labelled a, b, c, to correspond with the upper-case designation of the points. These angles don't have to be measured; because the co-ordinates of the triangle corners are known, the angles can be worked out. The measured angles, as already stated, are called α (alpha), β (beta) and γ (gamma), the first three letters of the Greek alphabet, to correspond with the angles a, b, c (α is on the opposite side of P from a, β is opposite b, and γ is opposite c). In the diagram the angles a, b and c are bisected by the lines joining P to the other three points, and this is perhaps a little visually confusing; the angle a, for example, is the whole angle between the lines AB and AC, and the same applies to b and c.

This may be the ideal situation, with P in the approximate centre of a triangle formed by the known points, but it doesn't have to be this way, and indeed the Tienstra method would be very limited in its usefulness if that were the case. Look at this diagram:

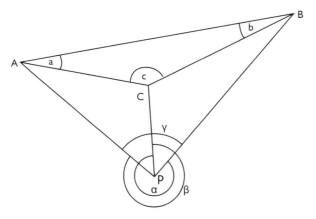

Figure 4.13 Tienstra's resection with the observer outside the triangle of known points.

Here point P is completely outside the triangle ABC, but the formula can still work, provided the lettering conventions are adhered to rigidly, something which requires a bit of concentration. Looking back at the last diagram for a moment, it can be seen that angle α is the one between lines BP and CP. Just as the three points at the corners of the triangle have to be lettered in clockwise order, so the angles have to be measured clockwise as well. This may not particularly seem to make sense at first, since in the first case angle α is the same size whichever way you measure it, but when P is outside the triangle ABC, things are quite different. Here angle α is still between the lines BP and CP, but when most people think of an angle they imagine something less than 180°, and this is much more. Following the clockwise convention, the line BP is taken as the starting point, and angle α is measured clockwise until the line CP is reached. In cases where P is outside ABC, some of the measured angles may be very close to being complete circles; in this case both α and β are very large, while γ is more conventional-looking. Obviously, great care has to be taken to get these angles right, or the results will be inaccurate by many orders of magnitude. However, as long as they are right, and the co-ordinates of ABC are correct, the formula will work every time.

Or almost. Going back to the basis of resection as a technique, it was shown that point P lies on two circles, one shared with A and B, and one with B and C. If it should happen that A, B, C and P all lie on the *same* circle (called by surveyors the *danger circle*), it would be impossible to determine the location of P; in fact, even if P is close to being on the circle which passes through A, B, and C it won't be possible to calculate a reliable location. The errors may either be gross, which is infuriating but at least obvious, or inaccurate but still plausible, which may in the long run cause more trouble, so it really is essential to take care to avoid the situation arising. Clearly, if P is inside the trangle safety is assured. If you have at least some idea of where P is, you may be able to decide in the field whether the danger circle situation is being approached, but if there is any uncertainty it would be better to choose a fourth point of known co-ordinates and measure an angle to this as well.

So, having acquired the necessary data, the calculation can proceed. The Tienstra formulae are fairly straightforward if you are in any way comfortable with numbers, and they can be carried out with the aid of just a calculator, but it has to be said that even then the business is somewhat time-consuming, and there are many opportunites to make mistakes. It's much better to create a spreadsheet which will perform the calculations, and any number of resections can then be performed just by entering the co-ordinates of the known points and the measured angles. I'm grateful to Dave Morgan of the IT Service at Durham University, who provided valuable help with the spreadsheet formulae, and introduced an element of elegance that was beyond me.

The algebraic formulae are logically given first, but you don't have to read them in order to construct the spreadsheet.

First of all, three terms are defined:

$$K_1 = 1/(\cot a - \cot \alpha)$$

$$K_2 = 1/(\cot b - \cot \beta)$$

$$K_3 = 1/(\cot c - \cot \gamma)$$

then the eastings and northings are calculated:

$$Ep = (K_1 E_A + K_2 E_B + K_3 E_C) / (K_1 + K_2 + K_3)$$

$$Np = (K_1 N_A + K_2 N_B + K_3 N_C) / (K_1 + K_2 + K_3)$$

E_A, N_A, etc. are the eastings and northings of the known points (Bannister *et al.*, 1998, pp.220–1).

	A	B	C	D	E	F	G	H	I	J	K	L
1	Co-ordinates and Bearings											
2	from point	easting	northing	to point	easting	northing	easting diff.	northing diff.	red. Bg. Deg.	Quadrant indicator	True Bg.	
3	A	310489.473	222795.215	B	311378.237	224051.887	888.764	1256.672	35.269	2.000	35.27	AB
4	A	310489.473	222795.215	C	312921.055	223313.469	2431.582	518.254	77.968	2.000	77.97	AC
5	B	311378.237	224051.887	A	310489.473	222795.215	-888.764	-1256.672	35.269	-2.000	215.27	BA
6	B	311378.237	224051.887	C	312921.055	223313.469	1542.818	-738.418	64.423	0.000	115.58	BC
7	C	312921.055	223313.469	B	311378.237	224051.887	-1542.818	738.418	64.423	0.000	295.58	CB
8	C	312921.055	223313.469	A	310489.473	222795.215	-2431.582	-518.254	77.968	-2.000	257.97	CA
9												
10	Calculted Angles											
11												
12		A	B	C								
13		42.699	99.693	37.608								
14												
15	Measured Angles											
16												
17		α	BPC									
18		β	CPA									
19		γ	APB									
20												
21		α	β	γ								
22		126.487	141.262	92.251								
23												
24												
25		α	β	γ	A	B	C			k1	k2	k3
26	radians	2.208	2.465	1.610	0.745	1.740	0.656			0.548	0.93	0.75
27	tan	-1.35	-0.8	-25.44	0.92	-5.85	0.77					
28	cotan	-0.74	-1.25	-0.04	1.08	-0.17	1.3					
29												
30												
31	EP	311677.516										
32	NP	223494.177										

Figure 4.14 A spreadsheet used to calculate Tienstra's resection.

This is a picture of the spreadsheet, complete with entered data. To facilitate data entry, all the cells which show calculated values are shaded in grey, while those into which numbers have to be typed are left clear.

Rows 1–8 contain the known point co-ordinates and interim calculated values used in calculating the bearings of the sides of the triangle of known points (these are needed in order to work out the angles within the triangle, which then appear in cells B13–D13). It would be possible to create more complex formulae and leave out some of the interim values, but as stated elsewhere, it's easier to type in simple formulae, and sometimes useful to be able to see various stages in the calculations.

Starting with row 3, column B contains the easting co-ordinate of point A, and column C contains the northing (typed in). This row is used to calculate the bearing of the line AB, so its starting point (A) appears in column A, and its end (B) is in column D. The co-ordinates of point B are actually entered in cells B5 and C5, and copied into E3 and F3. These last two cells contain the formulae

=B5
=C5

(remember that all formulae have to begin with the '=' sign, to show that they aren't just pieces of text).

Cell G5 contains this:

=E3−B3

which represents the difference in easting co-ordinates between the two ends of the line. This is called 'easting diff.' in the label in G2. Similarly, H3 contains the formula for the difference in northings co-ordinates:

=F3−C3

Of course, the easting and northing differences can be either positive or negative, depending on the relative positions of the starting and ending points of the line. The formula in I3 calculates the bearing of the line, but this is more complex than the ones entered so far:

=ABS(DEGREES(ATAN(G3/(H3 + 0.0001))))

One thing to take note of first are the 'nested' brackets, which separate parts of the formula. This is not the place to go into a description of how these work, but suffice it to say that they (obviously) have to be in the right places, and (equally obviously) there must be equal numbers of '(' and ')'. This may seem too obvious to state, in fact, but it's something that is very easy to get wrong. If you have an odd number of brackets an error message will be generated, but if you leave a pair out altogether you may just get a wrong result.

In algebraic form the *tangent* of the bearing is given by

tan Bg = easting diff. ÷ northing diff.

and then taking the *arctangent* (also written as tan^{-1}, especially on calculator keyboards) of the result would give the bearing. This spreadsheet formula does just this.

The function **ABS** calculates the 'absolute' value of whatever follows (i.e. it will ignore any minus signs); in this case there may be negative numbers generated, and we need to get rid of them.

The function **DEGREES** is needed because spreadsheets calculate their trigonometrical functions using radians, and this converts between the two. **ATAN** is the arctangent function, and **G3/(H3 + 0.0001)** means 'divide the value in cell G3 (the easting difference) by the value in H3 (the northing difference) plus 0.0001.

This formula gives the bearing of the line from A to B, but it isn't the bearing measured clockwise from north, rather it's the quantity known as the *reduced bearing*, the angle between the line AB and the north–south line *measured by the shortest route.* The next diagram shows what this means.

The diagram shows bearings from a central point to two others, one in the north–east quadrant, and one in the south-west. The reduced bearings of the two lines are shown using a dashed symbol, the true bearings are a continuous line. In the case of the point in the north-east quadrant the two bearings are the same.

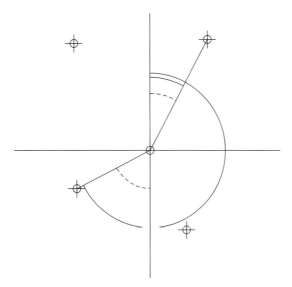

Figure 4.15 True and reduced bearings.

For the surveyor, who needs the value of the true bearing, this presents something of a problem. If the line AB has a true bearing (also called a *whole circle* bearing) of less than 90° the reduced bearing and true bearing have the same value; if the true bearing is between 90° and 180° it will be equal to 180° minus the reduced bearing; if the true bearing is between 180° and 270° it will be equal to 180° plus the reduced bearing; finally, a true bearing between 270° and 360° is equal to 360° minus the reduced bearing. It's possible, of course, to look at a plan of the points A, B, C and work out which calculation is appropriate in each case, but it isn't a very elegant way of doing things, and again is an area in which mistakes can be made. The solution here is to be found in cells J3 and K3. In the first of these, labelled 'quadrant indicator', is this formula:

=SIGN(G3) + SIGN(H3)

this uses the spreadsheet function (**SIGN**) which produces a value of 1 if the cell contains a positive number and −1 if the number is negative. Applying this function to the differences in eastings and northings can be used to show in which quadrant the line lies.

Cell K3 contains

=IF(J3 = 2,I3,IF(J3 = −2,180 + I3,IF(SIGN(H3) = −1,180 − I3,360 − I3)))

which gives the true bearing of the line. (This 'nesting' of the IF statements is a little tricky to get right, but if the syntax isn't correct (leaving out a bracket, for example) you will get an error message.) An explanation of how this works now follows, but understanding it isn't essential if you don't feel inclined.

The four quadrants in which the known point may lie are called 1st, 2nd, 3rd, 4th, and one result of the formula exists for each, i.e.

1   IF(J3 = 2,I6
    If relative easting and northing are both positive (1st quadrant), the result is 2, and the reduced bearing is equal to the whole circle bearing.
2   IF(J3 = −2,180 + I3
    if the relative easting and northing are both negative (3rd quadrant), the result is −2, and the whole circle bearing is equal to 180 + reduced bearing
3   IF(SIGN(H3) = −1,180 − I3
    if the sign of the relative northing is negative (and the 3rd quadrant, in which relative easting and northing are *both* negative, has already been accounted for in note 2) the second point must be in the second quadrant, and the whole circle bearing is equal to 180 − reduced bearing
4   360 − I3)))
    otherwise, quadrants 1, 2, and 3 being accounted for, the second point must be in the fourth quadrant, and the whole circle bearing is equal to 360-reduced bearing.

At the end of this first row of cells we now have the true bearing of the line AB. It may seem like a long way to get there, but once the formulae are entered this particular job need never be done again.

The next five rows are similar to the first, but have been arranged so that the point co-ordinates only have to be typed once (into the cells which have a clear background); where they occur in other cells they are copied from the 'input' cells, so that E3 contains

    =B5

and F3 has

    =C5

and so on. The formulae in columns G to K have simply been copied from the first row. One way to do this is to left-click the mouse on cell G3 then drag it to K3, then release the mouse button. A highlight will have appeared over the five cells, and there will be a small black square at the bottom-right corner of the rightmost cell. If you place the mouse pointer over this square it will change from a thick white cross to a thin black one, and if you now left-click and hold the button you can drag the highlight down to lower rows, and on releasing the mouse button the formulae will have been copied.

In cells B12–D12 the angles A, B and C are calculated by subtracting the bearings of the lines from each other. For example, B12 contains

    =IF(ABS(K3 − K4)>180,360 − ABS(K3 − K4),ABS(K3 − K4))

This again uses the ABS function to get rid of unwanted minus signs, and the IF function to prevent values of over 360° being generated. Cells C12 and D12 contain

    =IF(ABS(K5 − K6)>180,360 − ABS(K5 − K6),ABS(K5 − K6))

and

=IF(ABS(K7 − K8)>180,360 − ABS(K7 − K8),ABS(K7 − K8))

respectively.

On rows 15 and 16 are the labelled cells into which the measured angles α, β and γ are entered, along with a reminder of which angles these are in terms of the three known points.

On rows 21–24 is the next set of calculations, all much simpler than some of the preceeding ones. B22 contains

=RADIANS(H16)

which calculates the value of angle γ in radians, B23 has

TAN(B22)

to calculate the tangent of γ and B24 has

1/B23

which calculates the cotangent of γ (i.e. the reciprocal of the tangent). Columns C–G do the same thing for the angles α, β, A, B and C.

The values k1, k2 and k3 are calculated in cells I22–K22; in order they contain

=1/(E24 − C24)   =1/(F24 − D24)   =1/(G24 − B24)

The co-ordinates of point P are calculated in cells B27–28:

=(I22*B16 + J22*D16 + K22*F16)/(I22 + J22 + K22)
=(I22*C16 + J22*E16 + K22*G16)/(I22 + J22 + K22)

Note that when you are entering new data into the spreadsheet the calculations are updated after each new piece of information, so there will be times when some of the cells contain incorrect results, or even error messages, until all the new co-ordinates and angles have been entered.

Chapter 5

Application of surveying instruments

One of the things which inexperienced surveyors find most difficult is setting up an instrument (a total station or theodolite) on its tripod over a ground mark, most commonly a wooden peg in archaeological usage. This is in fact quite simple, but if the correct procedure isn't followed great difficulty may be encountered.

Centring and levelling the total station over a peg

1   Make sure the tripod head is approximately level, and position the tripod over the peg as best you can by eye. If you have a plumb line this *may* assist you (but in windy weather a plumb line can be more of a hindrance than a help). Have the tripod legs well spread out to give the instrument a stable platform. Press the feet of the tripod firmly into the ground, trying to keep your leg parallel to the leg of the tripod so that the point of the foot is going into a tightly fitting hole.

2   Place the instrument on the tripod, and tighten it (in most modern instruments there will be a vertical screw to clamp it in place).

3   There may be an *optical plummet* in the base of the instrument; this is a small eyepiece mounted horizontally, which gives a view through a prism which is along the vertical axis of the instrument. This will have a central mark in the field of view (either a small circle or the intersection of a pair of lines). A more modern alternative is a *laser plummet*, which projects a spot of red light at a point which again is a continuation of the vertical axis of the instrument. A laser plummet has to be switched on deliberately, and will be switched off automatically when the setup procedure is finished. (Each instrument will have its own way of doing this.) By rotating the *levelling screws* (three screws mounted horizontally at the corners of the base of the instrument), centre the optical or laser plummet onto the peg. You may need to move the screws individually and apparently randomly to achieve this, and of course it will make the instrument un-level.

4   The instrument will have a small circular spirit level (variously called a 'pond' or 'Bull's Eye' level); using this, adjust the length of the *tripod legs* until the bubble is centred. The instrument is now approximately level, and the plummet should still be centred on the peg. (If, during this procedure, the instrument becomes extremely un-level, so that it seems in danger of falling over,

stop immediately and return to step 1. If you have begun with the top of the tripod level, however, this situation shouldn't occur.)

5   In addition to the circular level, there will also be a long tubular spirit level (some modern instruments substitute electronic equivalents which are viewed on the main screen). Position the bubble tube so that its long axis is parallel to the line between any two footscrews.

   (a) Centre the bubble by rotating the two screws in opposite directions (as in the diagram). The bubble follows the movement of the *left* thumb.

   (b) Rotate the instrument through 90°, and centre the bubble again using the *third* footscrew. Note that each screw is used in only one part of this operation.

Repeat (a) and (b) above until the bubble remains centred in both positions.

6   It is likely that by this time the plummet indicator will have moved slightly from the centre of the peg. If so, *slightly* loosen the centre screw holding the instrument to the tripod, and slide the instrument sideways to remove any remaining displacement from the centre of the peg, then tighten the screw, and re-level using the procedure in 5 above.

   The instrument should never be moved so far sideways that its base overhangs the tripod head.

The instrument is now ready for use.

bubbles move this way

Figure 5.1 Procedure for levelling a theodolite or total station.

Correcting tape measurements for slope

Tape measurements are subject to a number of errors, as mentioned previously. Some of these can be mitigated by careful use; sag and lateral displacement by the wind can be alleviated by only using the tape for short lengths, when it can be held reasonably taut, or by taking measurements with the tape supported throughout its length. The steps taken to ensure precise measurement with steel tapes (such as the use of spring balances to ensure the correct tension, and temperature corrections) are unlikely to be employed in most archaeological situations. Supporting the tape along its length in practice means laying it on the ground, and while this achieves greater accuracy of linear measurement, obviously there will be a difference between the length measured and the true horizontal distance which is required for mapping, unless the ground is very level. Correcting this 'slope distance' to a horizontal distance requires either a measurement of the angle of slope, or of the difference in height between the two ends of the line.

If the slope angle is a, and the measured length is L, the horizontal distance is

$$L \times \cos a$$

e.g. measured length = 28.342m, angle of slope = 2.5°,

horizontal length = 28.342 × 0.999048221 = 28.315m

If there is a need to calculate the correction factor itself, this is given by

$$\text{correction} = -L(1 - \cos a)$$

In this case:

$$\begin{aligned} \text{correction} &= -28.342 \times (1 - 0.999048221) \\ &= -28.342 \times 0.000951779 \\ &= -0.0270 \end{aligned}$$

Clearly the correction is always negative, because the slope measurement must be greater than the horizontal.

The slope measurement given here is fairly approximate, as would be the case if it were measured with a device such as an Abney level. An adequate way of doing it would be for the observer to have an assistant at the far end of the line, to note some part of their clothing which was at the observer's eye-level and to use this as the mark to measure the slope. Alternatively a levelling staff, or a ranging pole with a piece of adhesive tape attached at eye-level, could be used. A much more precise measurement of the slope could be achieved with a theodolite, but when taking tape measurements over distances up to 30m (the standard tape length) the Abney level would suffice. In the example given, if the slope were measured as 2°24′30″ rather than 2.5° the calculated horizontal distance would be 28.317, a difference of only 2mm.

If a level has been used to measure the difference in elevation between the ends of the line, and this difference in elevation is called h, the correction is

$$\text{correction} = -[L - (L^2 - h^2)^{1/2}]$$

This contains a superscript ($^{1/2}$) which may be unfamiliar. Raising a number to the power of one-half is the same as taking the square root of the number, so the equation could be given as

$$\text{correction} = -[L - \sqrt{(L^2 - h^2)}]$$

If the measured length is 28.540 and the difference in elevation is 0.75m, the equation is:

$$\text{correction} = -[28.540 - \sqrt{(814.5316 - 0.5625)}]$$

$$= -[28.540 - \sqrt{813.9691}]$$
$$= -[28.540 - 28.530]$$
$$= -0.01\text{m}$$

If the elevation difference is less than 1 in 25 an approximation can be used (Bannister *et al.*, 1998, p.23):

$$\text{correction} = -(h^2 \div 2L)$$

e.g. $\text{correction} = -(0.5625 \div 57.08)$
$$= -0.00985\text{m}$$

Reading a Vernier

Once an essential part of the education of everyone studying any kind of science, learning to read a Vernier scale is something which few people now do. The purpose of this device is to make it possible to read an instrument with greater precision than is permitted by the physical size of the main scale. At one time the graduated circles of theodolites were read using Verniers, but they were superseded by other devices many decades ago. Some small instruments, such as Abney levels, still use them, however.

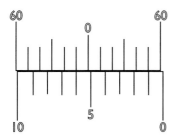

Figure 5.2 Example of a Vernier scale.

This diagram shows part of the scale of an instrument where the main (lower) scale is divided into degrees, and the Vernier is marked with divisions of 10 minutes (so from 0 to 60 is one whole degree). The size of the main scale means that it would be impossible to divide each degree into six parts, and to have these clearly visible (this diagram is of course much bigger than the scale would really be). The Vernier is designed so that six of its divisions cover exactly the same distance as five divisions on the main scale. It moves alongside the main scale as the instrument is operated. In the case of an Abney level it would move in one direction when measuring an upward inclination and the other way when measuring downwards; here it is assumed that the Vernier is moving from right to left. To take a reading, look for the position of the zero mark on the Vernier. It lies between the five and six degree marks on the main scale, so the size of the angle is somewhere between five and six degrees, and obviously closer to five than six. Now look to the left (the direction in which the Vernier scale was moving) and note which of its own marks corresponds most closely to a mark on the main scale. This is the ten minute mark, so this amount is added to the main scale reading, to give a total of 5° 10′.

Intersection

This technique is also called 'triangulation', which isn't inaccurate, but surveyors usually call it 'intersection', and this word avoids any confusion with the technique of 'trilateration' (which measures the lengths of the sides of a triangle), which is also often called triangulation.

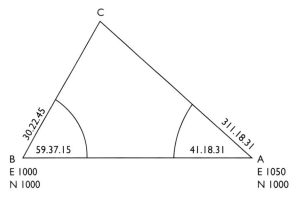

Figure 5.3 An example of intersection.

Points A and B are at either end of a baseline, and have the co-ordinates indicated (B = 1000,1000, A = 1050,1000). The two angles have been measured at A and B between the baseline and the unknown point C. The angular measurements needed to calculate the position of C are the bearings of AC and BC (later to be called α and β), however, so these need to be worked out first:

$$
\begin{aligned}
\text{bearing AC} &= \text{bearing AB} + 41°18′31″ \\
&= 270 + 41°18′31″ \\
&= 311°18′31″
\end{aligned}
$$

$$
\begin{aligned}
\text{bearing BC} &= \text{bearing BA} - 59°37′15″ \\
&= 90 - 59°37′15″ \\
&= 30°22′45″
\end{aligned}
$$

(In the case of AC the measured angle is added because it is measured clockwise, while the angle at B is anti-clockwise of BA and so is subtracted.)

The formulae for working out the co-ordinates of point C are some of those which may look daunting, but the quantities they contain are quite straightforward, and again the spreadsheet can be used to make matters easier. Here is the formula for the easting co-ordinate of C:

$$E_C = \frac{E_A \cot \alpha - E_B \cot \beta - N_A + N_B}{\cot \alpha - \cot \beta}$$

E_C means 'the easting co-ordinate of C', and similarly for the easting of A and B, and northings of A and B.

α and β are the bearings AC and BC

'cot' stands for 'cotangent', which is 1÷ (the tangent of an angle)

'$E_A \cot \alpha$' means 'take the easting of point A and multiply it by 1 ÷ the tangent of α'

So when numbers are entered we have:

$$E_C = \frac{(1050 \times -0.878788) - (1000 \times 1.70588) - 1000 + 1000}{-0.878788 - 1.70588}$$

$$E_C = \frac{-922.7274 - 1705.88}{-2.584668}$$

$$E_C = 1017.0000$$

To get the cotangent of α, for example, using a calculator will depend on the kind of calculator you have, but the operations necessary are to enter the angle (which is 311.3086111 in degrees and decimals), to take the tangent (−1.137931151), and divide 1 by this number (1 ÷ −1.137931151 = −0.878787788). Also depending on the type of calculator you have, the figures may vary slightly in some of the later decimal places.

To get the northings of point C:

$$N_C = N_A + (E_C - E_A)\cot \alpha$$

or

$$N_C = N_B + (E_C - E_B)\cot \beta$$

Using the first of these and entering numbers:

$$N_C = 1000 + (1017 - 1050) \times -0.878788$$

$$N_C = 1029.0000$$

This gives the co-ordinates of point C as E 1017, N 1029.

A spreadsheet solution

	A	B	C	D	E	F	G	H	I	J	K	L	M	N	O
1	Intersection														
2	Bearing is cardinal														
3															
4															
5	easting A	northing A	easting B	northing B		bg AB	bg BA								
6	1050.000	1000.000	1000.000	1000.000		270	90								
7															
8															
9															
10		angle at A			angle at B		l or r?	angle A	angle B	α	cot	β	cot	easting	northing
11	deg	min	sec	deg	min	sec									
12	41	18	31	59	37	15	r	41.31	59.62	311.31	-0.88	30.38	1.71	1017.000	1029.000
13	45	0	0	45	0	0	r	45	45	315	-1	45	1	1025.000	1025.000
14	45	0	0	45	0	0	l	45	45	225	1	135	-1	1025.000	975.000
15															

Figure 5.4 A spreadsheet used to calculate intersection.

The spreadsheet shown here can calculate the position of point C as described above, using the same relative positions of A, B and C. The user has to enter the co-ordinates of A and B, and the bearings AB and BA. It is possible, of course, to calculate the bearings as well, as in the resection spreadsheet on page 54. This would be useful if the points in the control network have been given co-ordinates in a larger-scale system, such as a national mapping grid, becasue it would be unlikely that the bearings would be exactly 90° or 270° as they are shown here. It's often the case in small 'divorced' surveys, however, that baselines are deemed to run east–west or north–south, and then the bearings are easy to work out, allowing the formulae to be simpler.

The user enters the co-ordinates and bearings in A5–G6, then the angles measured at A and B, as degrees, minutes and seconds, on row 12. Cell G10 asks 'l or r?' – the purpose of which is to determine on which side of the line AB the point C lies. As might be expected, 'l' is left and 'r' is right, and this is taken to be left or right *looking from point A*; it's up to the user to get this right.

Cell H12 contains

=A12 + (B12/60) + (C12/3600)

which converts degrees minutes and seconds into degrees and decimals (not essential, but it makes some of the other formulae shorter). Cell I12 similarly contains:

=D12 + (E12/60) + (F12/3600)

Cell J12 has

=IF(G12 = "r",$F$6 + H12,$F$6 – H12)

which calculates the bearing of the line AC (α); if G12 contains 'r', point C lies to the right of AB (seen from A) and so the measured angle is added to the bearing of AB (270°), otherwise the angle is subtracted. (Note that *any* other character, or indeed none, would cause the angle to be subtracted, but entering 'l' for points to the 'left' of the line will aid clarity.) K12 calculates the cotangent of the bearing (which has to be converted to radians first):

=1/(TAN(RADIANS(J12)))

Cells L12 and M12 do the same thing for the angle and bearing at B:

=IF(G12 = "r",$G$6 – I12,$G$6 + I12)
=1/(TAN(RADIANS(L12)))

Finally, formulae in N12 and O12 calculate the eastings and northings of C, as in the equations given above:

=(($A$6*K12) – ($C$6*M12) – $B$6 + $D$6)/(K12 – M12)
=$B$6 + (N12 – $A$6)*K12

The three pairs of angles entered in rows 12–14 show the example given above and two points at 45° to the baseline, one on the right and one on the left.

   Note that this spreadsheet is constructed on the assumption that intersections will only be attempted for points which lie between north–south lines running through A and B:

Figure 5.5 Suggested limits for the location of points by intersection.

This not only simplifies the formulae, but it's good surveying practice.

Trilateration

Many people call this operation 'triangulation', because it involves making triangles, but strictly speaking 'triangulation' should involve measuring angles, and this technique measures the sides only. Here 'trilateration' is used, although it's a less common term, to distinguish it from what surveyors call 'intersection', since by common usage both methods are called triangulation.

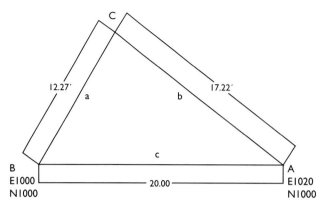

Figure 5.6 An example of trilateration.

In this example there is a baseline 20m long between points A and B, which have the co-ordinates shown. Point C has been measured as being 17.225m from A and 12.274m from B.

The first step in a trilateration calculation is in fact to work out the sizes of the angles in the triangle made by the three sides, using what are often called 'half-angle' formulae, all of which use a variable called 's':

$$S = \tfrac{1}{2}\,(a + b + c)$$

In this case, therefore,

$$
\begin{aligned}
S &= \tfrac{1}{2}\,(12.274 + 17.225 + 20) \\
&= \tfrac{1}{2}\,(49.499) \\
&= 24.7495
\end{aligned}
$$

There are three formulae which can be used to arrive at the values of the angles, one of which is:

$$\sin \tfrac{1}{2}A = \sqrt{\frac{(s - b)(s - c)}{bc}}$$

So in the above triangle angle A is:

$$\sin \tfrac{1}{2}A = \sqrt{\frac{(24.7495 - 17.225)(24.7495 - 20)}{17.225 \times 20}}$$

$$\sin \tfrac{1}{2}A = \sqrt{\frac{7.5245 \times 4.7495}{344.5}}$$

$\sin \frac{1}{2}A = \sqrt{0.103737627}$

$\sin \frac{1}{2}A = 0.322083261$

$\frac{1}{2}A = 18.78895856°$

$A = 37.57791712°$ (37°34′41″)

The formula for angle B is:

$$\sin \frac{1}{2}B = \sqrt{\frac{(s-a)(s-c)}{ac}}$$

$$\sin \frac{1}{2}B = \sqrt{\frac{(24.7495-12.274)(24.7495-20)}{12.274 \times 20}}$$

$\sin \frac{1}{2}B = \sqrt{0.241373583}$

$\phantom{\sin \frac{1}{2}B} = 0.491297856$

$\frac{1}{2}B = 29.42592164$

$B = 58.85184327°$ (58°51′07″)

The calculation now becomes an intersection of bearings, as the angles at A and B are known.

Bearing AC = 270 + 37°34′53″ = 307°34′53″
Bearing BC = 90 − 58°51′24″ = 31°08′36″

Easting of point C:

$$E_C = \frac{E_A \cot \alpha - E_B \cot \beta - N_A + N_B}{\cot \alpha - \cot \beta}$$

$$E_C = \frac{1020 \times -0.769586335 - 1000 \times 1.654887822 - 1000 + 1000}{-0.769586335 - 1.654887822}$$

$E_C = 1006.348$

Northing of point C:

$N_C = N_A + (E_C - E_A)\cot \alpha$

$N_C = 1000 + (1006.348 - 1020) - 0.769586335$

$N_C = 1010.506$

Trilateration using a spreadsheet

	A	B	C	D	E	F	G	H	I	J	K	L	M	N
1	Trilateration													
2														
3	length of baseline (side c):			20.000										
4	bg AB	270	bg BA	90										
5	easting A	1020	northing A	1000	easting B	1000	northing B	1000						
6														
7	side a	side b	s		sin half_A	A (degrees)	sin half-B	B (degrees)	l or r?	α	cot	β	cot	easting	northing
8	12.27	17.23	24.75		0.32	37.58	0.49	58.85	r	307.58	-0.77	31.15	1.65	1006.349	1010.504
9	9.97	12.5	21.24		0.21	23.98	0.26	30.64	r	293.98	-0.44	59.36	0.59	1008.577	1005.081
10	15.36	13.4	24.38		0.42	50.11	0.36	42.02	l	219.89	1.2	132.02	-0.9	1011.408	989.720

Figure 5.7 A spreadsheet used to calculate trilateration.

Here is an example of a spreadsheet solution to this trilateration problem.

The length of the baseline, bearings, co-ordinates and side lengths a and b have been entered from the keyboard. Cell C8 calculates the variable s:

=($D$3 + A8 + B8)/2

D8 calculates sin½A:

=SQRT((((C8–B8)*(C8–$D$3))/(B8*$D$3))
E8 calculates angle A in degrees:

=2*(DEGREES(ASIN(D8)))

F8 and G8 do the same thing for angle B:

=SQRT((((C8–A8)*(C8–$D$3))/(A8*$D$3))
=2*(DEGREES(ASIN(F8)))

Then the remaining cells contain the same functions as in the intersection spreadsheet:

I8   =IF(H8 = "r",$B$4 + E8,$B$4 – E8)
J8   =1/(TAN(RADIANS(I8)))
K8   =IF(H8 = "r",$D$4 – G8,$D$4 + G8)
L8   =1/(TAN(RADIANS(K8)))
M8   =(($B$5*J8) – ($F$5*L8) – $D$5+$H$5)/(J8 – L8)
N8   =$D$5 + (M8 – $B$5)*J8

Adjustment of levels

There is a tendency to assume, because modern methods of manufacture are so precise, and because the operation of a level is so simple, that measurements taken with a level will be 'correct', apart from the obvious degree of uncertainty associated with estimating fractions of a centimetre on the staff. There are, however, reasons why this assumption may not be true.

One, often neglected, is that the staff may not be straight. This may sound unlikely, but the very features which make a staff easy to manipulate on site – its small width and light weight, along with the other desirable feature, low cost – also make it vulnerable to damage, especially if handled carelessly. A serious bend in any one staff section would be likely to be noticed (it may even make it impossible to collapse the staff), but bending of the whole staff, perhaps by habitual carrying of the staff extended and in the horizontal position, is not unknown. Careful handling and visual inspection should avoid problems from this cause, along with the will to dispose of a staff which is no longer satisfactory, rather than keeping it at the back of the store for use in an emergency.

Another source of error is the failure to hold the staff vertically. Some types of staff are equipped with a small circular spirit level to assist in maintaining a vertical position, and it is possible to buy small devices with a circular level mounted in such a way that they can be clamped to the side of the staff by the hand. Hogg (1980, p.92) suggests that the use of such levels is unnecessary in ordinary levelling, though they are recommended for general use by others (e.g. Bannister *et al.*, 1998). Another way of avoiding errors caused by the slope of the staff is for the staff-holder gently to tilt the staff backwards and forwards along the line of sight, ensuring that it passes *through* the vertical position; the observer can then note the smallest reading on the staff, which will coincide with the staff being vertical. This does of course add to the time taken for each reading, and if the staff-holder allows the staff to wobble from side to side during the movement it can make observation more difficult, leading to a loss of accuracy and temper. It may be the case that if many (intermediate) levels are being taken over short distances from one instrument position errors caused by staff tilt can adequately be dealt with by a reasonable exercise of care on the part of the staff-holder, but if levels are being transferred over long distances, the instrument being moved often, more stringent precautions need to be taken.

When levels are being transferred, and the staff position is being used as both back- and foresight, care must be taken to choose a firm location for the staff, so that there is no danger of it sinking into soft ground, something which may go unobserved. If there are really no suitable locations, it is possible to use a *change plate*, which can be firmly fixed into the ground and will support the staff at the same elevation during the two reading operations.

'Assuming a tripod on firm ground with its legs well dug in, we can ignore the effects of tripod settlement' (Bannister *et al.*, 1998, p.92). If this situation always obtains, tripod settlement will indeed be insignificant, but it is still the responsibility of the surveyor to make sure that it does. Particularly in the case of excavations, perhaps, when a level is set up at the start of the day and left in place for intermittent use over a period of hours, there may be occasions when tripod settlement does become a problem, albeit one which may go undetected. In confined places, it may be difficult to set up the instrument in a position which isn't close to a thoroughfare, and apart from the immediate danger of the tripod being upset (especially if the confined space has led to the tripod being set up with the legs insufficiently far apart), the frequent passage of human feet and barrow-wheels close to the tripod feet may lead to differential settlement of the legs. The usual considerations of setting up the instrument should always be observed, even on awkward sites, and the tripod placed with its legs wide apart, feet well dug in on firm ground. If the only surface available is something as unyielding as concrete (often the case on urban sites), it's far better to go to the extra expense of buying a tripod stand (obtainable from about £40), into which the points of the feet are inserted, rather than trust to luck and assume that the legs won't slip.

When all these factors have been taken into consideration, there remains a more subtle one. A basic assumption about levels (and other instruments which have to be set up so that they are level) is that when a bubble is centred in a circular or tubular spirit-level, the line of sight through the telescope is also level. This is true when the spirit-level is in correct adjustment, but as Hogg notes (op. cit., p.93), although there is no very obvious reason why a level should go out of adjustment, they may nevertheless do so. Testing and adjusting a level is a simple process, and described in many books on surveying (e.g. Hogg, 1980; Bannister and Baker, 1994; Bannister *et al.*, 1998; Olliver and Clendinning 1978), but many archaeological surveyors seem reluctant to undertake it.

Figure 5.8 Method of checking the adjustment of a level.

To check the adjustment, create two marks (A and B) by driving pegs firmly into the ground between 50m and 100m apart, and set up the level midway between them. Now take readings to a staff placed on each point. If the level is correctly adjusted the line of sight will be horizontal, as shown by the solid line in the diagram. If there is maladjustment, the line of sight may be as indicated by the broken line, but since the level is midway between the two points the amount of error is the same for each reading, so the difference between them gives the true difference in height. The line AB is now extended, and the level moved to a position on the line as close to one of the marks as will still allow the telescope to focus on a staff held on it (shown as being to the left of point A). A reading is taken to the staff, and this can be taken as giving the correct height of the instrument above the point, since it is very close and errors of adjustment are likely to be small. With the height of the instrument known, it is now possible to work out what the correct staff reading at B *should* be. The staff is moved to point B, and, ignoring the spirit-level, the footscrews or other adjusting device are used to bring the horizontal cross-hair onto that value. The line of sight is now horizontal, and what remains is to adjust the *spirit-level*, so that the bubble is centred when, as now, the line of sight is horizontal. Exactly how this is done depends on the type of level being used. In older models, with a tubular spirit-level, there are usually small 'capstan' nuts at one end, the other end being pivoted, and by loosening one and tightening the other the tube can be adjusted. In automatic levels, there will be only a circular pond or bull's-eye level, which will have small screws placed around the perimeter.

Chapter 6

Surveying on a global scale

Satellite location

The use of satellites for establishing the location of points on the surface of the earth has been one of the revolutions in surveying. It might be argued that the first revolution was the discovery of the theories of geometry and trigonometry which made it possible to calculate or deduce quantities which would be very difficult to measure directly, for example the value for the circumference of the earth determined in the third century BC by Eratosthenes (Lewis, 2001, p.144). Perhaps the second was the appearance of instruments which could measure angles with great precision (Ramsden's telescopic theodolite of about 1785 could measure angles to a single second), and the third the development of electronic instruments which could determine distances with a similar degree of precision – first suggested as a technique in 1929, and coming into common use as a surveying tool in the 1980s (Bannister *et al.*, 1998). Satellite location doesn't require the surveyor to measure any angles or distances at all; co-ordinates are displayed instantly on a screen.

Inevitably, a system which demands so little of the surveyor (who should perhaps be called an observer) is itself extremely complex, and of course expensive, and like most complex expensive systems, and most uses of space technology, the origin of this system lies in the requirements of military planners. The satellite location system which is best known is GPS, the Global Positioning System, belonging to the United States Department of Defense.

It's usual to see this as a three-part system, consisting of the *space segment* (the satellites), the *control segment* (ground stations), and the *user segment* (the instruments used by surveyors). The satellites actually bear the name NAVSTAR (Navigation Satellite Timing and Range), the first of which was launched in 1978, though full implementation of GPS was delayed until 1993, partly as a result of the destruction of the space-shuttle *Challenger* in 1986. When using GPS, it's easy to forget that the instrument in your hand is only the very fringe of a web of technological complexity which is in some ways very fragile, and which depends for its continuation on not only the expenditure of very large amounts of money, but on global political stability. Although use of GPS has spread rapidly and widely into civilian activities, the system is designed for and controlled by the military, and there is no guarantee of its availability for other users.

GPS uses 24 satellites, orbiting the earth at a distance of 20,200km, each orbit taking 12 hours. At least 6 are 'visible' (to a receiver, of course they can't be seen by eye) from any point on the surface at all times. At least, this would be true if the earth was like a billiard-ball, and there were no objects on the surface to obstruct the signals.

The satellites are solar powered, with batteries to cover the periods of time when the sun is eclipsed from the position of the satellite. A vital requirement is the provision of accurate timing, and each satellite has four atomic clocks, two rubidium and two caesium. Signals are broadcast at two wavelengths, known as L_1 and L_2. The L_1 wavelength carries two code signals, the *precise* (P) code, which is restricted to military use, and the *coarse acquisition* (C/A) code, while L_2 has just the C/A code. Both wavelengths also broadcast a data message, concerning satellite position, time, and other system status information.

The *control segment* consists of five ground stations – a master station at Falcon Air Force Base in Colorado Springs, and four others at Ascension Island, Diego Garcia, Kwajalein, and Hawaii (all near the equator). Each station tracks the satellites and relays position information to the master station, where this is used to determine the precise position of each satellite; the onboard clocks are also compared with a master clock at Colorado Springs. Each satellite holds data about its position, which is broadcast in the message, but this is also updated every hour from the ground, giving the best possible position accuracy. Using the C/A code, it's possible to determine locations on the earth to within something like 10m, but for military reasons this accuracy was intentionally degraded, so that the simplest equipment could only obtain positions to within something like 100m. This technique of *selective availability* (SA) had two elements, *SA-dither*, whereby some of the satellite clocks were put out of phase by a certain amount, and *SA-epsilon* – each satellite broadcasting an incorrect position for itself. However, on 1 May 2000 the SA system was turned off, giving all users of GPS access to the more accurate positioning.

Finally, the *user segment* is what the user actually sees – the instrument in your hand. Essentially this consists of an antenna and receiver, which may be hand-held, mounted on a pole, in a backpack, or on a tripod. Along with these, there will of course be a data-logger and computing equipment.

There are two fundamental methods used to determine the distance between satellite and receiver – *pseudo-range* and *carrier-phase measurement*. Pseudo-range is the technique used by lower- and medium-range equipment, giving positions from about 10m to 'sub-metre'. The prefix 'pseudo' is used because the method depends on both accurate time measurement and synchronisation of the clocks in both satellite and receiver, the latter being impossible to achieve.

In outline, this is how it works. The satellite transmits a code signal (this is the C/A code), which repeats every millisecond; the receiver generates its own replica of this code. The receiver locks on to the satellite signal, and establishes the pattern of repetition. If the receiver were immediately adjacent to the satellite, since they both have clocks giving the same time (in theory) there would be no phase difference between the transmitted signal and that generated in the receiver, but since they are separated by thousands of kilometres, there is a difference in phase, and this is used to determine the time it has taken the signal to travel from the satellite, this then being converted into the distance (range), multiplying the time by the speed of light (the speed at which all electromagnetic radiation travels). This type of measurement is only possible using the coarse acquisition code, because of its short cycle; the precise code repeats every 38 weeks.

Since the positions of the satellites are known (being broadcast from the satellites themselves), having simultaneously obtained the distance to four or more satellites, the location of the receiver can be calculated by trilateration. In the case of the simplest instruments this location will be to about 10m, or perhaps a little less, partly depending on the disposition of the visible satellites. The GPS uses a Cartesian co-ordinate system called WGS84 (World Geodetic System), but most instruments are capable of converting these into local plane co-ordinates, which is much more convenient. Experiments carried out by the author have shown that if an instrument of the cheapest type is used to obtain co-ordinates for the same point several times over a period of about 30 seconds the reported positions will be contained by a circle of 5–10m diameter in most cases, but in at least one case (alongside a building which obscured a large part of the sky) the points covered an area 35m across. More complex equipment improves positioning accuracy by using a second receiver, whose position is already known. This receiver will be tracking the satellites itself, and calculating its position from their signals. The calculated position will differ from the known one by a certain amount, as a result of system errors (noise at the receiver, clock errors, and atmospheric effects), and provided the fixed receiver and the moving one are within a certain distance of each other (and therefore observing the same satellites), the effect of the errors will be the same in both locations, and can be used to improve the accuracy of the positions determined for the moving receiver. The fixed receiver has to broadcast this information continuously. In many countries beacon stations have been established to provide this service for purposes of navigation. The UK system is maintained by Trinity House (http://www.trinityhouse.co.uk), also responsible for lighthouses, and most of the beacons are in coastal locations, though recently two others have been constructed inland (Wormleighton in Oxfordshire, and Stirling in Scotland) as the demand for improved GPS accuracy has increased. In the United States there are many more beacons, and many others spread around the world, though coverage is patchy. In areas where suitable beacons aren't available, users can make use of commercial subscription systems which also provide differential GPS data (one example is the Landstar system from Thales, http://www.thalesresearch.com).

Even using data from fixed receivers, with pseudo-range measurement the accuracy of positioning is limited by the precision with which the receiver can align the two code patterns, and currently this means about ± 0.5m; not good enough for the provision of survey control points, but suitable for a number of applications. Many archaeological structures are rather poorly defined – earthworks, for example, and may be satisfactorily surveyed using instruments of this kind.

To achieve the highest accuracy, carrier phase measurement has to be used. In its principle of operation this is rather like distance measurement by EDM – it works by establishing the number of complete wavelengths of the transmitted signal between the satellite and receiver. The name results from the fact that it's necessary to strip off the binary code information which contains the data message. The technical details are quite complex, and a good description can be obtained from the University of Colorado, http://www.colorado.edu/geography/gcraft/notes/gps/gps_f.htm.

There are a number of ways in which carrier-phase measurement can be employed. One method uses *post processing*, in which data collected in the field by a roving receiver are compared at a later stage with those recorded by a master station at a known location, but the latest *real-time techniques* use two receivers in the field, one tripod-mounted to act as a master and in radio contact with the rover (or possibly several rovers at the same time). Five satellites have to be available for each measurement, rather than four, but the system can work with a distance of up to 10km between the receivers, and is rapid enough to be used in moving vehicles. Accuracy of positioning of the rover relative to the master or base receiver is to within a centimetre, so a survey of the average archaeological site could be carried out using just the real-time data and produce very satisfactory results. However, while the *relative* positions of the rover are known very precisely, the position of the base receiver isn't; it is receiving no differential information from any other receiver, and so has to rely on its own satellite observations to determine its location, and this can only be done to within about two metres. If the archaeological survey doesn't need to be precisely related to contemporary features of the landscape, the data generated in this way may be all that is required, but in many cases the whole survey will need to be more accurately located, and this is done by *post-processing*.

During the survey the base receiver can be made to record data from the satellites continuously for a period of hours, and this can subsequently be compared with data which have been recorded at known positions. In the UK the Ordnance Survey maintains a number of active GPS stations continuously recording satellite observations; for post-processing, a user can download from a web site data from the stations nearest to the survey area which relate to the period during which the base station was itself recording, and these are used to generate a high-accuracy position for the base station. The positions of the roving receiver during the whole survey are also adjusted as part of this process, so that every position in the survey will have the same absolute accuracy.

Once precise co-ordinates have been obtained for a control point, it is of course possible to use this point again, and when the base receiver is centred over it the precise co-ordinates can be entered from its keyboard, so that post-processing won't be needed again. There is in the UK another method of obtaining high-accuracy positions for base receivers, by means of the Ordnance Survey 'passive' GPS stations, of which there are about 900 (details are available from http://www.gps.gov.uk). These stations don't record any information, but their positions are very accurately known, and unlike the old triangulation pillars (which had to be placed in positions from which they had wide views of the landscape) they are located to be easy to access, often alongside roads. From the web site it is possible to find out which passive stations are close to the survey area and to look up the details of each (this includes sketch maps with distance measurements to prominent features, and in many cases photographs, which help to identify the precise location, and also an indication of whether the station can be reached by road vehicles). If a suitable passive station is available the base receiver can be centred over it, removing the need for post-processing. It may not be practical to leave the receiver on this station for a protracted period (often the passive stations are in very public places, and security becomes an issue), but it can be used to generate a precise position for a station which is close to the survey area, and which can then be occupied by the base instrument.

Everything said so far about satellite positioning has been in relation to 'GPS', which for most people is the same thing, but in fact there is another system, completely independent of GPS, but having a similar specification. GLONASS (Global

Navigation Satellite System) is the name of the Russian system (http://www.glonass-center.ru), which was constructed at the same time as the American one, and for the same military reasons. Where the NAVSTAR satellites orbit at just over 20,000km, the GLONASS units are at 19,100km, orbiting in 11hr 15min rather than 12 hours. Each GLONASS satellite also broadcasts on two wavelengths (again called L_1 and L_2), but these are different in each satellite. The master station is near Moscow, Golitsyno–2, and there are secondary stations around the world in areas which were formerly within the Soviet Union. On its own, GLONASS has five satellites visible at all times, and has better coverage than GPS in polar regions and below 50° latitude. Used in conjunction with GPS, there are 48 satellites, eleven of which can be seen at all times, and it might seem an obvious step to develop instruments which were capable of using both systems, but in fact this has only happened to a very limited extent, and most equipment uses GPS. In recent years there have been problems in maintaining the GLONASS system, and there are currently plans to replace the existing satellites with updated models (http://www.mosnews.com/news/2004/06/29/glonass.shtml).

These two global systems represent satellite navigation as it is now, but both were developed and are controlled by military authorities, and neither gives any guarantee that it will continue to be available to civilian users, despite the extent to which satellite positioning has become not only extremely useful but even essential to the safety of aircraft, for example. Partly as a result of this consideration, and also for political and financial reasons, a third global navigation system is planned by the European Union through the European Space Agency, called Galileo (http://www.esa.int/esaNA/galileo.html), and intended to come into operation in 2008. This will be dedicated to civilian use, and according to its designers it will exploit technological developments to produce a system which will be superior to either of the existing ones.

Ways of describing position

A discussion of the use of space-based location systems raises the subject of just how we can describe a position on the surface of the earth.

Anyone who has any sort of familiarity with map reading will also be familiar with the concept of map references using co-ordinates (sometimes called 'rectangular' or 'Cartesian' co-ordinates). The idea is that there is a point somewhere on the Earth's surface called the 'origin', and that the position of any other point can be described as being a number of metres east and a number of metres north of this point. (It doesn't have to be east and north, but this is conventional.) In the case of the maps of the UK produced by the Ordnance Survey this origin point is somewhere to the south-west of Cornwall, in the Atlantic Ocean. Extending north and east of this point is an imaginary grid of 100km squares, each one identified by a pair of letters, which can be used to give a rough location to any point within the UK. The city of Salisbury, for instance, lies within the square SU, the south-west corner of which is 400,000 metres east and 100,000 metres north of the origin. Not far from Salisbury, approximately to the north-east, is a burial mound known as Fussell's Lodge long barrow. Looking at a 1:50,000 scale map which contains both Salisbury and this barrow, it becomes obvious that there is also a grid of squares laid over it, this time with sides of 1000m, and the lines making up this grid are numbered at their ends. The information printed on the map tells you that if you want to describe the location of a point on the map you should take the line along the west side of its 1000m square and read the figures which are printed opposite to its north or south end, then take the line along the south side and read the figures printed opposite to its east or west end. Doing this for the barrow gives 19 and 32. The next instruction is to estimate how many hundreds of metres the point is from the west and south edges of the 1000m square; this gives 1 (or 2) and 5. The whole grid reference is therefore SU 191 325, and this is something which will be familiar to any UK archaeologist, or indeed any user of OS maps. It would be described as a 'six-figure' grid reference.

How many people who give references in this form think about what the figures actually mean? In some ways it doesn't matter, because to anyone who understands OS grid references they communicate useful information, but a fuller understanding is necessary if OS data are to be used effectively. Take '191'; it certainly doesn't stand for 'one hundred and ninety-one' of anything. Looking at the south-west corner of the whole map, there are some other figures which reveal the true meaning. The first figure written along the south side of the map (printed vertically, unlike the others) is 389000m, actually printed as $389000m$, which is the number of metres east of the OS grid origin. One thousand metres to the east is printed 90, then 91, standing for 390000 and 391000 metres. Figures follow up to 99, then the next one is 00. The '99' stands of course for 399000m, and since the major square divisions of the OS grid are 100km (100,000m), this means that we have reached the end of one (it's actually ST) and the beginning of another (SU). The '00' figure therefore actually stands for $400000m$. Going further east along the edge of the map, the figures continue to increment: 01, 02, 03, etc., until we reach 19, the line marking the west side of the square containing Fussell's Lodge barrow. This line, then, is $419000m$ east of the grid origin. In a similar way, it can be established that the line on the south side of the barrow's square is 132000m north of the origin. We can now add the estimated figures to each part of the grid reference, to give $419100m$ east and $132500m$ north. The convention of quoting references in the form SU 191 325 can save space, but it involves using numbers in a slightly odd way. Note also that in a purely numerical form both easting and northing end in '00' – they are correct to the nearest 100m, which means that this grid reference defines a 100m square, and every point within that square would have the same SU 191 325 reference, though if we had a larger-scale map we could give a longer reference, which could define a 10m (eight-figure), or even 1m (ten-figure) square (or come to that 0.1m or 0.01m).

Many people reading this may feel that the point is being laboured, and that everyone reading this book will already be familiar with the information. My excuse is that I am drawing attention to the complexity of something which *is* so familiar that most of the time we don't think about what it means.

The whole area covered by the OS National Grid is 700,000m by 1,300,000m, and this grid is conceived of as a plane. Convenient in many ways, as it makes it easy to define the relative positions of points on the ground in terms of 'metres east and metres north', but of course the surface of the Earth isn't flat, and while we can ignore this fact over distances of even several thousand metres, it can't be ignored over the whole OS grid area. How does this flat plane relate to the curved surface which actually exists?

Going back to the map sheet, there are some more figures printed along the edges, such as 'Lat 51°N' and 'Long 1°35'W'. These refer to another co-ordinate system altogether, and are what are called 'geographic co-ordinates'. They are of course the global co-ordinate system of latitude and longitude, measured in degrees north or south of the equator and east or west of an arbitrary line of longitude which for historical reasons is one passing through Greenwich in south-east England. The notional position from which these degrees are measured is the centre of the earth.

Going from a position on the earth's curved surface to a flat plane involves a mathematical process known as 'projection'. Imagined simply, this means devising a shape which can be made to fit round the earth (a cylinder, for example, which is used by the Ordnance Survey), and onto which points from the curved surface can be drawn. An analogy which is often used is to imagine a light source at the centre of a sphere round which the cylinder is wrapped; a point on the surface is marked by making a pin-hole, so that a beam of light will shine through the hole and make a spot on the cylinder, which can also be marked. This is done for as many points as required, then the cylinder is opened out to make a flat rectangle and the spots where the light beams touched the cylinder now have a projected position which can be described by measuring distances 'east' and 'north' of one corner of the rectangle. (Map projection is of course much more complex, and many more shapes than the cylinder can be used.) The projected positions of course are distorted representations of those on the spherical surface; you can't make a curved surface flat without distorting it. All maps – flat representations of a curved surface – are distortions of reality. Projections may be devised to maintain the shape of areas on the ground, but in that case the size of those areas must be distorted; size may be maintained, in which case shape must be distorted. Some projections (such as the famous Mercator projection) are designed to maintain true directions from one place to another (vital when navigating at sea), but then shape *and* size of areas must be distorted. Of course, the amount of distortion depends on the total size of the area being represented on the projected surface. The United Kingdom is a fairly small area of the earth's surface, and can be projected onto a single plane without introducing unacceptable distortions; large countries must use more than one projection (in the USA each state has at least one projection of its own, and most have more than one), and any map which depicts the whole world in one projection must have gross distortions in many parts. To take the example of the Mercator projection again, frequently used for producing rectangular maps of the whole world, this is a cylindrical projection in which the cylinder is deemed to touch the earth around the equator and to have its long axis running north–south. In a projection such as this distortion is zero at the equator and increases as you move north or south. Many people are aware that while on Mercator maps Greenland appears to be larger than Australia this is a reversal of the truth; Australia is the larger, but because Greenland is further from the equator its size is more distorted. Antarctica represents even greater distortion; while the continent is roughly circular it appears as a strip of land running along the southern edge of the map, and the south pole – a point – appears as a line. In fact, a modification of the simple cylindrical projection is needed even to show the pole at all. This may make the Mercator projection seem less than useful, but the problem lies not with the projection but with the size of the area being mapped. Mercator projections are used for mapping many parts of the earth, and very successfully. The Ordnance Survey of the UK uses what is called a 'transverse' Mercator projection because in this case the cylinder is oriented east–west, and touches the surface along the line of longitude 2° west of Greenwich (this line is called the 'central meridian').

Where does this fit in with the subject of archaeological surveying, where most sites are no more than some tens of metres across? For surveys conducted using tapes, compasses, theodolites or total stations, a consideration of the size and shape of the earth and its projection onto a plane surface may indeed be irrelevant, but as soon as the surveyor begins to make use of satellite location (GPS) even using the simplest equipment he or she is tapping into a system of observation which looks at the world from a distance of 20,000km, and from here it looks very different from the view we have on the surface.

(Before going further, it is worth mentioning that English Heritage has produced, in association with the Ordnance Survey, a very useful guide to the use of GPS in archaeology, which would also be a valuable introduction to anyone wanting to use and understand the subject of satellite navigation (*Where on Earth are We?*, English Heritage, 2003). This can be obtained from English Heritage (e-mail to customers@english-heritage.org.uk) or downloaded as a pdf file from the Ordnance Survey web site (http://www.ordnancesurvey.co.uk).)

The first major consideration in the construction of any global mapping or navigation system is the shape of the earth's surface. A photograph taken from space shows it to be something very much like a sphere, but careful measurements have shown (long before the age of space fight) that the equatorial diameter exceeds the polar diameter. This would imply that the earth is a 'spheroid' or 'ellipsoid', a shape made by rotating an ellipse about one of its axes. Many attempts have been made to calculate the diameters of the ellipsoid, based on measurements made in different parts of the world, and these have produced different results, because the earth isn't a perfect ellipsoid any more than it is a perfect sphere, and in national mapping schemes the practice has been to choose the ellipsoid which is the best fit to the part of the earth being mapped. In the case of the OS survey of the UK the reference ellipsoid which has been used is that calculated by Airy in 1830, and based on this was generated the system of plane co-ordinates which most people call the National Grid, known more formally as Ordnance Survey Great Britain 1936 (OSGB36). This allows two-dimensional positions to be defined, and it is supplemented by another system of measuring elevations to give the third dimension. The latter is 'ODN', 'Ordnance Datum Newlyn', and uses as a reference the mean sea-level observed at Newlyn in Cornwall between 1915 and 1921. This datum was manifested through the existence of physical markers ('bench-marks') on solid structures such as buildings, which were also marked (along with their elevations) on OS maps. All elevation values on OS maps of mainland Britain, whether contours, spot-heights or bench-mark values, are related to ODN, although there are other datums used for the Isle of Man, Shetland, Orkney, St Kilda, the Outer Hebrides and the Scilly Isles (English Heritage, 2003). This multiplicity of datums reflects the fact that even over such a relatively small area as the UK, a universal datum can't be applied. (In fact, modifications also had to be made to the OSGB36 in the region of St Kilda in order to keep distortions to within the specified limits.) The physical bench-marks have not, for the most part, been rigorously checked since the 1970s, and can no longer be relied on for precise work, since movement of the bench-mark may have occurred, but heights can now be determined using GPS. It's also interesting to note that while most people who were aware of them thought of bench-marks as being at least semi-permanent, in fact they (along with every other point on the earth's surface) can move up and down (relative to the centre of the earth) by as much as a metre in a day, under the influence of the tidal effects caused by the sun and moon (Leica Geosystems, 2003).

The standard way of referring to the position of any point on the ground within the UK is still to give three dimensions in metres, two (eastings and northings) referring to distances from the origin of the OSGB36 co-ordinate system, and one (height) being relative to ODN. GPS, however, being a global system, has to use a global system of reference. The traditional system of latitude and longitude was based on observations of astronomical bodies. This could yield precise results, but called for lengthy and careful observations and some complex mathematics (Pugh, 1975; Allen *et al.*, 1968). GPS uses something called the World Geodetic System 1984 (WGS84), an internationally agreed global framework of co-ordinates within which points are located by values of latitude, longitude and 'ellipsoid height'. The latter is a vertical datum like ODN, but instead of being related to a physical phenomenon like average sea-level it refers to a mathematically defined ellipsoid surface, so that ellipsoid height may differ considerably from ODN or any other national vertical datum. In fact, WGS84 values of latitude and longitude are different from those defined astronomically as well, though not by very large amounts (up to a few hundred metres), but this is only a matter of convention. There is no absolute way in which the equator or the Greenwich meridian is 'zero', these are arbitrary values and any others would do just as well (Leica Geosystems, op. cit.). It has been found convenient for the WGS84 system to resemble the traditional latitude and longitude so that, for instance, 54°N 1°W refers to a similar location in both systems, but obviously for any accurate kind of work it is essential to know which is being used.

WGS84 co-ordinates are what are produced by any GPS instrument, but any GPS device, even the simplest, can display or record co-ordinates in another reference system, depending where on the earth the receiver is. In the UK the device can display OSGB36 eastings and northings and ODN heights, for example. There is a problem, though, with converting from WGS84 (based on mathematics) to any system which refers to positions of things on the physical surface of the earth, and that relates to the fluid nature of that physical surface. The continents are constantly moving with respect to each other, and the UK moves with respect to the WGS84 datum by about 25mm per year (English Heritage, op. cit.), too much to be ignored by precise surveying. Fortunately, while the UK is moving in this way so is the rest of Europe, and it has been possible to devise another reference system to cover this whole area, within which co-ordinates don't change. This is the European Terrestrial Reference System 1989 (ETRS89), and it is this, not WGS84, which is the basis for the Ordnance Survey national system of GPS location. Most other countries in Europe also use ETRS89.

This potentially confusing array of reference systems reflects the fact that the earth is a complex and dynamic system, and that no one global co-ordinate framework can be adequate for all purposes. The required degree of accuracy is a governing factor. If a position needs to be known only to the nearest metre (or worse) GPS co-ordinates in WGS84 can be converted to OSGB36 plane co-ordinates without introducing unacceptable error, but for greater accuracy ETRS89 must be used, and the user of GPS equipment for anything more than low-accuracy work must be aware of the differences. UK users of survey-grade (one centimetre) GPS equipment will be using OS data to correct their observed locations anyway, either by downloading RINEX (Receiver Independent Exchange Format) data from active GPS stations or by placing their reference receiver on one of the passive stations, and in this case the user will be obtaining ETRS89 co-ordinates for all their survey points, and these can be converted to OSGB36 eastings and northings using the Ordnance Survey Definitive Transformation (OSTN02) and to heights above mean sea-level with the National Geoid Model (OSGM02). The latter is a model which relates GPS ellipsoid heights to those measured from sea-level. Anyone in the UK who is buying or hiring survey-grade GPS equipment will also be acquiring software to process the data, and will need to be advised on the specific use of both hardware and software by the supplier, but they must be aware of, and be sure that their system is making use of, not only WGS84, but ETRS89, and OSTN02 and OSGM02 if they are converting co-ordinates to OSGB36.

The abundance of information of which the user of high-accuracy GPS needs to be aware may seem daunting, but while it needs to be included in a book of this kind it is information which may hardly touch the lives of many successful archaeological surveyors. The average archaeological site is extremely small compared with the size of the earth, and simple assumptions, such as the earth being flat except when we can see that it isn't, will serve quite well. We must seek to produce accurate surveys, but what matters most is the relative accuracy with which the shapes, sizes and relationships of archaeological features are expressed, and this accuracy can be achieved even using simple equipment. The location of the whole 'site' can be defined much less precisely without seriously damaging the whole of the work. A single-receiver GPS location of one survey point, accurate to within a few metres, and a compass bearing defining north to within a degree or so, will enable the site to be plotted acceptably on a map base at a scale of 1:10,000. In most cases this will be more accurate than measuring offsets from features such as field boundaries, which may not in reality bear much resemblance to the infinitely thin line with which they are shown on the map, although even this information is usable, as is a compass resection, provided enough landscape features can be identified. Higher-accuracy GPS really becomes a benefit when work extends over large areas, or when time is of the essence, in the commercial world of archaeology or in special cases where work has to be completed rapidly, as with the inter-tidal zone where the archaeological material may only be exposed for short periods and leaving site markers is impractical.

Alternative co-ordinate systems

Anyone with sufficient resources, and sufficient will, can create their own co-ordinate system, to cover a small area (which is easy) or a very large one (much more difficult and expensive). In February 2000 *The Washington Post* published an article recalling the time in the nineteenth century when the American government created its own system with a zero meridian running through the US Naval Observatory on 24th Street in Washington (see http://www.surveyhistory.org/attitude_and_longitude1.htm). This failed as an alternative to the existing meridians through Greenwich and Paris for navigators, but was used by land surveyors, so that the prominently square boundaries of many western states are all designed to be in round numbers from the American Meridian at 24th Street. The eastern border of Wyoming is exactly 27° west of

24th Street, that of Arizona is 32° west. The American Meridian was abandoned in 1884, when the Greenwich Meridian was accepted as the international standard. Another co-ordinate system devised in the United States has, however, continued in use, and it's one with which all surveyors should be familiar, the Universal Transverse Mercator system (UTM).

The UTM system

Surveyors working in the UK, the United States, or a number of other countries, will be operating in an environment in which high-accuracy surveys have been carried out and where up to date digital data sets are available, within which surveys of a scale suitable to archaeology can conveniently be fixed. The digital maps may themselves be used as a source of co-ordinate information, or co-ordinates in the local grid system may be calculated by conversion from GPS data. This is not the situation everywhere in the world, however. In some countries there may be no digital map data available (even in western Europe digital data for some countries have only become available in the last few years), either because they don't exist at all, or because the authorities don't *make* them available for sale. In others, even paper maps may be hard to acquire at scales useful for survey work, or the maps which do exist may not have any co-ordinate information printed on them, or this information may be inaccurate. Locating your survey within the national survey system may be very difficult in these circumstances.

The use of GPS is of course of great importance if you are working anywhere away from a readily accessible national co-ordinate system. Using survey-grade equipment the whole of your survey can be conducted with the satellite data, and the fact that your co-ordinates are in WGS84 latitude and longitude rather than grid metres doesn't really matter. The problem occurs if you are using simple GPS devices to obtain co-ordinates for just a small number of points and the rest of the detail is to be captured using other methods. It isn't at all easy to work in latitude and longitude over distances of a few hundred or thousand metres. For this reason, long before the advent of satellite navigation, a grid system was designed to cover the whole of the earth's surface, and this is known as the Universal Transverse Mercator (UTM) grid. The original use of this system, like many mapping systems, was military, but it was adopted after World War II for the intensive mapping programmes which were taking place in various parts of the world (Olliver and Clendinning, 1978).

As already discussed, it isn't possible to have a single projection system for the whole world without introducing huge distortions over most of the area, and the UTM doesn't attempt this. It uses a transverse Mercator cylindrical projection, with the axis running east–west, using 60 different central meridians to create 60 zones each covering 6° of longitude and extending from 80° south to 80° north. The central meridian of each zone is in the centre (this may sound obvious, but the central meridian of the *projection* wouldn't necessarily have to be in the centre of the grid zone, though of course this is the best arrangement since distortion increases as you move away from the central meridian either east–west or north–south). To avoid negative easting co-ordinates the central meridian of each zone is assigned an easting of 500,000m. As far as northings are concerned the zones are each divided into two parts. In the northern, the equator is zero, and co-ordinates increment northwards; in the southern, the equator is assigned a value of 10,000,000 and co-ordinate values decrease as you go south. This means that in each zone the same co-ordinate location can occur in both north and south parts, so the hemisphere must be specified. The zone numbers start at 1 in the Pacific Ocean 180° east (or west) of Greenwich (which is itself on the boundary between UTM Zones 30 and 31). Sometimes a further subdivision of the zones is employed, into segments 8° from north to south, making a total of 20 in each zone, and these divisions are designated by letters, beginning with C in the southernmost and continuing to X in the north. A further subdivision into 100,000m squares is also used, with two-letter designations, constituting the Military Grid Reference System (MGRS).

The UTM can be very useful, but care is needed in its use, especially in areas which cross zone boundaries.

For a normal size of archaeological survey it should be satisfactory to use GPS co-ordinates output as UTM metres (even simple instruments will do this) for, say, the ends of a baseline, and then to make this the basis of your survey in which you measure co-ordinates and distances in metres as usual. If you only have a very basic GPS, and hence locations to within several metres, it may be better to get co-ordinates for a single point and use a compass bearing to obtain the direction of north, or to get a bearing for a line whose ends are sited as appropriate for your survey. If local mapping doesn't give you any information about how to make an allowance for magnetic variation and so determine the direction of true north, it is possible to obtain global information about magnetic variation from a web site run by Ed Williams at http://williams.best.vwh.net/magvar.html, or to download a simple program which will run on your own PC to do the same thing.

There may be circumstances in which you have co-ordinates for an existing point in latitude and longitude, and wish to convert this to UTM but don't have GPS available. A very useful spreadsheet has been created by Professor Steven Dutch of the University of Wisconsin-Green Bay http://www.uwgb.edu/dutchs/UsefulData/UTM-Formulas.HTM which will perform this calculation (as well as UTM to latitude/longitude).

Chapter 7

Using CAD software

There are many different CAD packages available today, some commercial, some which can be downloaded from an internet site at no cost. Some of them are intended for very specific purposes, such as designing gardens or electrical circuits, and may be difficult to employ more generally; others have a limited set of facilities. As with all other kinds of software, developments are rapid and difficult to predict, and the potential user has to make judgements about the suitability of any particular product, especially if significant cost is involved. The instructions given here relate to *IntelliCAD*, the closest approach I have been able to find at affordable cost to what has become the 'de facto industry standard', AutoCAD. As far as possible, descriptions will be of generic facilities, so that individuals may have a chance to adapt them to other software. (A relatively recent arrival in the free software arena is *A9CAD*, from A9TECH of Redmond, in Washington USA, web site http://www.a9tech.com/, a capable package which supports many AutoCAD commands, and works with the AutoCAD dwg file format, but in its present version it doesn't offer all the facilities which are really needed to handle survey data.) This is a brief introduction to some of the basic facilities of CAD; more details are given in the case studies.

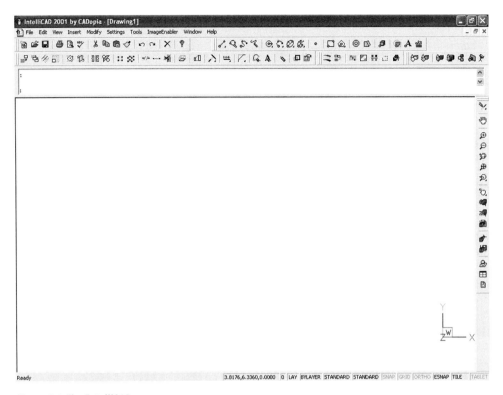

Figure 7.1 The IntelliCAD screen.

The CAD screen has several elements. Across the top, as in most software, is a menu of commands, below which is a toolbar with buttons which give access to a range of functions. In CAD packages there are usually a very large number of functions for drawing and modifying various kinds of objects, far too many to be accommodated on a single toolbar, and so others exist in the background, and can be called onto the screen as required. To do this, right-click the mouse over an existing toolbar to see a list of all those available. How many toolbars you can have active at any one time depends on the size and resolution of your screen.

Below the toolbar is the largest section of the screen, the drawing area, and between the two is another space, where commands may be typed using the keyboard. It isn't necessary to click the mouse in this area to activate it; anything typed will appear there automatically, whatever else is happening at the time. When carrying out a drawing operation, it will often be the case that the user has a choice of several ways to proceed – using the menu, clicking a tool button, or typing a command. In what follows I will indicate what seems to me to be the best way to operate, though after their own experiences individuals may well differ.

Co-ordinates

The drawing area (and indeed an infinitely large area around it) is covered by a co-ordinate grid, in the same way that any piece of landscape is associated with a co-ordinate system. Co-ordinate values can be specified as positive or negative, and to any desired degree of precision. Angles and distances can also be entered, again as precisely as is appropriate.

This infinite co-ordinate field is known as the World co-ordinate system, but one of the great strengths of CAD is its ability to create any number of other co-ordinate systems to suit the user's purposes. Imagine the case of a traverse control network, with many 'legs', and following a complex route, perhaps through the buildings of an urban landscape. Any point on the traverse could be made the origin of a new system, with the adjacent leg being the horizontal axis. Points of detail can then be located by specifying *x* and *y* distances from the origin of this new system.

When plotting the results of a survey the surveyor has a choice of how to proceed. Elsewhere it has been argued that the most precise results may be obtained by calculating co-ordinates from field measurements of angle and distance; this is likely to be the most efficient method, as will be described below, but a CAD package can be used as a sophisticated and highly accurate way of plotting angle and distance directly.

A simple drawing example

A survey has been based on a control structure created using steel tapes. The first measurement was the length of a line between two points called A and B, and this line is taken to be running east–west, the co-ordinates of A (the western end) being E1000 N1000; the length of the line is 28.56m.

Click on the **line** tool, or type **line** and press **enter**. The prompt becomes:

    Start of line:

Type 1000,1000 (no spaces) followed by the **enter** key to locate one end of the line at A. A line appears connecting point A to the mouse pointer, and the prompt becomes

    Angle/Length/<End point>:

mirrored in a pop-up menu (called **Line**), which has options

    Angle Length Cancel

It would be possible to work out the co-ordinates of point B (1028.56,1000) and type these in, but it's often more useful to be able to give the position of one point relative to another, so instead type

    @28.56,0   <enter>

which means 'starting from the last point drawn, move 28.56m east and 0m north'. The line will be drawn, but the command remains active for the drawing of more lines, and the prompt and the menu will have changed; the menu has

    Angle/Length/Follow/Undo/<End point>:

while the menu has a different command, Done, as the last one. End the line by right-clicking the mouse or pressing Done in the menu box. It may be that the line isn't visible in the drawing area, so press the **zoom extents** tool button ⊕ .

The next survey point, C, has been located by tie measurements of 19.98m from A and 33.02m from B, while point D is 32.03m from A and 11.91m from B. These need to be plotted next. In a manual drawing the procedure would be to create arcs centred on the two points A and B with radii equivalent at the plotting scale to the tie distances. The IntelliCAD version being used has various tools for drawing arcs, but not one which allows you to specify the centre from which the arc is drawn and its radius. Instead the circle command has to be used, with the option **circle-center-radius**, the first circle tool on the toolbar. To begin drawing the first circle, centred on A, click on this tool, or type

    Circle <enter>

The prompt options are

    2point/3point/radTanTan/Arc/Multiple/<Center of circle>:

with the last being the default, as usual. The centre of the circle needs to be exactly at point A, and this is where one of the useful facilities of CAD can be employed. Before trying to click the mouse on point A, *double*-click on the **ESNAP** button at the bottom of the screen (OSNAP in AutoCAD). This opens the Drawing Settings dialogue with the Coordinate Input tab, and here you will find **Entity snap modes**. 'Snapping' in CAD means connecting one drawing object *exactly* to some part of an existing entity, and since point A is at one end of the line already drawn check the **Endpoint** box and click **OK**. The mouse pointer should now show an additional mark like a long pin, and when you click the mouse with the pointer near to the end of the line at A the snapping facility will ensure that the point selected becomes exactly the end of the line, not just a point somewhere near it. Having clicked on this point, the prompt will offer

    Diameter/<Radius>:

At which you can type **19.98**, and the circle will be drawn.

Now repeat this sequence using point B and the radius 33.02. Notice that when you have specified the centre point, the prompt line will show the last value used for a radius (i.e. 19.98); if you wanted to use this again you could just press **enter**, but since you don't just type the number 33.02.

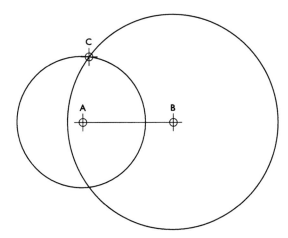

Figure 7.2 Initial plotting of a simple survey using CAD software.

You will now have two circles, which of course intersect at two points; it's up to the surveyor to know which of these is the right one, just as it would be if the survey were being plotted on paper. Provided the field notes are adequate and the locations of the survey points have been appropriately chosen with respect to each other, there shouldn't be any real difficulty about the choice.

The next step is to draw a line between point A and point C. Give the line command, and make the first point on it A. The next point is at the intersection of the two plotted circles, and to make sure the point is located exactly we need to use the ESNAP tool again, this time clicking on the **Intersection** option, which will add another shape to the mouse pointer, this time a circle with a point on it; click the mouse on the (correct) intersection between the two circles to complete the line.

To satisfy yourself that the new line really does connect to the end of the original line and the intersection of the circles, use the **zoom window** tool to zoom in close to the relevant points. When doing this to the intersection you may notice an odd effect. The parts of the circles you can see may not look like circles at all, but straight line segments, and the end of the new line may not appear to connect to the intersection point. This is to do with the way the screen has been re-drawn, and if you type the regen (regenerate) command the circles will assume their correct shape and the new line should connect properly.

When the line has been plotted the circles have no further use and can be deleted. Click on each one in turn (the solid line symbol will change to a broken one to indicate that they have been selected) and press the **delete** key on your keyboard. There may be a few dots left on the screen in the position of the deleted circles; these are not part of the drawing and will disappear on their own in the end, but they can be removed immediately by typing **redraw** or **regen**, or using the redraw tool.

Next, repeat these steps to create a new point (D) and draw lines joining it to point B, and point C to point D.

When the lines have been constructed and the second set of circles deleted, the drawing should look like this:

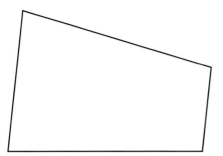

Figure 7.3 Four lines plotted using CAD.

This represents the lines between the survey points, but we may also actually want to plot the points themselves, and this gives an opportunity to explore the subject of CAD **layers**. As explained elsewhere layers can be used to group drawing objects together, so that they can be given different properties (colour, for instance) or be made visible of invisible as required. Everything drawn so far has been included in the default layer **0** (zero), and the name of the layer appears at the bottom of the screen in a box to the right of the one which shows the co-ordinates of the current cursor position. Next to it, again to the right, are two other boxes, both containing the word **BYLAYER**. The first of these indicates the current drawing colour, the second the current linetype, and both are by default set to be those which apply to the layer (i.e. zero). It's possible to set a layer to have a particular colour, which will then apply to all objects on that layer, although individual objects can be selected and given a different colour, and the same applies to line types.

First of all, create a new layer to hold symbols for the four points A–D.

Double-click on the **0** box at the bottom of the screen, which will open the **IntelliCAD Explorer – Layers** dialogue. This will show that there is one layer, called 0, that its colour is white, and its linetype **continuous**. There are other attributes as well, with which we are not concerned at the moment. Click the **New** tool button at the top left of the box. Another line is added, for a layer called **NewLayer**, colour **white**. The layer name is open for editing (or if it isn't, double-click on it), so type a new name (perhaps 'points') and press **enter**. Double-click on the layer colour, and choose a suitable one from the 256 available.

The original layer 0 has a tick next to its name, showing that it is **current** – i.e. any new objects will be added to this layer. Make sure that the name 'points' (or whatever you have called it) is highlighted, then click on the tick symbol on the toolbar, which will make this new layer the current one. (Alternatively, right-click on the layer name, and select **current** from the menu which appears.)

Close the Explorer dialogue box.

To create a point, type **point**, or use the point tool. The prompt changes to

Settings/multiple/<Location of point>:

For the first point, click the mouse anywhere on the screen, and you will see that the default point symbol is not necessarily going to be useful, being the smallest possible dot. To change this, use the commands

Tools | Drawing Settings

and click the **Entity Creation** tab. In the field labelled **Change settings for:** select the option **Points,** which will produce an array of point symbols from which you can select a new one. Click **OK.**

Give the point command again, and place symbols at the four points defined by the lines you have already drawn. This time, after giving the command type **m** at the prompt to choose the multiple points option, or click the **Multiple points** in the menu box, so that you can position all four points without having to give the command again.

Depending on the point symbol you have chosen, your drawing may now look something like this:

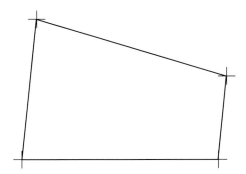

Figure 7.4 Lines and points plotted in CAD.

Because the lines and points are on different layers, we can choose to display them both together, or individually, by turning them on or off, or **freezing** and **thawing** the layers. Double-click on the **current layer** box at the bottom of the screen, and open the Explorer dialogue. Along with the names of the layers are their attributes, one of which is labelled **On/Off,** currently set to **On** for both of them. Click on the word 'On' which is against the name of layer zero, and it will change to 'Off'. Close the dialogue box. The drawing now looks like this:

Figure 7.5 Drawing with the 'lines' layer turned off.

Open the Explorer again, by clicking on the current layer box, and click on 'Off' against layer zero to make it 'On'. Look at the attributes of the layers again; one of them appears to be **All . . .**, but if you were to expand the name field (there's no need to actually do this) you would see that it really says **All Viewports** (viewports are a feature of CAD software that allow multiple views of the same model, but they won't be discussed any further here). The settings in this field look like **Tha . . .**, but again this is a truncation, this time of **Thaw**. If you click on this word it will change to **Fro(zen)**, and if you then close the dialogue the frozen layer will have disappeared. There are technical differences between turning a layer off and freezing it, but they aren't important at the moment.

The last thing to do to this simple drawing is to add some text labels to the points. To add a simple piece of text (in this case just one letter), the command **text** can be used; for larger amounts, **mtext** allows the entry of multiline text, and both commands are replicated on the toolbar. Use the **text** command, which produces a range of options at the prompt:

Text: Style/Align/Fit/Center/middle/Right/justify/<Start point>:

Just click the mouse at the point where you want the text to appear. This will change the prompt to

Height of text <1.5>:

You can set the height of the text by typing a new number (the units will be the same as the drawing, so '5' would produce text 5m high), but the mouse pointer is also now anchored to the text insertion point, so you can specify the text height by moving the mouse until the line is as long as you like. In this drawing a height of 2 might be appropriate. The next prompt is

Rotation angle of text <0°>:

Which you can accept by just pressing **enter,** and then you will be invited to enter the **text** itself. The text produced will be of a rather crude appearance, being the sort that was designed many years ago to be drawn by plotters which used liquid ink or ball-point pens, and when more complex fonts meant a large overhead in plotting time. Other fonts can be produced by using the commands:

Settings | Explore Text styles

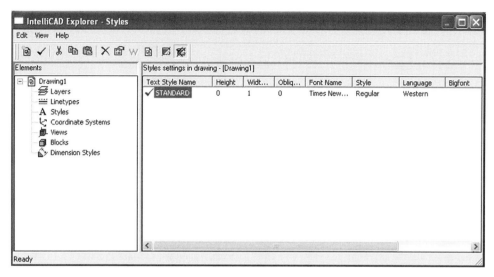

Figure 7.6 IntelliCAD text styles window.

Initially there is only one style visible, STANDARD. To create a new one, click on the **New Item** icon (extreme left of the toolbar), or use **Edit | New | Style**.

'NewStyle1' appears on the right-hand side, with a series of attributes (height, width, etc.), which don't have to be filled in; the **Font Name** will still be **txt.shx**, but a double-click on this item brings up a list of available windows fonts. A **right-click** on the **Text Style Name**, followed by **Properties**, brings up the **Style Properties** dialogue box, in which a new font can be selected, and where a sample of the font will appear. Right-clicking on **Text Style Name** also allows you to rename it, or make it current.

txt.shx   Poor Richard
Times New Roman   *Vivaldi*

Figure 7.7 Some text styles.

This is a small selection of text styles which may be available.

Printing a CAD drawing can be a complex process, involving multiple views of the same data, perhaps at different scales, on the same page. Obtaining a single view at a specific scale, however, isn't such a problem. In IntelliCAD the commands

File | Print . . .

Bring up this dialogue box

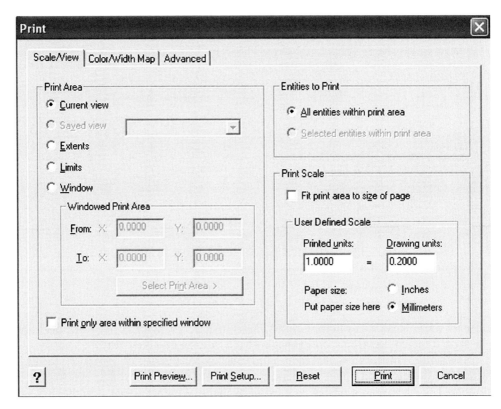

Figure 7.8 IntelliCAD print dialogue.

To print the current contents of the screen, leave **Current view** checked (the default). Under **Print Scale**, checking the box **Fit print area to size of page** would do what it suggests, making the drawing as big as possible given the size and shape of the page. (Clicking **Print Setup** would give access to the usual Windows controls for changing the printer, paper orientation, etc.) Usually, in the context of a survey drawing, a specific scale would be required, and this is slightly complicated, but only slightly. There isn't a window into which to type '1:500' as might be expected, but instead a relationship between drawing and printing units has to be created. In the **User Defined Scale** area are two fields labelled **Printed units** and **Drawing units**, and below these options of Inches or Millimetres for the page units. Either type is acceptable as a way of describing the page size, but assuming the survey to have been conducted using metres, the option millimetres is the most convenient to use. An equation of one printed unit to one drawing unit (1mm = 1m) would give a scale of 1:1000, while the figures shown above, 1mm = 0.2000m, represent 1:200. For any other scale, take the desired figure and divide it by 1000; e.g. for a scale of 1:5000 enter 1 printed unit = 5 drawing units, or for 1:750 1 printed unit = 0.75 drawing units.

Clicking **Print Preview** will show you what the output will look like, while clicking the **Advanced** tab gives access to two other useful facilities:

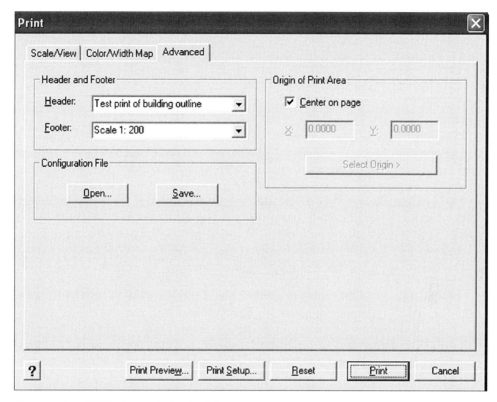

Figure 7.9 IntelliCAD advanced print facilities.

The **Center on page** option gives a better balance than the default, which locates the drawing in the lower-left part of the page. The **Header** and **Footer** fields can be used to enter text which is to appear at the top and bottom of the page. In addition to free text there are some standard options such as date, date and time, user name, etc.

Clicking **Print** produces the hard copy.

As stated above, this is a very simple approach to what can be a much more sophisticated process.

Photographic surveying using CAD

Apart from their general usefulness in recording landscapes, buildings and other structures, photographs contain a great deal of information about the relative positions of objects, and in some circumstances this can be recovered and used to produce plans of things which are too difficult, time-consuming or hazardous to survey in a traditional way. Photographic surveying has been a recognised technique for many years, at least since 1895 (Deville, 1895; Atkinson, 1995). The method has quite a lot to offer, and perhaps deserves more attention than it gets. Certainly the advent of CAD software and digital cameras has opened up new possibilities for it.

Any photograph contains information about the relative directions from the observer to the objects which appear in the photograph. If photographs of the same objects are taken from two locations, and if they can be correctly oriented with respect to each other, it's possible to project a line from each observer position through an object in the photographs and form an intersection which gives the position of that object. This technique has been used in standard surveying practice, and special *photo-theodolites* were constructed to enable very precisely oriented photographs to be produced, though these were very heavy and expensive and seem not to have been used much. In fact, it's quite possible to use ordinary cameras, and while the results may not be enormously accurate they can be good enough to provide approximate locations and extents of objects of interest, especially when time is short, or when conditions are difficult or dangerous. Wright (1982) gives details of using photographs to augment plane table surveys, and Wright and Dahl (1995) show how the technique was applied to the survey of glaciers in Greenland, using a theodolite and a popular make of 35mm camera. Atkinson (1946) also discusses the use of photographs in plotting archaeological features in difficult locations (such as pits exposed in quarry faces). The camera has to be used on a tripod, and made as level as possible, and the centre of the photograph must be defined by a recognisable object whose location is known or can be determined. Some reflex cameras are capable of being fitted with special focusing screens on which a graticule of some sort has been imposed, and this makes it fairly easy to direct the centre of view to a particular point. Others (especially the more modestly priced digital cameras) may have a simpler pointing device, often consisting of four lines, two vertical and two horizontal, in the shape of a cross, but with the ends of the lines not touching.

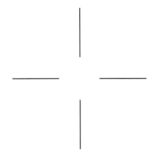

Figure 7.10 A typical pointing device in a camera viewfinder.

In a case like this it will be advisable, if at all possible, to choose an object with a vertical component to be the reference for the centre of the photograph (part of a building, for example).

Before photographs can be used for this purpose, some information about the camera has to be obtained first, in order to establish exactly where the observer position is in relation to the photographic image. This position is also known as the projection centre of the photograph, and Wright (op. cit.) describes a technique for finding it when working with photographic prints and a plane table (in all the cases referred to above photographic prints were used). The camera is set up on a tripod, as level as possible (a small spirit level balanced on the the camera can be used for this, though some more sophisticated tripods have spirit levels built in, and levels can also be obtained which fit the camera's flash shoe). A photograph is taken of a number of clearly identifiable objects which are distributed somewhere close to the horizontal line running through the middle of the print; Wright suggests that the easiest way to do this is to take a photograph across a lake, in which case objects close to the shore will also be close to the centre line of the photograph. A plane table is also set up at this point, and the directions to these objects are plotted on tracing paper or drawing film. When an enlarged print has been produced the plot of the lines is placed over it and moved around until the lines all lie over their respective objects. (This will be familiar to archaeological air-photograph plotters who use the 'paper-strip' method.) The point where the lines converge now indicates the location of the projection centre, and a line drawn from this point to touch the centre line of the photograph at right-angles defines what is known as the 'principal point' of the photograph. In traditional film cameras the principal point usually isn't, as might be expected, the centre of the photograph as defined by lines running between the mid-points of opposite sides (Wright explains that this is a result of having to accommodate the film-winding mechanism inside the camera). Atkinson suggests a similar exercise using a row of stakes set out on a line about 100m away from the camera. As an alternative to the plane table, angles between the identifiable objects in the photograph could be measured with a theodolite, and then plotted on the drawing film.

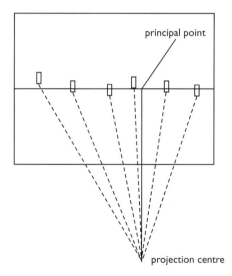

Figure 7.11 Finding the principal point of a photograph.

If the size of the print were reduced to the size of the negative, and all the lines in proportion, the length of the line from the projection centre to the centre of the photograph would be the same as the focal length of the lens. Provided the prints used are all of the same size, and a lens of the same focal length has been used, the projection centre will be the same for all of them. In order to locate unknown points at least two photographs will obviously have to be used, and these must be taken from known locations. In addition, the bearing of the centre of the photograph must be known so that it can be correctly oriented. This can be achieved by centring the view on an object whose position is already known from existing map data (or one which can be visited with a GPS unit), or by measuring the angle between it and the baseline between the two photograph stations. The photo stations can now be plotted on a drawing, and the photographs placed so that their projection centres are on the stations and their central points are on the correct alignment. This permits lines to be plotted through points of detail which will intersect at the correct locations of those points (some more detail of how to do this is given below).

Images from digital cameras have to be treated rather differently. The images can certainly be imported into suitable software packages (e.g. CAD packages), and lines plotted at appropriate angles to represent the directions to a series of points near the centre line of the image, but for once it's actually more difficult to manipulate these so that the lines pass through the points correctly. However, this process doesn't have to be gone through, because the principal point can be taken to be the position where lines between the mid-points of opposite sides intersect, i.e. the 'middle' of the photograph (EOS Systems Inc., *c.* 2005). This gets rid of one problem, but another remains, that of establishing the location of the projection centre, and for this the size of the image in the camera needs to be known (equivalent to the negative size in a film camera). Film cameras have traditionally been known by the size of the negative which they produce – '35mm' (a rectangle 24 × 36mm), '6cm' (square) etc. – but digital cameras of similar appearance may actually use sensors of different sizes, and manufacturers' literature doesn't always make it entirely obvious what this is. Sensor sizes are measured in millimetres, length × width, but a camera handbook will often refer to a '1.1/8‴' or '1.2/7‴' sensor. Some common sensor sizes are:

1.2/7″ equivalent to	3.96mm ×	5.27mm
1.1/8″	5.32mm ×	7.18mm
2/3″	6.60mm ×	8.80mm
4/3rds	13.50mm ×	18.00mm

(Digicaminfo, *c.* 2005). Some software packages, such as Photomodeler from EOS Systems (referred to in greater detail in the case study of the Barnard Castle Butter Market) are capable of calculating the size of the format from information obtained from photographs and other measurements, but the documentation supplied with the software also explains how to do it using simple methods (EOS Systems, 2000). The camera is set up on a tripod, levelled, and pointed squarely at a wall, to which a sheet of A4 (or similar) size paper is attached so that its centre is in the middle of the camera's field of view, as in these diagrams:

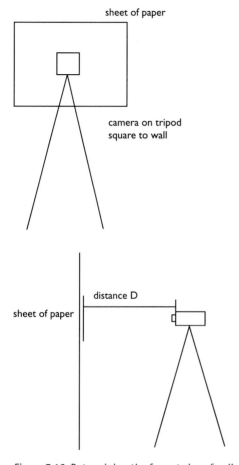

Figure 7.12 Determining the format size of a digital camera (after EOS Systems, 2000).

The paper should fill about 75 per cent of the image area. Obviously this will depend on the distance of the camera from the wall, and on the focal length of the lens (the focal length is also used in the calculation); on most digital cameras a zoom lens is fitted, and the easiest way of determining the focal length is to use it either at minimum (wide-angle) or maximum (telephoto) focal length, since these figures are written around the outside of the lens. Between these two settings there is no direct way of reading the exact focal length being used, although, in more recent cameras at least, the information is recorded along with the photograph, and can be read by certain software packages, such as Adobe Photoshop® or utility software which may sometimes be supplied with a new camera. (This information is part of what is sometimes called the EXIF file, standing for Exchangeable Image File format, which uses pieces of metadata with other file formats such as JPEG and TIFF to record shutter speed, aperture, focal length, focusing and metering methods and other things (CoolUtils. com, 2005).) It will also be necessary to measure the horizontal distance from the paper to the imaging chip in the camera, which is called 'D' in the diagram. (Obviously you can't see the chip, but the recommendation given is to measure to a position 'just behind the back of the lens'.)

A photograph of the paper is now taken, and the image transferred to a PC where it is opened in an image processing program. You now need to know the size of the image of the paper as a proportion of the whole image. The total size of the image will be visible somewhere on the screen in something like this form: '2048 × 1536 × 16 million', which gives the number of pixels in terms of columns and rows and the number of colours used. Co-ordinates in a digital photograph have 'x' first (the column number) and 'y' (the row) second, as in normal surveying practice where the easting is given before the northing, but while the position of the origin (0,0) of a co-ordinate system is usually at the bottom left, in an image it's at the top left, so a high row number refers to a row towards the bottom of the image. (I mention this because it has sometimes confused me.) The size of the paper can be determined by placing the mouse pointer over one corner, say the top left, and observing the row and column co-ordinates which will appear somewhere around the edge of the screen, then moving to a diagonally opposite corner, such as the lower right, and doing the same thing again. If the first position gives 266, 197, and the second gives 1782, 1339, then the image of the paper is 1516 pixels (1782 − 266) by 1142 (1339 − 197). It will be necessary to zoom into the image to obtain these co-ordinates.

All the parameters needed have now been obtained, and they are given the following names:

Focal length of lens	f	(millimetres)
Distance from camera to paper	D	(mm or inches)
Size of paper in x direction	Px	(mm or inches)
Size of paper in y direction	Py	(mm or inches)
Size of whole image in x	Sx	(pixels)
Size of whole image in y	Sy	(pixels)
Size of paper image in x	Nx	(pixels)
Size of paper image in y	Ny	(pixels)

The values D, Px and Py may be in either millimetres or inches, but obviously they must all be in the same unit. As the focal length is in millimetres, the size of the format will also be in millimetres.

The x-dimension of the format (width) is calculated by

$$w = (Px \div D) \times (f \div Nx) \times Sx$$

and the y-dimension (height) by

$$h = (Py \div D) \times (f \div Ny) \times Sy$$

So in a case where the parameters were

Focal length of lens	7.2mm
Distance from camera to paper	497mm
Size of paper in x direction	297mm

Size of paper in y direction	210mm
Size of whole image in x	2592
Size of whole image in y	1944
Size of paper image in x	1662
Size of paper image in y	1141

The calculations become

$$W = (297 \div 497) \times (7.2 \div 1141) \times 2592 = 6.71\text{mm}$$
$$H = (210 \div 497) \times (7.2 \div 1141) \times 1944 = 5.18\text{mm}$$

When the size of the format has been determined, it's time to turn to a CAD package.

A rectangle is drawn to represent the format, using the real dimensions; a central line is then drawn, joining the mid-points of the vertical sides (use the **midpoint** option of ESNAP to facilitate this). This central line indicates the plane in which the image has been formed (although it will be viewed as if laid flat), and a vertical line from the midpoint of this line (the principal point of the image) of a length equal to the focal length of the lens gives the position of the projection centre of the image.

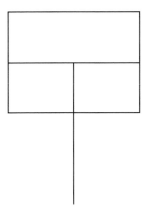

Figure 7.13 CAD drawing of a frame to accept photographs.

It would be best to use a fixed focal length lens for this work, but most digital cameras, other than the still expensive digital single-lens reflex models, have zoom lenses. It is possible, as mentioned above, to find the actual focal length used to create any image, but it might be better, in order to avoid confusion, to stick to one focal length, and in the case of most cameras this would probably mean choosing one end of the focal length range (probably the shortest). This frame can be saved as a drawing file and subsequently inserted into other drawings for work with particular sites. The insertion points in the receiving drawing should be marked with a point symbol first. It should be noted that in CAD software the default point symbol is just a dot the size of one pixel; when the point drawing tool is selected IntelliCAD produces a menu which includes a **Point Settings** option which allows an alternative symbol to be selected. Another way of achieving the same thing is to use the commands **Settings | Drawing Settings** and in the **Change Settings for**: field choose **Points**. (Versions of AutoCAD I have used up to 2004 don't give an option of changing the symbol at the time that the points are being created; the commands **Format|Point Style** have to be used.) Changing the point symbol in either of these ways affects *all* the points in the drawing, including those which have already been created. Point symbols are created with a size relative to the screen, and don't change in size when the view is zoomed in or out. (This may not appear to be the case, however. If point symbols become larger or smaller on zooming, the command **regen** – for 'regenerate' – should be used, which will return them to their correct size.) When the points have been marked the frame can be inserted.

There are different ways of copying the frame from its own file into the receiving file, but this is one which I have found to work reliably in IntelliCAD. Select all the elements in the frame, either by clicking on them individually, or clicking and dragging the mouse to create a window which includes them all. Right-click and select **Copy**. The command line prompt becomes

Multiple/Vector/<Base point>:

Click on the projection centre (the point at the far end of the line joined to the centre of the image frame). The prompt changes to

Displacement point:

Either move the mouse up to the command menu and choose **Window** (this pulls down a menu in which the names of all open files are visible, and the correct one can be chosen), or press ctrl-tab (hold down the control key and press the tab key) to switch between IntelliCAD windows. A moving copy of the image frame will appear in the receiving drawing window, with a line linking it to the co-ordinate position from which it has been copied. Click the mouse onto the point which represents the point from which a photograph was taken, and the copy will be added to the drawing at this location.

The frame was created using the correct measurements for the size of the format and the focal length, but these were in millimetres while the co-ordinate system used to define the position of the photo stations is almost certainly based on metres. This will mean that the frame appears very small. There is no problem about increasing the size of the frame, as long as the line representing the focal length is increased at the same time; then as the frame gets bigger the projection centre gets further away from it, so that angles plotted through the frame will remain the same. It isn't possible to say what is the ideal size for the frame, as this depends on the overall size of the survey area, but obviously it musn't be so large that the frames for two photographs overlap. Experiment will usually be necessary, but a starting point might be a scale increase of 50–100 times. To carry out the scaling operation, select all elements in the frame (including the line representing the focal length), right-click and select **Scale** from the menu; type the scale factor (e.g. 50), and press **enter**.

Having scaled the frame, it has to be oriented. In order to do this correctly it's necessary to project the line from the projection centre through the rectangular image frame so that it can be made to intersect with the reference object which is being used. An ordinary line could be used, but there would be a problem with maintaining a straight line from the projection centre, through the mid-point of the centre line and beyond for perhaps a considerable distance. Instead of a normal line, therefore, a special kind of line, called a **ray**, is used. This is a line of infinite length, which is defined only by a starting point and a direction. The IntelliCAD command for drawing this object is **ray**, or the menu sequence **Insert | Ray**. The first point will be the projection centre, and the direction will be the principal point; when these points have been entered with the mouse an infinite line will extend through the photo frame, as in this diagram.

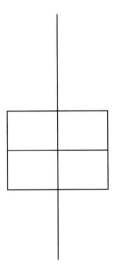

Figure 7.14 Image frame with projected centre line.

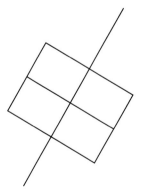

Figure 7.15 Rotated image frame.

The whole structure can be rotated by selecting each part of it as before, by left-clicking or dragging a window, after which a right-click allows the **rotate** command to be chosen from a menu. The command line will prompt for a **rotation point,** at which the projection centre is left-clicked, and then the objects can be rotated using the mouse, until the ray intersects the reference object. The frame is now correctly oriented, and the ray can be deleted.

To add a photograph, the **ImageEnabler** toolbar has to be made visible (do this by right-clicking over one of the visible toolbars and choosing its name from the menu. The ImageEnabler bar looks like this:

Figure 7.16 IntelliCAD image enabler toolbar.

The icon on the left (actually composed of strokes of red, yellow and blue) is the control to **attach raster image**, and clicking it allows the selection of an image file, after which this appears:

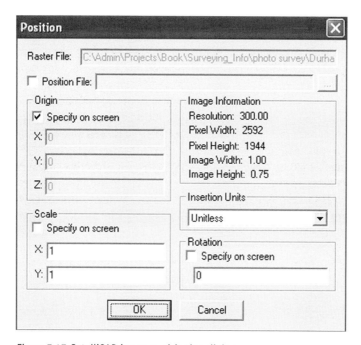

Figure 7.17 IntelliCAD image positioning dialogue.

Leave the **Origin** box checked, but uncheck **Scale** and **Rotation**. The image will need scaling and rotating, but this is more easily done when it's visible on screen. Click **OK** and then click the lower-left corner of the image frame (or what was originally the lower-left corner before rotation) to attach the image to it. When this has been done the command prompt is

Scale Factor <1>:

It may be as well at this point to enter the same factor as that by which the photo frame was scaled; it won't be correct, but if the scale factor is left as 1 the image may be so small that it isn't visible. The result of this operation may look like this:

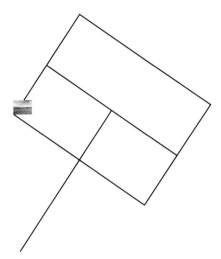

Figure 7.18 Initial appearance of photographic image in a CAD drawing.

Now select the image by left-clicking, right-click to get the menu, and choose **Scale**. The prompt is for a **Base point:**, which needs a click on the corner of the image where it joins the frame. The prompt changes to **Base scale/<Scale factor>:**, at which you should type **B**. The prompt changes to **Base scale <1>:**. Don't type anything, but left-click on the lower left corner of the image, and with the prompt showing **Second point:** click on its lower-right corner. The prompt is now **New scale**. Move the mouse to the original lower-right corner of the image frame, and left-click. The result should be

Figure 7.19 Photographic image correctly scaled.

Select the image again, right-click and choose **Rotate**. With the prompt **Rotation point:** left-click on the lower-left corner of the image. The prompt becomes **Base**

angle/<Rotation angle>:; left-click the lower-right corner of the image frame, which should produce this:

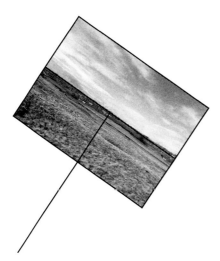

Figure 7.20 Photographic image rotated to fit frame.

When first inserted (and at other times as different operations are performed), the image will appear to be on top of the photo frame and other lines, and this will be inconvenient. This can be resolved by selecting the image (it will appear covered by grey hatched lines) then clicking the icon at the right of the ImageEnabler bar (the **DrawOrder** tool; this brings up a menu including the command **Send to back**, which will cause the vector objects to re-appear.

   The diagram below shows the method of plotting the direction of a point of detail. The point is shown by a circle with a cross through the centre (this is one of IntelliCAD's standard point symbols). It would be inaccurate to plot a line (or in fact a ray) from the perspective centre through this point, because it isn't in the plane of the photograph represented by the centre line. Instead, draw an ordinary line from the detail point (it doesn't necessarily have to be marked with a point symbol) to the centre line, having changed the ESNAP setting to **perpendicular** (and removing all the other snap settings). With this setting, as the mouse approaches the centre line the yellow symbol for a perpendicular snap will appear, and when this is showing a left-click will cause the end of the new line to be attached to the centre line at a point where the angle between the two is exactly 90°. A ray can now be plotted from the perspective centre through the intersection of the two lines, and this gives the correct bearing of the detail point from the observer's position.

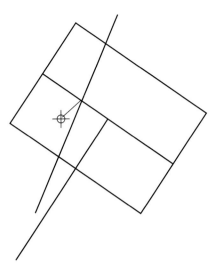

Figure 7.21 Plotting a ray through the photograph.

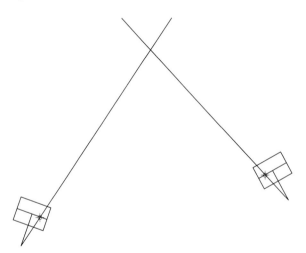

Figure 7.22 Intersection of rays plotted through two photographs to locate a point.

Plotting the bearing of the same point on two photographs as described gives a pair of intersecting rays which define the true location of the point, which can be marked with a point sysmbol, while the rays are deleted.

Chapter 8

GIS in archaeological mapping

Much has been written in the last 15 years about the application of GIS (Geographic Information Systems) to archaeology (a good recent summary can be found in Wheatley and Gillings, 2002). As with many new concepts which achieve rapid popularity (in their discussion, at least, if not in their use) there has grown to be a degree of difference in the way the three-letter-acronym 'GIS' is employed. Some people consider themselves to be 'using GIS' if they are running a software package which calls itself GIS (as many of them do, including those of major companies), whatever they may be using the system for. Others would wish to make a distinction between 'mapping' or 'cartography' and 'GIS', seeing the latter as necessarily involving some sort of spatial analysis and the creation of new sets of data from those which have been imported into the system in their existing form. Examples of this kind of analysis might range from determining the average distance from stone circles to sources of water, to relatively complex statistical considerations of the visibility characteristics of archaeological sites, such as the work on long barrows carried out by Wheatley (1995) or that on mesolithic sites by Lake and Woodman (2000). Some teachers of cartography have complained that the rapid adoption of GIS software has led to a decrease in the quality of maps generated by students who are faced with too much choice and complexity, and forget that simplicity may be an aid to communication ('Give students 40 text fonts and they'll use them all on the same page' one such teacher was heard to complain at a GIS conference in the 1990s). Sometimes complexity is entirely justified. The analysis of earthworks at Stapely Hill by Fletcher and Spicer (1992) was an elegant model of how this kind of work might be developed (although seldom emulated), but understanding the results requires a high level of understanding on the part of the reader. In most cases, when displaying archaeological information we are looking for something which will communicate rapidly and effectively with the viewer.

The types of software already considered are very useful indeed for those purposes for which they are intended, and between them are capable of producing almost any kind of map we could imagine, but they don't necessarily make it easy to do so. The surveys portrayed have been deliberately straightforward, but the nature of archaeological information (or many other kinds of information recorded in the field) is seldom so simple. A scatter of points on a map may represent sites drawn from a county sites and monuments record, and we may well want to show them all using the same kind of symbol because they come from the same source. On another occasion we might want to show prehistoric sites as black dots, Roman ones as red triangles, medieval ones as blue squares, and post-medieval as green hexagons; or again we might need to differentiate between barrows, enclosures, pillow mounds, cist burials and chapels. All of these different kinds of information would today probably be stored in a database system of some kind, where they could readily be accessed and used as a basis for sorting or querying the whole set of data. Displaying these attributes graphically using a CAD package, for example, would be very cumbersome, though it could be done, but it is far better to use something designed for the purpose, and this is where GIS software comes in.

The differences between various kinds of graphical software which can all be used to produce 'maps' of some sort have been summarised by Eiteljorg *et al.* (2002). The particular importance of GIS for the current purpose is that while most users and consumers of GIS products are familiar with seeing information expressed in the form of maps, a GIS is much more of a database than anything else, but a database designed with a particular emphasis on the graphical expression of information, and this makes them very suitable for the sort of task outlined above.

A problem faced by the individual wishing to make use of GIS, similar to that confronting would-be CAD users, is the cost of software: the packages produced by the major companies in the field are all priced in thousands of pounds. Some companies do produce free software, but normally this has considerable limitations on what it can do. ESRI (the Environmental Sciences Research Institute) produces the widely used packages Arcview and ArcGIS (and formerly Arc/Info) costing large sums of money, but also has free software called ArcExplorer which can be downloaded from its web site (http://esri.com). This package is fine for its purpose, but it's really only designed as a data viewer.

Two other packages must be mentioned. SPRING is an excellent and very comprehensive GIS and image-processing system, produced in Brazil by the Instituto Nacional de Pesquisas Espaciais (National Institute for Space Research); it can be downloaded free from http://www.dpi.inpe.br/spring/english, but while there is a version in which the menus and commands are in English, the documentation is entirely in Portuguese (with large parts also available in Spanish). The producers wish to have an English translation, but at present funds are not available to support this. TNTLite is a free version of the TNT software produced by Microimages of Nebraska, USA (http://www.microimages.com/). Again it is a very comprehensive package, and while the Lite version has limitations, these are mainly in the form of the size of files or images which can be manipulated, and the software can in fact be used quite effectively for many archaeological purposes. Both packages are perhaps *too* comprehensive for the purposes of this book, but are well worth looking into, although investigating SPRING needs linguistic skills which I don't possess.

The software described here is another free program, Christine GIS, produced by Josef Genserek (www.christine-gis.com). This software is under development, and currently (2005) has fairly limited spatial analytical capability, but it makes an excellent tool for management and display of data, and is well suited to use with survey information. It's also remarkably small by current standards; the download file is only about 1.5Mb, and installation requires only 3Mb, though presumably this will increase somewhat as functions are added.

Components of Christine GIS

When first loaded, the Christine window shows the usual menu and toolbars (initially with only a small number of options), and below this two main areas. The larger right-hand division is where data will be displayed, and on the left is a description of the structure of the current *project*. GIS software often uses this concept of a project, which consists, potentially, of a number of different elements, defined here as *views, tables,* and *scripts*. Views are graphical displays which most people would describe as maps; tables are data arranged in rows and columns; scripts are essentially programs which can be used to automate GIS operations and to add functions. At the top of this list of elements is **Project.cri,** which is the default name of the project. This is in fact a text file, which contains a list of instructions to the software about the views, tables, and scripts which are contained within the project, as well as other details. It's important to realise that the project file does not itself contain any data; these will remain in the external files which are used by the project, so copying the project file from one computer to another will only result in disappointment!

A significant problem faced by the user of free GIS is that of data formats. The major packages all have the ability to import data in many forms, and to save in others, but in general the free products don't (an exception is TNTLite, which will import many formats, though there is no export capability). Nor do the surveying package *Terrain Tools* (free version) or *IntelliCAD* export data in any GIS format. *Christine* GIS uses one of the most widely used GIS file formats, ESRI's *shapefile,* and data must be translated into this form first. Searching the internet will reveal quite a number of free programs which will convert shapefiles into dxf files, but conversion in the other direction is much more rare; in fact, the only program I have discovered which will do it (outside the major GIS packages) is *Cad2Shape* by Guthrie CAD/ GIS Software of Adelaide, South Australia, and this costs about $A200 (http://www.guthcad.com.au). There is a way of creating shapefiles using free software, but this involves going via the medium of another format, the ESRI *generate* file. This is actually a plain text file, which contains the co-ordinates of the objects to be created, and it can easily be made from a spreadsheet file which has been used to calculate co-ordinates from field measurements, or it might consist of co-ordinates given in, for example, a sites and monuments record. A generate file might look like this:

```
1010,409000,510000
2102,390200,512000
3321,390000,512400
1245,392090,512490
3544,399000,513000
6036,399200,513400
2045,399200,513400
1731,408630,514200
2644,412490,514580
1674,410690,514740
3946,406230,515210
1623,419630,515750
```

```
1232,405480,517110
3168,392450,517890
1696,412960,524100
end
```

Each line contains a numerical label identifying a point, followed by the co-ordinates of the point, all separated by commas (no spaces). The word 'end' must appear on the line after the last co-ordinate pair.

The program used to convert this to a shapefile is **gen2shp**, produced by Jan-Oliver Wagner (http://www.intevation.de/~jan/gen2shp/gen2shp.html). This is a DOS program, consisting of a single file called **gen2shp.exe**. It doesn't run in the Windows environment, but has to have a special window opened for it. In Windows 98 this is done with the commands

Start | programs | MS-DOS prompt

And in Windows XP with

Start | All Programs | Accessories | Command Prompt

The window which opens will have a black background and white text, saying something like

---

Microsoft® Windows 98
  ©Copyright Microsoft Corp 1981–1999

C:\

Or

Microsoft windows XP [Version 5.1.2600]
  © Copyright 1985–2001 Microsoft Corp.

C:\

The last line indicates that the root directory of Drive C: is 'current'; to change to another one (which must contain the file gen2shp.exe and the generate file) type the full path like this:

cd \ph\temp\gen2shp   (or whatever the path is)

'cd' means 'change directory', and it's followed by the appropriate path to the data. When you press **enter** after the above command the prompt changes to

C:\ph\temp\gen2shp

or whatever it may be, to show that this directory is now active. If you now type

```
gen2shp   <enter>
```

a short welcome text will give you information about how to use the program. As an example, if the generate file above was called **sites.gen** (the file type should be .gen), and you wanted your shapefile to be called *sites* you would run the program with a line like this:

```
gen2shp sites points < sites.gen
```

(note the < character). The program will run and three files will be created, called **sites.shp, sites.shx,** and **sites.dbf,** together making up the shapefile *sites*.

The word 'points' tells the program what kind of features are in the file; it could also be 'lines' or 'polygons'. A generate file for lines might look like this:

```
1
23431.017,561392.639
23560.128,561485.599
23640.176,561504.966
23769.287,561488.181
23959.079,561517.876
24115.303,561485,599
24210.845,561352,615
24351.576,561297.097
end
2
23424.561,561368.108
23396.157,561281.604
23393.575,561214.467
23432.308,561138.291
23582.076,561078.900
23720.225,561089.229
23881.613,561068.571
24048.166,560994.979
24190.187,560996.270
24283.147,561028.547
24382.562,561127.962
24368.360,561266.111
end
end
```

The first line in the file contains an identifying number for the first line feature, followed by as many co-ordinate pairs as are needed to define it. After the last pair comes the word 'end', to indicate the end of the line, then another number to show the start of the next line, then its co-ordinates, then 'end' to show the end of the line, followed by another 'end' to indicate the end of the file.

A generate file for polygons is very similar to a line generate file, e.g.

```
1
0,0
1,0
1,1
0,1
0,0
end
2
10,10
10,11
11,11
11,10
10,10
end
end
```

but in the case of each feature the last co-ordinate pair is the same as the first, closing the figure. Note, however, that when running the program gen2shp you *must* give the feature type as 'polygons' not 'lines', or the features created will only be recognised as lines.

Coming back to the file of points, having created a shapefile, it needs to be added to a view, but the new project doesn't yet have any, so right-click on the word **Views** in the project area, and choose **New View** from the menu. Any set of data which can be displayed in a view is called a **Theme**, so adding the shapefile is done using

View | Add Theme

or by right-clicking *in the legend area* of the view and choosing **Add Theme** from the menu. When initially displayed, the theme appears as scattered very small point symbols, which can be changed by using the commands

Theme | Properties

or by right-clicking on the name of the theme in the legend area and choosing **properties** from the menu.

This important function controls the display of the theme in a number of ways, but for the moment all that is needed is to click on the **Point symbol** tab, which gives access to the range of symbols available. There are 39 basic shapes

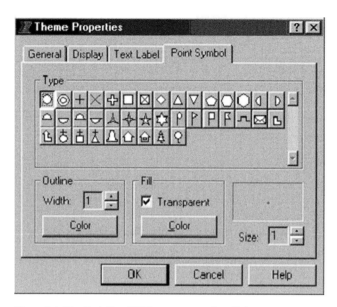

Figure 8.1 The Christine GIS theme properties dialogue.

which can be rendered in a variety of ways. The **Outline** field controls the thickness of the line used to draw the cross symbols, or for the outline of the others; the colour can also be chosen here. The **Fill** field controls the colour of the interior of the shapes (obviously it has no effect on the crosses), but if the **Transparent** box is checked (which is the default) the setting has no effect, and the interior will be empty. If there are many symbols close together it may sometimes be better (if not aesthetically pleasing) to use transparent symbols so that it will be obvious where they overlap, as opaque symbols may just merge together and obscure the situation.

This problem of overlapping symbols is one which occurs frequently, not only within a dataset but also, of course, when two or more datasets are displayed together. The order in which themes are drawn reflects the order in which they were added to the view – the first one is 'on the bottom', and if a later theme overlaps with one of its features that of the earlier theme will be obscured. It's possible to alleviate this to an extent, as already mentioned, by using transparent symbols, but there will be cases when it's positively desirable to have some features 'on top' of others, as in the case of a group of polygons shaded or coloured to reflect, say, national or other administrative boundaries, while the locations of archaeological sites need to appear above them.

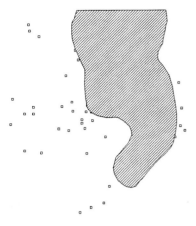

Figure 8.2 A set of points overlapped by a polygon.

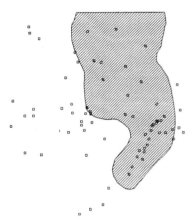

Figure 8.3 Points overlying a polygon.

In Figure 8.2 a group of points (sites) was added to a view, followed by a polygon representing, say, part of a national park boundary. In Figure 8.3 the same data sets are displayed in reverse order, polygon first, points second. Clearly the second plot contains more information, and would in most cases be the one that was required. Obviously it's easy enough to ensure that the right one is put in first, but it might be more difficult if there were many themes in the view. Fortunately, it's also easy to change the display order of the themes. One way is to click on the theme to move and use

Theme | Order | Move to Top   (or Move to Bottom)

Alternatively, just left-click on the name of a theme in the legend area of the view and drag it up or down to the desired position.

These two diagrams illustrate another point which is worth bearing in mind when looking at someone else's digital maps (or even your own). The hatched shading pattern of the polygon is obviously opaque, but it might not always be obviously so; it might be mistakenly assumed that because it consists of 'lines' the spaces between them are just that – spaces – and that anything beneath the polygon would be visible, which in this case would be erroneous. It is possible to make this kind of shading transparent (there's a simple check box labelled 'transparent'), and sometimes this may be a useful thing to do, to make themes beneath it visible, but it does depend on the type of symbols beneath, as sometimes it just produces confusing interference patterns.

Having explored the method for choosing one satisfactory symbol, it's time to turn to using the attributes of the points to determine how each should be represented. A point is of course characterised by its position (a 'spatial' attribute), but it will also usually have what are known as 'non-spatial' attributes. Assuming our set of points to be archaeological sites, their non-spatial attributes might include a name, site type, period, and perhaps many others. When the shapefile is created, part of it is something called an 'attribute table', which can be viewed by clicking on the name of the theme in the legend area and choosing

Theme | Table

Doing this with the shapefile called **sites** produces this:

sites_id
1010
2102
3321
1245
3544
etc.

i.e. just the identifying number of the point. The co-ordinates don't appear, as in GIS terminology they aren't normally classed as attributes. Note that the column of numbers has a title, **sites_id**, made by taking the name given to the shapefile and adding **_id** to it. Any other attributes have to be placed in another file, which might be called *site_attribs.txt* (the name isn't crucial, but it must have the extension .txt), a text file in which commas have been used to separate the data which will fill the new table fields. When creating comma-separated files containing the attributes, a minor annoyance may be encountered because of the fact that while Christine GIS expects comma-separated files to have a *.txt* extension to their name, as far as some other applications (such as Excel) are concerned the expected file extension is *.csv* (comma-separated value), and in many cases even if you give *.txt* as part of the file name, *.csv* will be appended as well (as in *sites.txt.csv*). The file has to be re-named using Windows Explorer. (Some GIS software will accept tab-separated files, which in Excel have an extension of .txt, but these don't work in Christine.) As an alternative, enclosing the whole file name in double quotation marks (e.g. "site_attributes.txt") will prevent *.csv* being added.

These are the fields in the file **site_attribs.txt**:

```
Sites-id,type,period
1010,round barrow,BA
2102,long barrow,Neol
3321,round barrow,BA
1245,coin,Roman
3544,chapel,medieval
6036,palstave,BA
2045,round barrow,BA
1731,hammer,modern
2644,pottery,Roman
1674,pottery,Roman
3946,enclosure,medieval
1632,pottery,modern
1232,crop mark,unknown
3168,coin,Roman
1696,metal fragments,unknown
```

The first line gives the names for what will become fields or columns in the attribute table; note the crucial presence of a field called *sites_id*, which matches the first field in the existing attribute table of the shapefile; this will be used to create a link between the two tables.

At the moment, however, the file containing the table of attributes can't be used by the software, because it isn't yet part of the project. In the area to the left of the Christine screen there is a list of all the project components (Views, Tables and Scripts). Right-click on **Tables** and choose **Open Tables**. This opens a dialogue in which you can choose a file to open. By default Christine will be looking for files in the dBase III format, with *.dbf* extensions (dBase was an important database software package, and the format is still much in use – a .dbf file is a part of all shapefiles). In the field **Files of type:** choose **Delimited text (*.txt)**. The file **site_attribs.txt** should be visible in the list and can be opened. You will be asked by the software which character is used to delimit fields, and at this point you type a comma in the appropriate place and click OK. The file will be opened in a new window, with the first line used as the field names. With this table active, click on the commands

Table | Merge Tables

This produces a dialogue in which you can make the following selections.

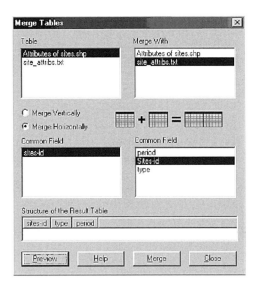

Figure 8.4 The merge tables dialogue.

In the field **Table** click *attributes of sites.shp* and in **Merge with** click *site_attribs.txt*.

Beneath these fields there is a choice of merging horizontally or vertically; we need *horizontal*, because we are going to add new fields to the existing attribute table, rather than extending it downwards by adding rows.

In the two fields called **Common Field** click *sites_id* – note that sometimes the field names may appear in upper case in one table and lower case in the other, but this doesn't matter. A **Preview** button can be used to show what the structure of the merged table will look like.

Finally click **Merge**. A single table window will be left open, showing a table which contains all the fields from the two original tables. The merged table is removed from the project.

Depending on how the text file of attributes was created, the above instructions may or may not succeed. In merging tables it isn't necessary for the common fields to have the same name, but they must be of the same *type*. In databases various different field types are recognised, some of them being *number* (having numerical values), *string* (any combination of characters, possibly digits and letters, but not having a numerical value), *Boolean* (containing just 1 or 0, perhaps indicating presence or absence), and *date* (which can be used in calculating the passage of time). It may sometimes happen (for reasons which may not be clear) that a field in one of the tables, which you consider to contain a number, is interpreted by the software as being a string, while in the other table the same characters occur as a number, and the only sign that this is the case may be that the field which is a number is aligned to the right, while the string is aligned to the left. In these circumstances, it will be impossible to merge the tables using these two fields as common. In the example given here, the file of attributes was created using a text editor, and the site numbers have become character-strings, while in the attribute table of the shapefile they are numbers (if the attribute file had been created in a spreadsheet the numbers would still be numbers).

Remedial action is possible, but it requires the creation of a new field in one of the tables.

Open the table *site_attribs.txt* (right-click on its name, then **Open**), if it isn't open already, and choose

Edit | Add Field

In the **Field Definition** box which appears enter the name for the field (in this case *site_no*, though this is the user's choice) and select the type *number*. The default width of 16 (characters) can be accepted, and the number of decimal places should be zero (again the default). Click OK.

Now *left*-click on the name of the new field which has appeared in the table; this will produce a drop-down menu, from which the option **Calculate** should be chosen. This produces a dialogue called **Calculate Value for Field [site_no]**.

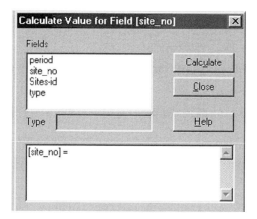

Figure 8.5 Dialogue box used in calculating values for fields in an attribute table.

This contains a list of all the fields, and at the bottom an area within which the calculation will be defined. Initially this area contains the characters *[site_no]=* which should be completely deleted and replaced with this:

[Sites-id].AsNumber([site_no]);

(the semicolon at the end is part of the command, and *must* be present; also note the presence of a full stop after [**Smr_id**]). Click on **Calculate**, and the new field will be filled with strings of characters which are visually identical to those in the field Smr_id, but which have a numerical value and can be used in merging the two tables together (but this time choose **sites_id** in the table of attributes, and **site_no** in the text file).

Instead of performing the calculation described above, it would also have been possible to change the numerical value of the field in the existing attribute table into a string, in which case the calculation would have been:

[Sites_id].AsString([site_no]);

(The formulae given here are simple examples of the use of a *scripting language*, referred to above, something which can be used in most GIS to automate repetitive tasks or to add functions to the software, but this subject is entirely beyond the scope of this book.)

Now that the non-spatial attributes are in place, they can be used to alter the appearance of the SMR theme.

Changing the theme legend using attributes

Right-click on theme, choose **properties**. Change from **single symbol** to **unique values** and choose the field in the attribute table which will be used to decide on the choice of symbol. All the categories will initially be given the same symbol, so you have to set each one individually (double-click on the required symbol to make changes to it). The button labelled **Initialize** will reset all symbols to the default, so take care with this, especially if you have a lot of categories. When all the changes have been made and OK clicked the appearance of the theme will change to reflect the categories and their associated symbols. In the legend area of the view you will also see the category symbols set out. This is mostly a useful thing, but if you have several themes, each of which has a large number of categories, the length of the symbol lists will be considerable, and it may be difficult to find a particular one. Legends can optionally be hidden using

Theme | Legend | Hide/Show

This can be applied to just one theme, or to several at a time, depending how many are currently selected, but note that this command works as a toggle; if you highlight several themes, some of which already have their legends hidden, these will become visible again, while those which were visible will become hidden. In order to avoid confusion it may be better to work with just one theme at a time.

This is the result of changing the theme legend to reflect the categorisation of sites by period.

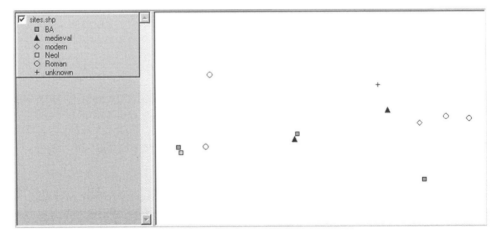

Figure 8.6 A set of points with symbols indicating non-spatial attributes.

Reading attribute information

One way of viewing the attribute information for a point is to use the information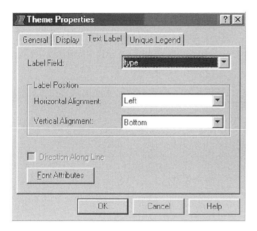
button. When this tool is selected the mouse pointer changes to reflect its icon,
and now when clicked on any feature in the theme a window opens in which the whole
of the record in the attribute table can be seen. Only one record can be seen at a
time.

Labelling themes

Items from the attribute table can be used to label the features in a theme, either
individually or all at once. The field to be used for labelling is chosen by right-clicking
the theme name and choosing **Properties**.

Click the **Text label** tab.

Figure 8.7 Changing a text label.

In **Label Field** choose the field from the attribute table which contains the label text,
and in **Label Position** set the placing of the label relative to the point. **Font Attributes**
allows you to choose font, colour, size, etc.

To label all the features at once, choose

    Theme | Auto-label

and the selected text will appear in the chosen position next to each point. Some GIS
software has the ability to recognise overlapping labels and leave some of them out,
but Christine can't do this at present, nor can you delete individual labels if they
clash.

The size of text is fixed relative to the screen, so while zooming in will move the
points further apart, and perhaps make the labels more easily visible, the text will
remain the same size (as of course will the point symbols); if larger labels are needed
you will have to change the font attributes.

An alternative to wholesale labelling is to use the label tool 🔲 , after which a left-click of the cursor will place a label next to each point in turn. All the labels can be removed from the active theme using

Theme | Remove Labels

You don't have to confine labels to the text items which appear in the attribute table. (These may not always be very informative to all users of your data, if for example you have abbreviated or numerical codes for attributes which would be better described using words.) The label text can be changed by opening the properties dialogue again, clicking the **Unique Legend** tab, and for each category click in the **label** field, delete the current piece of text, and type something new.

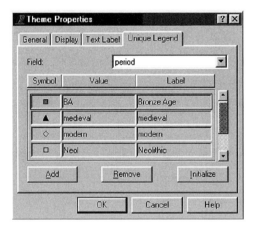

Figure 8.8 Defining a legend based on attributes.

Note that when you have changed the label in one category, you have to use the **enter** key to move to the next one down. If you click the mouse in the next field the label you have just changed will be reset to its original value. When you have entered the last label you have to press **enter** again, or that label isn't changed. Click OK to enable the changes. The legend can be saved to be used on future occasions (it could be very laborious to have to do it each time you use a theme); use

Theme | Legend | Save

The legend is saved in a file with the extension *.leg* and once this has been done it can be called up again to be used in any theme which has the same attribute values. To do this you have to make sure that the theme you want to work with has been highlighted in the legend area of the view, then use the commands

Theme | Legend | Load

Looking at parts of the data

Of course, in many cases you won't want to view the whole of the data set at the same time, for example when there are many features close together which can't be distinguished. A number of tools allow you to change the scale of the view:

Figure 8.9 Tool buttons for changing scale.

The two four-arrow tool buttons zoom in or out by a fixed amount (×2), keeping the centre of the view in the same place. The left-hand button zooms out so that all features are visible, the second from the left zooms to all active themes, and the third from left zooms so that all the selected features of the theme are visible. There is also a button like a magnifying glass which can be used in two ways: either click on a point of your choice to zoom in by the same fixed amount, using the click-point as the view centre, or click and drag to define a window which becomes the approximate extent of the view. When the view extent is less than the full extent of all features, the pan tool (looking like a hand) can be used to move the view around the data set.

Selecting features from a theme

When dealing with large or complex data sets it will often be the case that it is necessary to extract some of the features, perhaps those of a particular period, to display on their own. In a database it would be possible to perform a query to carry out this process, and in a GIS it would be the same. The command

Theme | Query

can be used to select part of a theme in this way, but in Christine GIS (unlike some other GIS software) the selected features appear on screen in a different colour, but the other features remain visible in their original symbols. If it is desired to display only the selected features, this has to be done through the **Theme Properties**. Click on the **Unique Legend** tab, then in turn on each of the categories which it is required to remove, and click the **Remove** button. When OK is pressed, the theme will have changed so that only the desired features are visible. If this selection is one which is needed often (all of the prehistoric sites, for instance), it will be worth saving this legend as well, in a file called *preh.leg*, perhaps, so that it can be used again easily. It may be worthwhile to do this for each of your periods, so that you have a legend for each. You can add a shapefile as a theme in a particular view as often as you like, so if you have seven periods you can add the shapefile seven times, and apply the appropriate period legend to each, so that you have a set of themes which can be turned on and off in any combination which suits the current purpose.

Overview map

A particular facility which Christine has is the **Overview Map**. This is a small map which appears at the bottom of the legend area when it has been enabled with

> View | Overview

(it can be turned off using the same command sequence). This is of little use if you are always going to be looking at the whole of your data set, but if you zoom in on part of it this area will be shown on the overview as a red rectangle, which can assist in understanding what the map is showing. Individual themes can be selected for inclusion in the overview by highlighting them and then using

> Theme | Use in Overview

(or by right-clicking on the theme name). The overview is included in printed output if it is enabled.

Scaling a view

Although the features in the shapefile are defined by co-ordinates, the view initially has no scale, because no units are associated with the numbers. The command

> Theme | Properties

allows the correct units to be selected (metres in most surveying contexts, though centimetres, millimetres, kilometres, miles, feet and inches are also available, as well as decimal degrees – these are very useful if your data include GPS locations which haven't been converted to grid co-ordinates). You can also change the name of the view and its background colour (and that of the overview if there is one). When the view has been given units it now also has a scale, and this is displayed in the small window at the top right of the view window; at first this will probably be something inconvenient like 1:24761, but you can click the mouse in the window, delete this figure, and replace it with, for example, 1:25000, followed by the **enter** key (you only type the figure *25000*). The scale you set will be used when printing the view.

Printing

Printing is very straightforward, although some may find it restrictive, as the current version of the software gives the user little in the way of options.

> View | Print

will start the process (or use the familiar printer button on the toolbar), and click OK. The printed page has a border line within which are a window for the view (also with a border) and one for the legend, scale (printed as a ratio, not a scalebar), statement of the map units, and the date. At the top is the name of the view as it has been set, and along each of the view borders is a figure which represents the co-ordinate values of eastings (left and right sides) and northings (top and bottom). The view will appear on the page approximately as it does on the screen, given the fact that the screen window may be a different shape from the view area on the page. If the overview option is enabled the small map will be printed at the bottom of the page to the left of the legend.

Exporting a view

An option which has appeared in the most recent version is the facility to export a view in the form of a Windows bitmap image. The image will show the view as it appears on screen, and it is produced using

View | Export

This image could be inserted into another kind of file – a word-processor document, for example – which may enable the user to produce a customised page for printing, though the legend and overview map don't appear.

Chapter 9

The shape of the ground

All surveyors will be concerned with describing the general shape of a piece of terrain, in addition to capturing details of other features of the landscape which exist on the surface. The most usual way to convey this information is by the use of *contours*, lines joining points of equal elevation. Steep slopes will be shown by the contours coming close together, more gentle ones by the lines being further apart. In most presentation maps contours are shown by a broken or dotted line symbol, or in a colour which is not too obtrusive (such as the familiar brown used by the Ordnance Survey in its Landranger 1:50,000 scale maps). Contours on small-scale maps give only a general idea of topography (the Landranger contours, for example, being accurate to ± 3m) and for many purposes it will be necessary to undertake custom-ised surveys with a much greater vertical accuracy. Contour surveys may be con-ducted in a number of different ways, but they always require the expenditure of a considerable amount of effort, which may not always be repaid. The most convenient way of capturing the shape of a ground surface is by the use of GPS equipment with sub-centimetre accuracy, but in this case time and effort are replaced by considerable financial cost.

In archaeological surveys of earthworks, however, contours may not successfully convey the desired information, as the artificial changes in slope are often very slight, and they may also follow a very complex pattern, especially in the case of multi-phase structures. Bettess (1992) refers to some of the problems of interpreting contours from archaeological earthworks, and Fletcher and Spicer (1992) give an even more extreme (though by no means unparalleled) example of slight earthworks resulting from mul-tiple phases of activity of different kinds. (They also present an ingenious way of analysing this complexity.) As Bettess points out, contour lines without information about their height are virtually useless, but on the other hand labelling them adequately may be difficult to achieve without making a drawing very cluttered. In a digital mapping environment it's easy enough to employ a colour scale to indicate elevation values but in publications it won't always be possible to use colour, and in the case of complex earthworks even colour may not serve to produce a map which can easily be interpreted.

A further consideration is the choice of contour interval, the vertical distance between contour lines. In order to capture the detail of slight archaeological earth-works a close interval will often be needed (perhaps 10cm), but it's frequently the case that these artificial changes in slope will be superimposed on much larger-scale natural changes, in which case a close interval will simply generate a mass of contour lines which blur together, while a larger interval may make the archaeological information disappear altogether, or frustratingly appear only in some places.

Finally, it isn't as easy as might be supposed to map archaeological earthworks by means of spot heights. A bank running across a field may be perfectly visible to the experienced observer, but it is unlikely to be uniform in profile throughout its length; in many places it may actually show no difference in height from the local 'background' elevation, and even closely spaced contours may not reveal the shape which the observer 'knows' is there.

Hachures

Hachures are a graphical form of representation which allow the communication of information about changes in surface height, often with great subtlety, but which don't depend on any elevation values which have been measured in the field, only on lines which indicate changes in slope. The general form of the hachure is that of a long thin triangle or a line with a triangular head, drawn at right-angles to the line representing the top of a slope, the broad end being at the higher end and the length of the hachure indicating the horizontal distance between the top and bottom of the slope. The form of the hachure is completely within the control of the individual producing the survey map, and this is at once their strength and their weakness. They can be used to indicate the presence of features which can be seen to be present, but which are difficult or impossible to capture through measurements of elevation, and variations in their size and shape can indicate subtle differences in the nature of slopes within the survey; on the other hand there are few universally agreed conventions about their use, and they contain no information about numerical differences in elevation. Hachures may give a quite unrealistic impression about the earthworks on a site, and can't safely be used on their own, but must be accompanied by at least some spot height values, profiles, and/or photographs. Much has been written about the use of hachures (e.g. Taylor 1974), and not only by archaeologists. The First Edition Ordnance Survey maps used hachures to show relief, although by the early twentieth century writers such as Usill (1900) did not refer to their use, and while Parry and Jenkins (1946) include hachures as suitable symbols for embankments and cuttings, their use is not discussed in any way. Use of them by the OS is now confined to conventional symbols for features such as railway cuttings. Certainly modern textbooks (e.g. Bannister *et al.*, 1998), ignore them, and perhaps their undoubted virtues are now only appreciated by archaeologists, with their unusual requirements in surveying.

While hachures can undoubtedly be used with subtlety, one thing is true of hachures drawn using conventional techniques; they require the exercise of considerable skill on the part of the draughtsperson, for there may be a very large number of hachures in a single plan, and each one has to be created with the same care as all the others, and to give the correct impression of the shape of the earthworks, the size, shape and angle of the hachures must be precisely controlled. Personal preference will determine the exact type(s) of hachures used. Bettess (op. cit., p.53) expresses something of a dislike for those which are drawn with a mechanical regularity, and this argument has much to commend it – after all, the earthworks being represented are unlikely to be nearly so regular themselves – but there are few things so dismal to contemplate as a poorly executed hachure plan, and in the absence of a really skilled person, my personal preference would be for regularity, even in plans created conventionally.

In a CAD environment, it's possible to create anything which can be imagined, and certainly any kind of hachure can be created, and then copied as many times as needed at whatever size is desired. This doesn't make the process anything like automatic, however, as each hachure still has to be placed and scaled individually, which takes some time. The more sophisticated CAD packages can be programmed to carry out repetitive or complex tasks (in the case of AutoCAD using the language called AutoLISP, which can also be used with IntelliCAD), and while the subject is beyond the scope of this work, a simple application of programming can make the production of hachures considerably less time-consuming than it might otherwise be.

To create a program in AutoLISP requires only a text editor; a simple one such as Windows Notepad is ideal, as the text must be saved without any formatting, but WordPad, Word, or any other word-processing software can be used, as long as the file is saved using a 'text-only' option.

The following is a sequence of instructions for drawing hachures:

```
;Program to draw hachures
;
; convert an angle in degrees to radians
(defun dtr (a)

   (* pi (/ a 180.0))

)
; Acquire information for hachure
(defun hachinf ()
   (setq sp (getpoint "\nStart point of hachure. Press ESC to quit:"))
   (setq ep (getpoint "\nEndpoint of hachure:"))
; set dimensions of hachure head
   (setq length (distance sp ep))
   (setq hfwidth (/ length 15))
   (setq hdlength (/ length 2.5))
   (setq tlength (- length hdlength))
   (setq hangle (angle sp ep))
   (setq width (* 2 hfwidth))
   (setq angle1 (+ hangle (dtr 90)))
   (setq intang1 (atan (/ hdlength hfwidth)))
   (setq angle2 (- hangle (- (dtr 90) intang1)))
   (setq slength (/ hdlength (sin intang1)))
   (setq intang2 (atan (/ hfwidth hdlength)))
   (setq angle3 (+ hangle (dtr 180) intang2))
   (setq angle4 (+ hangle (dtr 180)))
)
; Draw hachure
(defun drawout ()
```

```
    (command "pline"
       (setq p (polar sp angle1 hfwidth))
       (setq p (polar p angle2 slength))
       (setq p (polar p hangle tlength))
       (setq p (polar p angle4 tlength))
       (setq p (polar p angle3 slength))
       "close"
    )
)
; Draw hachures many times
(defun hach ()
    (setq numhach 1000)
    (setq counter 1)
    (while (<= counter numhach)
       (hachinf)
       (drawout)
       (setq counter (+ 1 counter))
    )
)
```

The text above should be saved in a file with the extension *.lsp* to its name, for example *hachure.lsp*. The lines which start with a semi-colon are included only as information for the human reader; they have no functional significance and could be omitted. To use the program, open your CAD package, and type

(load "hachure")   (assuming your file of commands to be called *hachure.lsp*)

then type

(hach)

In both cases the brackets must be included. On giving the command **(hach)** a prompt will appear on the command line, like this:

Start point of hachure. Press ESC to quit:

At this point place the mouse at the point which is to be the centre of the head of the hachure and click the left-hand button; the prompt changes to

Endpoint of hachure:

which is chosen in the same way. The hachure is now drawn, and the prompt changes again to invite the first point of a new hachure. The program will draw up to 1,000 hachures before stopping, but at any time pressing the ESC key will stop it. The hachures are a permanent part of the drawing, and can be treated just like any other object (placed on different layers, coloured, etc.).

Figure 9.1 Hachures produced using CAD software.

A number of hachures representing a section of ditch, drawn using the above LISP routine, might look like this.

Terrain modelling

Contours

Larger scale landscapes will normally be displayed differently (although early editions of Ordnance Survey and other national maps did use hachures). Traditionally, variations in terrain elevation have been conveyed by means of contours, lines representing the occurrence of points of equal elevation above some chosen datum, such as mean sea-level. The alternative of a three-dimensional visualisation of the surface was used relatively little, being rather difficult and expensive to use, and was mainly reserved for specialised display purposes. In the context of computerised data processing, terrain models are normally generated in a completely different way (see below), and if contours are needed they are generated as a secondary product. Contour lines are relatively easy (with practice) to plot by hand and eye through a set of points with elevation values, while creating a three-dimensional surface is much more difficult to achieve using manual methods; computers, on the other hand, find it easier to produce the 3D model. Any kind of terrain model of course, like any other survey, is only as good as the set of data on which it is based, and it is up to the surveyor to collect a sufficient number of data points, in the right parts of the landscape, to achieve a model which is sufficiently close to reality to satisfy the purpose of the survey.

Contours exist as lines which could be surveyed on the ground. Bettess, 1992, gives a description of this operation, called 'contour chasing', in which points of equal elevation are found and marked, and subsequently located by a separate surveying operation. This has advantages if manual plotting methods have to be used, but it requires a great deal of time spent in the field. A better system, also described by Bettess and by Olliver and Clendinning (1978) is that of grid levelling, in which a grid of suitable size is set out on the ground and the elevations of its nodes determined with a level or by tacheometry, contours at regular values then being interpolated between them.

Olliver and Clendinning (p.137) suggest that grid levelling, with squares of 10 or 20m, is suitable for 'very small' areas, up to about 200m², and, very importantly, *having no detail*. Bettess makes the point that a grid survey, in which the points are set out on a rigid plan which can take no account of the nature of the terrain is always likely to fail to capture the detail of significant features, such as small streams; a smaller grid interval might solve this problem, but only at the expense of multiplying the number of data points – and the amount of fieldwork – many times.

The usual method of contouring is to choose strategic points, such as summits and breaks of slope, along with a general carpet of other points, and to determine the three-dimensional position of these to use as the basis of interpolation. Points collected in this way can also be used for the creation of other kinds of terrain model. When plotting contours by hand an important consideration is the *contour interval*, the vertical distance between the lines. This needs in part to be a function of the nature of the terrain and in part determined by the scale at which the contours are to be displayed, but Olliver and Clendinning make some suggestions as to suitable intervals for level or 'moderately undulating' ground:

Scale	contour interval
1:500	0.25m
1:1000	0.5m
1:2000	1m
1:5000	2m
1:10,000	5m
1:25,000	10m
1:50,000	25m

In the case of computer plotting of contours from an existing model it's very easy to change the vertical interval until the appearance of the contours gives the best impression of the nature of the terrain.

Terrain surfaces

Contours provide a visually satisfactory way of representing the surface of a piece of landscape, but they remain a series of lines, with no data in the spaces between them, and this is a severe limitation when it comes to analysis of the characteristics of the surface with Geographic Information Systems (Wheatley and Gillings, 2002). It also makes it impossible to produce coloured and artificially illuminated views of the landscape which can be much more informative than two-dimensional contours.

Complete surfaces can be generated from field measurements in two ways. The first is to generate a grid of points, the node separation being determined by the scale of the landscape, and to calculate elevation values for the nodes using the actual values determined in the field. This involves the selection of a number of real elevation values for each grid node and the application of a formula which takes account of the distance between the spot heights and the location of the node. Some systems choose the nearest (for example) eight real points (diagram on the right below), while others define a number of segments radiating from the node position (typically four or eight) and choose at least one spot height from each segment (diagram on the left).

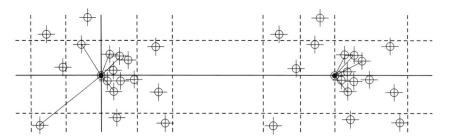

Figure 9.2 Interpolating an elevation grid from field measurements.

The other kind of terrain surface is what is usually called a TIN (Triangular Irregular Network). This uses the original data points, and joins them together to form a continuous surface of triangular facets. The algorithms used for this process attempt to construct what surveyors call 'well conditioned' triangles (i.e. where the angles have similar values), but inevitably their shapes will vary, as of course will their size, depending on the distribution of the original data points, and the last points to be joined may create very long and thin facets. This is an example of part of a TIN model:

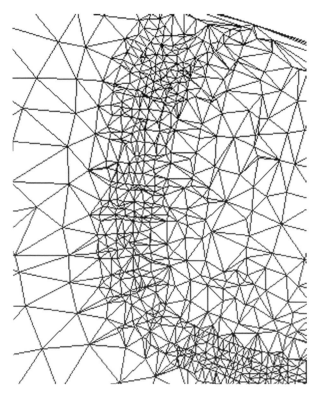

Figure 9.3 A TIN elevation model.

A feature of TINs is that the outer perimeter is by default 'convex', which means that if you are trying to create a model of an island, for example, which has concavities in its outline (bays), these will be filled in with triangles unless a special polygon is made from a feature representing the coastline and this is used in the TIN-formation process to confine the creation of triangles to the inside.

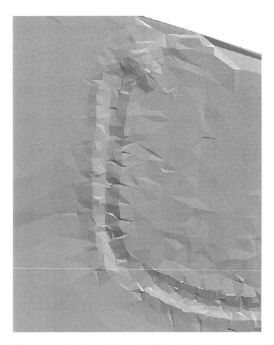

Figure 9.4 Overhead view of TIN model, with artificial illumination.

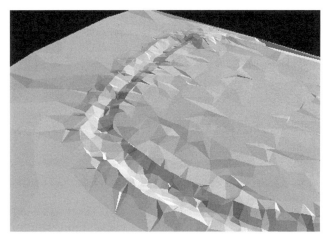

Figure 9.5 TIN model viewed from an angle.

TINS are normally viewed with the surfaces filled with solid colour and artificial illumination used to add an impression of depth. The may also be displayed as three-dimensional surfaces from different directions and elevations, which can have a strong visual impact, and a vertical exaggeration factor can be used to give greater prominence to slight changes in elevation.

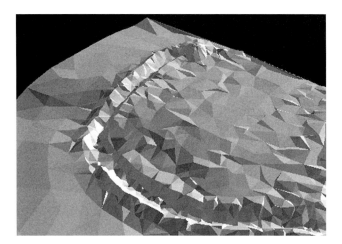

Figure 9.6 TIN model with vertical exaggeration.

It should also be noted that despite a high density of information, as is evident from the number of triangles in the TIN, this model is far from perfect, and an even larger number of points would need to be captured in order to improve it.

Chapter 10

Sources of digital map data

The main focus of this book is on the acquisition of spatial information by means of survey in the field. Ways have been described in which individual surveys can be placed within the framework of a wider co-ordinate system to enable others to locate the site, and to make it possible to combine the data from a number of surveys carried out by different people or at different times. Often, it would be desirable to overlay the survey data onto a base of contemporary mapped data, and this is also possible provided the co-ordinate system used for the survey is the same as that used for other mapping. What is often a problem is the provision of the 'other' data. In many countries digital map data are unobtainable as a product of a national mapping agency, sometimes for political or security reasons. In others, such as the UK, the data are readily available from the Ordnance Survey, but at a price which is likely to be daunting to the individual or, say, an amateur group (at least for the larger-scale data sets). Those working in the United States are in a much more favourable position, as large quantities of data produced by the United States Geological Survey (USGS) can be downloaded from web sites free of charge, while others come on CD at a quite modest cost. (A more detailed description is given in the case study of a site in New Mexico.) Workers elsewhere who need extensive coverage of large-scale data have no choice but to pay for it, either in time or money, but smaller-scale data can be of use in showing the locations of sites or in producing wide-scale distribution maps, and there are some sources of data of this type which are available to anyone at no cost.

ESRI world basemap data

ESRI (Environmental Science Research Institution) is one of the leading producers of GIS software (their products include Arc/Info, Arcview and ArcGIS). They are also, via their web site (http://www.esri.com/data/download/basemap/index.html), major suppliers of digital map data.

The world map database provided by ESRI is inevitably limited in its content, being intended for use at scales no larger than 1:1,000,000, but its scope makes it useful, because it is a source of data for every part of the world. The data layers are in the form of shapefiles, and include coastlines, national boundaries, major roads and railways, rivers, water bodies and contours. This is a map of part of western Europe, showing national boundaries, major cities and main roads and railways:

Figure 10.1 ESRI 1:1,000,000 scale map data for western Europe.

This map of the north-east of England shows the maximum amount of detail available, and has urban areas, major and secondary roads, and contours.

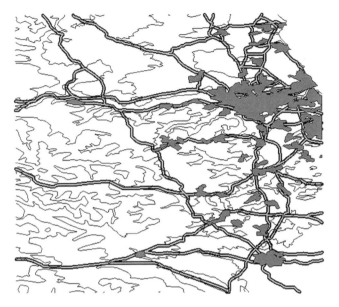

Figure 10.2 ESRI map data for north-east England.

As these data are supplied as shapefiles they are readily usable in any GIS software; in this case Christine GIS is being used again.

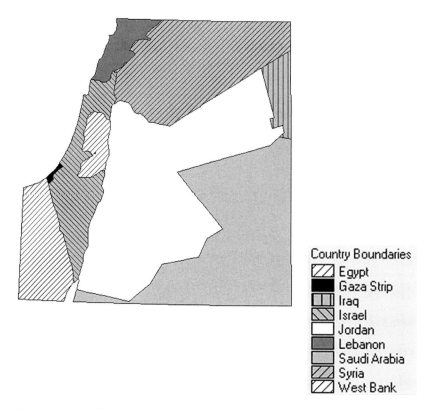

Figure 10.3 ESRI digital data for the eastern Mediterranean.

The map above shows national boundaries in an area to the east of the Mediterranean, centred on Jordan. Below details of other kinds have been added.

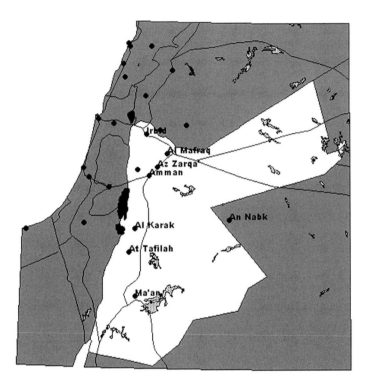

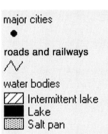

major cities
●

roads and railways
∕∖∕

water bodies
▨ Intermittent lake
■ Lake
▦ Salt pan

Figure 10.4 Map of Jordan and surrounding countries, showing major cities, roads and water bodies.

Shuttle Radar Topography Mission (SRTM) data

The Shuttle Radar Topography Mission is a cooperative project between NASA, the National Geospatial-Intelligence Agency (NGA) of the US Department of Defense and the German and Italian space agencies. It is managed by NASA's Jet Propulsion Laboratory, Pasadena, California (NASA, 2005). It began in February 2000 with an 11-day flight of the Space Shuttle Endeavour. Using a specially modified radar system (Synthetic Aperture Radar, or SAR) elevation data were acquired of over 80 per cent of the Earth's land surface, between the latitudes of 60° north and 56° south. The equipment consisted of two radar antennae, one in the shuttle's payload bay and another on the end of a 60m extendable mast; a technique called radar interferometry was used to turn the two images into terrain model data. The total amount of data collected was 8.6 Terabytes, equivalent to over 14,000 CDs, and two years were needed to process the data to the point where they could be used generally (NASA, 2004).

SRTM data have been processed to produce terrain models of the USA which have a resolution of about 30m, and of the rest of the world for which coverage is available at a resolution of 90m. These can be used to produce quite startling visualisations of landscapes, which can have other types of data overlaid on them (such as satellite images, ratser map data, GPS waypoints, etc.). They are a very useful resource for workers in countries where national mapping does not include digital terrain models, where such models are expensive, or where copyright restrictions make it difficult to disseminate the product of your own work if it includes data purchased from a government agency. They are not perfect, however. Most if not all of the files have missing data, which become visible in the form of irregularly shaped vertical sided holes in the terrain surface. Some parts of the earth's surface were overflown less often than others in the course of the SRTM mission, and in consequence have more missing data. Visualization software such as **3DEM** (by Visualization Software, see below) is capable of patching these holes by interpolation using calculations based on adjacent data points and producing a realistic-looking surface, but of course the missing data remain missing. Coastlines are on the whole rather poorly represented, at least compared with the highly artificial solid (and essentially non-existent) line which we are used to from most kinds of map. It's easy to see when visiting the coast that not only does the division between land and sea move about with time, but that the division is far from being clear-cut; SRTM probably gives a more realistic rendering. Similarly, water surfaces don't appear as flat, and, depending on the shading system employed, they may appear to be speckled with small dots of 'land'.

SRTM data may be obtained via the USGS 'seamless' server at http://seamless.usgs.gov/.

Using SRTM data

The SRTM data can be viewed using a free software package called **3DEM**, a product of Visualization Software LLC by Richard Horne (obtainable from http://www.visualizationsoftware.com/3dem.html). This useful package not only reads SRTM data, but a number of other formats, and in fact it will read any topographic data organised by rows and columns. It will also output terrain models in a number of formats suitable for use in GIS, and save images of its models in bmp, jpg, tiff, png and other common file types.

To use all the functions of 3DEM software it may be necessary to alter some of your PC's settings (Richard Horne, pers. comm.). You will soon find out if this is required because the software will crash as soon as you try to do anything other than an initial two-dimensional display. If this happens:

- Right-click the mouse somewhere in the Desktop area and select **Properties**.
- In the **Display Properties** window click the **Settings** tab, then the **Advanced** button.
- The title and contents of the window which appears now will vary depending on

the exact configuration of your hardware, but there will be a tab labelled **Trouble-shoot**, and you should select this one.

• You will now see this:

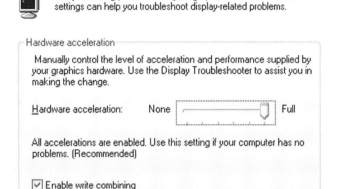

Figure 10.5 Changing hardware acceleration settings to use 3DEM software.

On the line beginning **Hardware acceleration** you have to move the slider control from **Full** towards **None**; how far you need to move it may be a subject for experimentation, but on most PCs I have used it has been necessary to move the slider four spaces to the left. (Some people may feel doubtful about making this kind of modification, and I probably did at first, but I have never known it to cause any problem, even when I have forgotten to re-set the hardware acceleration level after using 3DEM.) When you click OK after changing the setting the screen will go black for a moment.

Opening files in 3DEM

Use **File | Load Terrain Model**. The type to choose is **SRTM data**, the files of which have the extension **hgt**, but 3DEM will read a number of other useful terrain model formats, notably the United States Geological Survey **DEM** format, and **GeoTiff** files. The latter are different from normal tiff files, which may contain any kind of image, in that they contain georeferencing information, and this particular variety of GeoTiff contains elevation data rather than an image. Those with more wide-ranging interests may note that 3DEM can also read information about the surface of Mars from the Viking Orbiter and MOLA systems.

SRTM files have names of the form **N54W002.hgt**; N54 means 54 degrees of latitude north of the Equator, and W002 means 2 degrees of longitude west of the Greenwich meridian, being the location of the south-west corner of the tile of data. You can select a single one, or highlight a group to give a combined model. This image comes from a combination of N54W002, N54W003 and N54W004, and covers much of the north of England and a small part of south-west Scotland.

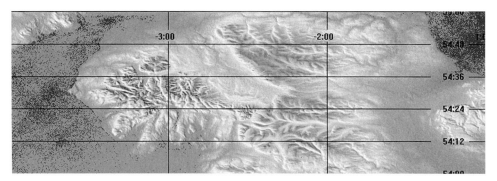

Figure 10.6 SRTM data for the north of England.

The strange appearance of the sea is very evident, but the topography of this fairly rugged part of the UK is clearly defined. A co-ordinate grid showing degrees of latitude and longitude is overlaid, but this can be turned off. (The default shading scheme uses colours, and these can be customised; the grey scale image is for publication purposes only.)

To those familiar with Ordnance Survey maps of the UK, the most striking thing is that the shape of the landscape looks wrong – it seems compressed from north to south. This of course is because the image isn't based on the OS map projection, and is expressed in degrees and not metres. The command **Operation | Change Projection** allows a change to be made, but only to the UTM (Universal Transverse Mercator) system. This global system of grid co-ordinates is discussed elsewhere. Choosing this option produces a request to **Choose UTM Ellipsoid** and a choice of WGS84, WGS72, NAD83 and NAD27. WGS is the World Geodetic System, appropriate to any part of the Earth's surface, while NAD is the North American Datum. The choice of ellipsoid may be determined by any data which is intended to overlay on the surface, as the reference ellipsoid must be the same. In this case WGS84 would be appropriate. The image changes to look like this:

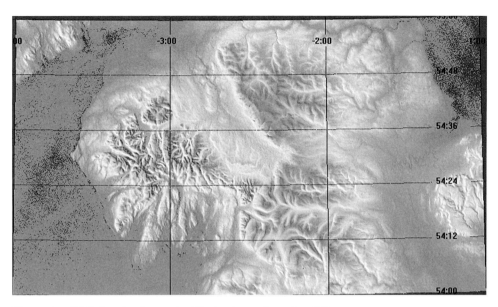

Figure 10.7 SRTM data for the north of England transformed to UTM system.

The shape of the landscape is now more familiar, but the co-ordinates are still in latitude and longitude, and the graticule lines are curved rather than straight.

A useful thing to do is to change the declared elevation of sea-level, to get a better definition of the shape of the coast. This can be done using **Color Scale | modify Scale**. The window which appears allows many changes to be made to the colours used in shading the surface (the elevation classes and colours used may be individually defined and saved for future use), and permits the use of conventions to denote forest cover or snow on higher ground.

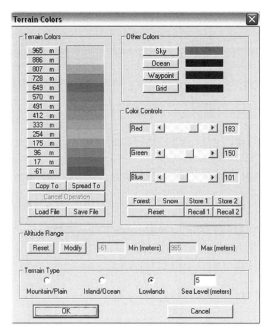

Figure 10.8 3DEM dialogue box for changing terrain colours.

To change the sea-level, just enter a figure other than the default '0' in the field at the lower-right; using 5 changes the appearance of the map to:

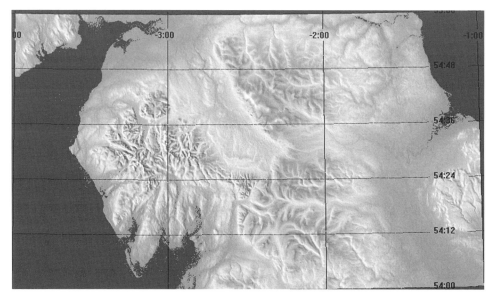

Figure 10.9 SRTM data for the north of England, with modified sea-level.

There is still a speckled appearance in the estuaries and around some islands, but the distinction between 'sea' and 'land' is much clearer.

The above images are saved using the commands **File | save Map Image**, but they don't reflect the exact appearance of the screen, which is this:

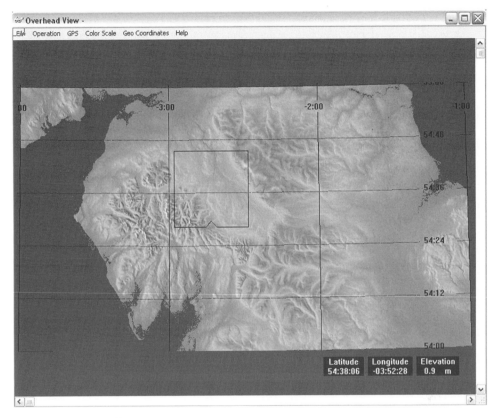

Figure 10.10 3DEM software screen.

The figures at the lower-right give the current position of the mouse pointer, and the small black square shows the area which will be imaged in a three-dimensional view. This square can be moved around the screen by left-clicking the mouse, at which the square will jump so that the middle of the lower side (where the notch is) is at the position of the mouse. The square can be re-sized or rotated by clicking and holding the mouse on any part of its perimeter and moving as needed. When the square has been sized and positioned to your satisfaction the command **Operation | 3D Scene** begins the process of creating the scene. A number of parameters have to be given (defaults exist):

• **Projection Type** The default is **Color**, but alternatives are **I/L** or **R/B**, which produce interlaced or red/blue stereo images for viewing with LCD shutter electronic glasses or red/blue glasses.

- **Projection size** is the size of image in pixels, the default being 640 × 480, the maximum 1024 × 768.
- **Observer's Altitude** can be set in metres, provided that the **Terrain position** is set to **Near** and not **Far**.
- **Terrain illumination** allows entry of the azimuth (direction) and altitude of the light source.
- **Terrain Vert Mag** (terrain vertical magnification) exaggerates the elevation of surface features to make them more visible.
- **Terrain resolution** governs the size of features which will be visble. **Min** gives the 'smoothest' surface, but renders quickly, **Max** shows more detail but may take minutes to produce the image.
- **Terrain type** controls the colours which will be used in rendering to imply a division into mountain and plain, islands and ocean (with blue used for zero or low elevations) or lowlands, which is best for landscapes in which large areas are close to sea-level and the island/ocean option may lead to inappropriate colouring of the sea and land.

Positioning the square like this (looking from the edge of the Pennines towards the Lake District):

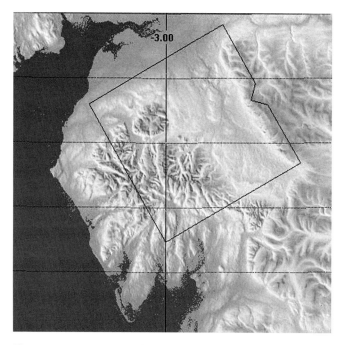

Figure 10.11 3DEM screen showing 3D imaging area.

with an observer elevation of about 2500m, maximum terrain resolution and mountain/plain colouring produces this scene:

Figure 10.12 View of SRTM surface with observer elevation of 2500m.

Elevating the observer to 15,000m gives this:

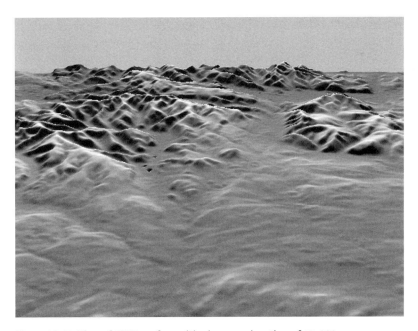

Figure 10.13 View of SRTM surface with observer elevation of 15,000m.

The 3D scene appears in its own window, within which the command **Operation** can be used to vary the appearance; one of the most useful options is **Change Position**, which allows interactive fine tuning, moving the observer up and down, forward and back, and rotating the view left and right. The scene can also be saved in various graphical formats.

In the main map window the command **Operation | View Flyby** opens a window in which the observer automatically moves over the surface, using the current viewing parameters, while **Operation | Animate Flyby** saves the flyby in a movie in AVI or MPEG format.

In addition to the colours which 3DEM generates to render the surface, it's possible to overlay a range of image files, such as satellite data or raster maps showing surface features. (More detail of overlaying raster data sets on terrain models is in Chapter 16.)

Chapter 11

The Butter Market, Barnard Castle, County Durham

The town of Barnard Castle lies on the River Tees in County Durham (the river formerly marked the boundary between County Durham and Yorkshire). The castle which gives the town its name began to be built in the early twelfth century by the Balliol family, and when Bernard Balliol gave land to the townspeople a market was established. The town has been of considerable significance over the years, but most of the extant buildings date to the post-medieval period (the bridge over the Tees, built in 1569, is still a major route across the river). One of the best-known buildings in the town is called the 'Butter Market', an octagonal structure built in the eighteenth century and given to the town in 1747 by Thomas Broakes (http://www.keystothepast.info/k2p/usp.nsf/pws/Keys+to+the+Past+-+Home+Page). Apart from acting as a location for the sale of dairy products, the building became the town's administrative centre, incorporating the elements of town hall, court and jail.

As a subject for the surveyor, the Butter Market offers a number of challenges.

Figure 11.1 Photograph of the Butter Market.

While being fairly regular in form, the projecting lower storey, with its many columns and half-hidden internal features, rendering impossible access to the upper floors, would make many kinds of classical surveying difficult, but features outside the building make matters worse. It lies on what is still a very busy route, and acts as a traffic island; on either side of the road, particularly on the west, there are narrow pavements and the fronts of numerous shops and other small businesses. Setting up an instrument on a pavement would be a practical impossibility, and crossing the road to access the building itself would be very hazardous. Any kind of 'hands-on' survey, apart from requiring permission from the local authority, would involve interrupting the flow of traffic, which would involve in addition the police, traffic-management contractors, negotiations with business proprietors, and a great deal of time and money.

The approach adopted was to produce a three-dimensional model based on photographs, using PhotoModeler® software from EOS Systems http://www.photomodeler.com/ or http://www.photarc.co.uk/. The advantages of this method are that it can be implemented using standard cameras, either film (scanning prints or negatives) or digital; it requires minimal contact with the structure (only one distance needs to be measured in order to give scale to the model), and the time which needs to be spent on fieldwork is very small compared with most other techniques. This isn't to say that it is an effortless technique. Like any other it has to be learnt, and initially progress in modelling may be slow. Archaeological buildings, too, may present special problems when compared with newer ones. In order to locate a point in space the technique relies on being able to identify that point in (usually) at least three photographs, and this is more difficult than it sounds, especially when stonework is eroded or discoloured, and the identification becomes problematical. The small amount of time in the field may be balanced by considerable amounts of time spent in front of a computer, though this is of course in many respects less stressful, and the work can proceed in any weather, or indeed in the dark (this may sound humorous, but those who have conducted any kind of outside work at the latitude of County Durham will be aware just how little useful daylight there can be at some times of the year). It may be pointed out that while the technique employed here requires, in effect, a dedicated set of photographs to be taken (given that they must all use the same camera and focal length of lens, and must give adequate coverage of the building), there are circumstances in which it may be possible to produce reconstructions of buildings or parts of buildings from even a single photograph, opening up the possibility of modelling historic buildings which are no longer in existence, and of which few photographs exist (Bottrill *et al.*, 1998).

Pairs of photographs are worked on together, the operator first marking a series of points in each photograph, then identifying the correspondence between them. The points may be just that – individual points – or points marking the ends of lines, and then surfaces can be constructed between the lines and points. This photograph shows a number of points, lines and surfaces on one photograph, though of course more images have been involved in their creation.

Figure 11.2 The Butter Market with lines and surfaces created using PhotoModeler.

It's obvious that no attempt has been made to capture all the detail in the building. As with all kinds of surveying, a decision has to be made as to how much detail is needed, and this is related to the use to which the final product is to be put. Photographic survey is unusual in that large amounts of detail are captured in a very short time, so that there is scope to change from a simple model to a more detailed one after the fieldwork has been completed (provided there has been sufficient photographic coverage to ensure that the additional detail points are visible in sufficient images), but additional detail still takes time to create, and it is usually best (especially in the case of beginners) to start with a simple model to capture the outline features; including too much detail from the outset is only likely to lead to confusion. When a number of points have been marked on three photographs the project can be 'processed', at which time the software will produce a report on the quality of the links between images and give an estimate of the accuracy which has been achieved, along with suggestions as to how to improve it (such as identifying points on additional photographs). As the project progresses three-dimensional views may be generated, such as this one.

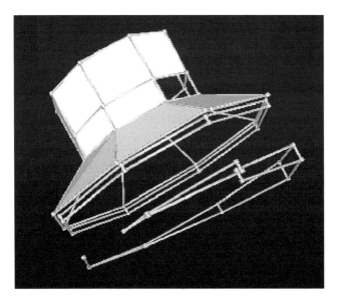

Figure 11.3 A stage in the construction of a 3D model.

Ultimately, when a complete series of surfaces has been developed, the original photographs can be applied to the surfaces as 'textures', which can give a very vivid impression of the real structure, though in many cases obstructions such as bushes growing at the bottom of the walls – or in the case of the Butter Market, litter bins – can rather spoil the effect as they are smeared over the building.

Another option offered by PhotoModeler is output of the model as a dxf file, which means it can then be taken into a CAD package for further work. This is what has been done here, after the outline of the building had been captured from images. A fairly early stage in the CAD model is shown here, in which a start has been made on modelling the columns as cylinders. (PhotoModeler can model cylinders, but it is somewhat involved, and was not attempted in this case.)

Figure 11.4 PhotoModeler 3D model transferred into IntelliCAD.

The flat surfaces were produced using PhotoModeler. The image in Figure 11.4 shows a 'rendered' version of the model, in which light and shade effects have been used. More information on rendering is given in Chapter 15, p. 251. The columns are simple cylinders, but some parts of the building defy this kind of modelling, and may have to be approximated. The metal top to the open 'lantern' is one of these. Its profile is something like this:

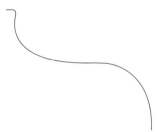

Figure 11.5 Estimated profile of the top of the Butter Market.

which can be created in CAD using the **polyline** tool. (Note that the **spline** tool, which fits a mathematically defined curve to a series of points isn't suitable in this case.) This line can be developed into a surface using the **revolved surface** tool, which requires the construction of a line to act as the axis of revolution, like this:

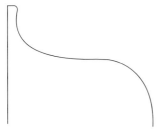

Figure 11.6 Profile of the lantern with a line to act as the axis of rotation.

The command to create the surface is **revsurf**, or use the ⚙ button on the surface toolbar. The command will respond with

Select a linear entity to revolve:

at which the operator must click the polyline, and then with

select the axis of revolution:

(click anywhere on the vertical line).
  The prompt then asks for the

Angle to begin surface of revolution <0>:

(just press **enter**), and the

degrees to revolve entity (+ for ccw, – for cw <360>:

(ccw stands for counter-clockwise, cw for clockwise; the default is to revolve through 360°, which is required, so just press **enter**).
  The surface produced will look something like this:

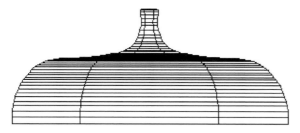

Figure 11.7 Surface produced by the rotation of the profile.

Its exact appearance will depend on the setting of one of the *system variables*, something which many users of CAD have never had to really think about, but in this case it becomes necessary. If the surface is produced as described above it will have six segments, because the variable called **surftab1** (the last character is a figure '1', not a letter 'l') has a default value of six. It can be changed by typing

surftab1 *space*

As soon as the space bar is pressed the command line shows

New current value for surftab1 (2 to 32766) <6>:

(six is the current value); type

8 <enter>

This has to be done before the surface is created. The surface will now look like this (viewed from above right):

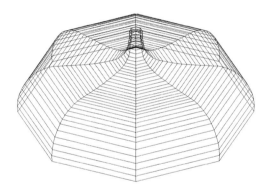

Figure 11.8 Revolved surface with eight segments.

A model of this kind, showing the main surfaces, might suffice for some purposes, and if this is the case it could be completed with only a little more work. There are other features, though, which will probably be needed, such as the windows and 'alcoves' in the upper part of the building. These are far from easy to capture in PhotoModeler as they don't offer projecting features which can be identified on three photographs. It is possible, however, once a suitable face has been constructed, to trace the outline of features onto that face as a two-dimensional drawing. This drawing can then be output with the rest of the model into the dxf file, and again this may be a sufficient record for some purposes. Going further, to create the appearance of real three-dimensional openings in the building, requires considerably more work.

AutoCAD® and other CAD software offering the facility of creating solid models (including the more expensive versions of IntelliCAD®) allow structures to be *subtracted* from each other to create holes of simple or complex shapes, but since the emphasis here is on keeping software costs low an alternative approach is used, making use of surfaces.

To begin with, the 2-dimensional outline of, for example, a window, is needed. This may be imported from PhotoModeler or drawn in the CAD software. The outline must consist of polylines, and this presents an immediate problem, as polylines may only be drawn in the *xy* plane. (There is such a thing as a 3D polyline, but this is much less flexible.) To get round this it is necessary to create a new **User Co-ordinate System** (UCS). In this diagram

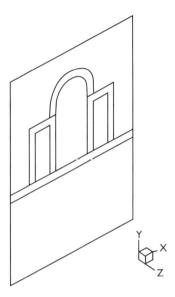

Figure 11.9 A vertical face showing a new user co-ordinate system (the *y*-axis is now vertical).

a series of polylines has been drawn in the plane of a vertical surface. Note that the *xyz* symbol shows the *y* dimension as being vertical, which has permitted the drawing of the polylines. This was achieved using the **UCS** command:

UCS <enter>

and selecting the **3 point** option from the pull-down menu which appears, or by typing

3 <enter>

(the command prompt and menu show a number of other options which are too complicated to describe here). Three points have to be specified, which are

new origin (click on the lower-left corner of the rectangular surface)
point on positive *x*-axis (click on the lower-right corner)
point in *x*–*y* plane with positive y value (click upper-left corner)

All drawing commands will now be executed within this co-ordinate system until the command

UCS <enter>
W <enter>

is given to restore the **world** co-ordinate system, in which all points are ultimately specified.

In fact, two sets of polylines have to be constructed, as shown here.

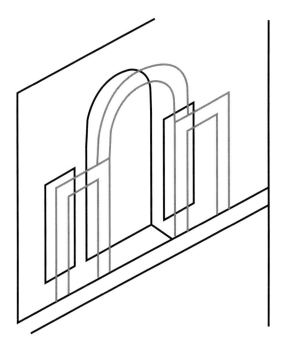

Figure 11.10 Two sets of polylines drawn as a stage in the construction of window openings.

The lines shown in black were created first, using the new UCS; they were then moved away from the drawing plane with the command **move**. The entities to be moved are selected (click on each in turn), then a **base point** (click on any point of the selected polylines), then when the command prompt is

Displacement point:

Type

@0,0,–0.2

to move the polylines away from the drawing plane by 0.2m (the *z* axis is now at 90° to this plane). The lines shown in grey were then created. Two other lines were also drawn, attached to corners of polylines like this:

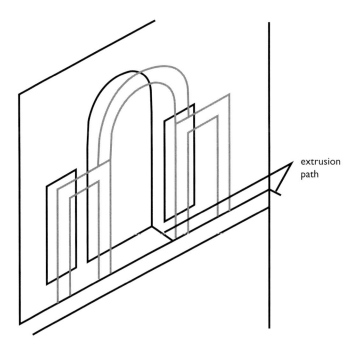

extrusion
path

Figure 11.11 Drawing showing paths for the extrusion of surfaces.

These lines will act as paths along which the polylines will be *extruded* to make surfaces. (After giving the line command, click on a polyline point for the first point, then use **@0,0,0.2** for the second.)

As an example of extrusion, first of all consider the narrow horizontal rectangular moulding which runs across the centre of the rectangular surface. This has a very short extrusion path. Type

   tabsurf <enter>

or use the ▦ tool on the surface toolbar, then select the object to extrude, then the extrusion path. Take care here. When selecting the extrusion path it's essential to click on the path close to the point where it joins the object being extruded; if you click closer to the other end of the path the object will be extruded the wrong way. The extruded surface should look like this when viewed in a rendered model:

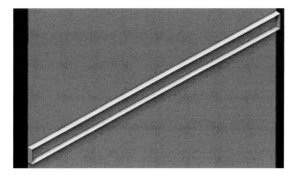

Figure 11.12 Extruded surface of wall moulding.

The object created is hollow; in software supporting solid modelling the extrusion would have an 'outer' surface. To produce the required effect in this version of IntelliCAD you now need to draw another polyline round the outer edge of the extruded surface; rendering the model should now produce:

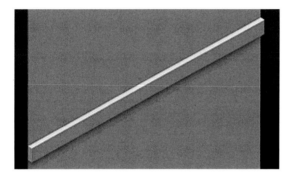

Figure 11.13 Extruded surface closed by the addition of a polyline.

Creating extruded surfaces from the features around the window openings can be done in the same way, as shown below, but there remains the problem of the flat surface of the wall surrounding the openings. As mentioned above, software which supports solid modelling makes this job easier, by allowing the construction of solid shapes which overlap in co-ordinate space and subtracting them from each other, but this isn't possible with surfaces. What has to be done is to fill in the spaces around the openings with a series of surfaces which taken together make up one complex surface. In the diagram the edges of most of these surfaces are shown as broken lines; these are the simple type of surface created with the command **3dface**.

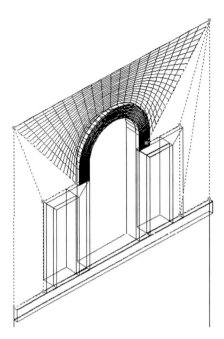

Figure 11.14 Window opening surrounded by 3D faces.

They can be made between any three or four points. In this diagram the vertical rectangle is just made up of lines, with nothing between them.

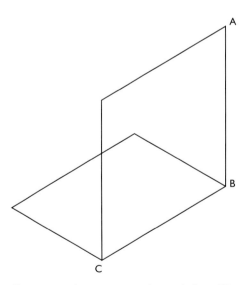

Figure 11.15 An open rectangle consisting of lines.

Giving the command **3dface** produces a command prompt

Invisible edge/<First point of 3dface>:

Clicking the mouse on point A will start the creation of this face, and the prompt will change to ask for more points. (Invisible edges can be used in cases where it is required to have a surface but not to have a definite wireframe entity representing the edge; I have not myself ever made use of them.) If the mouse is clicked on A, B and C in that order, and the command ended by two right-clicks or pressing **enter**, the result looks like this:

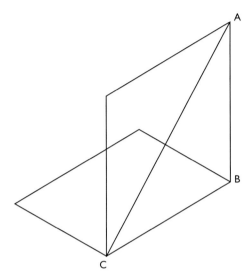

Figure 11.16 A 3D face constructed between three points.

Giving the command **hide** shows that the face really is there:

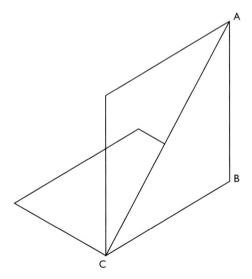

Figure 11.17 A 3D face shown by the use of the 'hide' option.

After point C had been clicked the prompt would have changed to

Invisible edge/<last point>:

indicating that one more point can be used in creating the face. If point D (in the next diagram) had been clicked a four-sided face would have been created, and it's then possible to go on clicking more points as desired; the complete sequence A, B, C, D, E, C (right-click) would produce this:

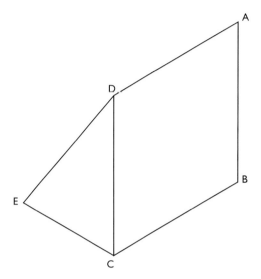

Figure 11.18 Four-point and three-point 3D faces.

The other face, above the head of the window, is more complicated as it involves curved edges. It is in fact a 'Coons surface', the creation of which is described in Chapter 15, where it is used to model a roof with a curved edge. A Coons surface can be made between any four edges as long as their end points join up to make a complete circuit, and it can exist in a plane, as here, or be a complex three-dimensional curve.

When all the surfaces are complete, a rendered version looks like this:

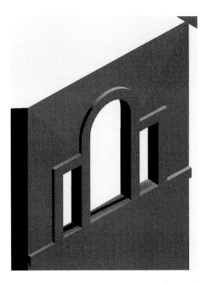

Figure 11.19 Rendered version of completed window.

The lighting has been changed using the control on the render toolbar, to give emphasis to the window openings and the upper surfaces of some of the extruded features, although of course in a full model the interior would be dark. In the version of IntelliCAD used here the lighting options are less sophisticated than in some other software, but they can still be used to produce subtle effects. The basic options include 'sunlight', side light, spot light, side and rear main light with a filler, and 'eyelight' (an effect rather like a camera flash), and all can be customised to change the horizontal and vertical angle of the light direction, its colour and intensity.

Some of the walls of the upper storey of the building have window openings like these, but alternate faces have an alcove opening with a curved inner surface and a top forming a quarter-hemisphere. The curved wall is easy enough to create, first of all drawing a semicircle and then extruding a surface to the appropriate height.

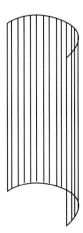

Figure 11.20 Semicircle extruded into a surface.

The top of the opening was made by copying the semicircle and bisecting it with a line from its centre. (The ESNAP setting **centre** can be used to snap a line to the centre of a circle or part of a circle, though to actually snap to this point the mouse has to be placed close to the perimeter of the circle, not the centre, something which seems a little confusing at first.) A polyline was then drawn, starting at one end of the semicircle and, using the **arc** option, a second point was placed on the curve of the semicircle and a final point at the end of the bisecting line (as shown by the cross-and-circle points in the diagram). The semicircle was then deleted, leaving a quarter-circle curve and a radius line.

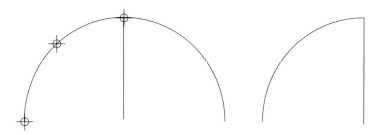

Figure 11.21 Creating a quarter-circle polyline.

These shapes have had to be created in a two-dimensional plane, as the drawn elements can't be created in three dimensions. Now they have to be rotated so that the plane formed by the two lines is vertical, and this is done with the command rotate3d. The command is given first, the the user is prompted to select the objects to rotate (left-click each one, right-click to end selection), after which the prompt is:

Select axis by: Entity/Last/View/Xaxis/Yaxis/Zaxis/<2 points>:

The last, as always, is the default, so all that has to be done is to left-click on the end of the curve and the straight line to give the end points of the axis. The prompt now asks for a rotation angle, which should be 90 or −90, depending on which end of the axis was selected first. To create the quarter-sphere the command to use is **revsurf** (revolved surface), as used to create the shape on the top of the lantern (also available from the **Draw3d** toolbar with the 🐾 button). The prompt asks for a

Linear entity to revolve:

which is the curved line, and at

Select the axis of revolution:

the radius line is clicked. At

Angle to begin surface of revolution <0>:

press **enter,** and the number of

degrees to revolve entity (+ for ccw, − for cw <360>:

will be 180 this time. The result is as in this diagram. The vertical line can be deleted, and the curved surface moved to fit on top of the extruded surface created previously.

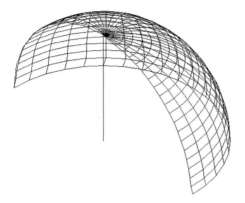

Figure 11.22 Half-hemisphere surface created by revolving a quarter-circle polyline.

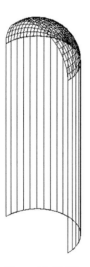

Figure 11.23 Wire-frame version of the complete alcove.

Figure 11.24 Rendered version of the alcove.

The finished wire-frame and rendered versions are shown here, the latter in its final position and surrounded by flat surfaces as were created round the windows.

The above account describes all the drawing operations which were necessary to complete the model of the Butter Market at this level of resolution. Below are two images of the whole model, a three-dimensional wire-frame representation and a rendered version.

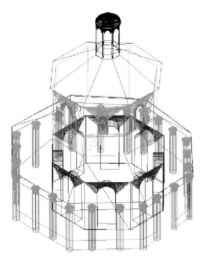

Figure 11.25 Wire-frame version of the complete model of the Butter Market.

Figure 11.26 Rendered image of the model of the Butter Market.

Some elements have been left out of the wire-frame version in order to aid clarity.

The model is essentially based on the photographic model, but some parts of the building have proved difficult to represent in this way, and have been approximated. The pillars, for example, as mentioned above, while they are about the correct size have been created as cylinders and not as accurate representations of the originals. The capitals, too, are regular revolved surfaces, and give a general indication of their appearance. Nor, of course, does this model show any of the many variations from what was the original intended appearance of the building caused by weather, accident, repairs and maintenance over a period of over two and a half centuries.

Chapter 12

The Boeotia field survey project

An archaeological field survey of this large province of central Greece began in 1979, conducted mainly by members of the Universities of Bradford and Cambridge (and latterly the University of Durham). The part of this survey which is discussed here, bordering the ancient city of Thespiae, was surveyed in the mid-1980s (Bintliff, 1997; Bintliff and Snodgrass, 1985).

The survey area represented is just over 3000m across from east to west, and it was subjected to intensive fieldwalking over several summer seasons. Transects were established to (ultimately) cover the whole landscape.

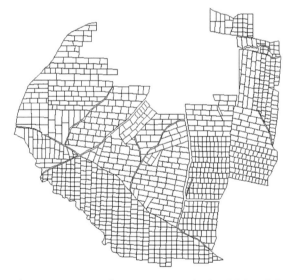

Figure 12.1 Layout of survey transects in the vicinity of Thespiae city.

The size of the transects varied somewhat because of topographic factors such as the size and shape of present-day fields, location of roads and tracks, etc. The boundaries of the transects were located with total stations. Each transect was surveyed by people walking along lines 15m apart, scanning a notional 2m wide strip and counting every sherd which could be seen within this strip. Small amounts of pottery with diagnostic features (i.e. which could be dated) were collected for later analysis. As always, the ground surface was variably visible; in some places there was bare soil, in others stubble or a thin growth of weeds, yet in others there were standing crops, and some areas were completely covered with concrete.

Another variable was transect area, and of course so were the counts of ceramic material. The latter varied from zero (eleven transects out of 1180) to 11,280. Counts of dated sherds (of very much smaller magnitude) were other variables. Given the nature of the data, a GIS is the most appropriate kind of software to use to display it. In this case the use of Christine GIS will be described, but any other GIS could be used.

The image above was obtained by adding the polygon shapefile (called OFF-SITE.SHP) to a view and using a **Single Symbol** display. To obtain a first map of the basic ceramic counts (the attribute table field is called CERAM), use

Theme | Properties

Click the **General** tab and change **Classification Options** from **Single Symbol** (all polygons are the same) to **Intervals**. It wouldn't be appropriate to use **Unique Values** in this case, as while there are many different values of the variable CERAM, they all represent the same thing, i.e. the number of ceramic sherds. Unique Values should be used where different values of a variable represent different things, such as site type, in which case we would want to differentiate clearly between the classes of the variable – blue for round barrow, red for long barrow, or whatever it might be. In order to display the variation in the value of ceramic counts, we need to *classify* the variable into groups of values, and then shade these in a way which reflects greater or lesser value rather than a qualitative difference.

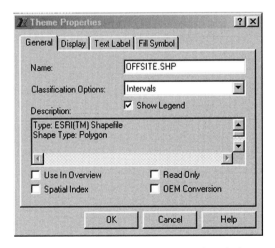

Figure 12.2 Christine GIS theme properties window.

Figure 12.3 Choosing a database field for classification of the transects.

As soon as the Intervals option has been chosen, another window opens in which the field to be used for classification can be chosen (CERAM). Click OK in this window, but before clicking OK in the Theme Properties window, click the **Intervals** tab (which isn't visible until a field has been chosen, and so doesn't appear in the image above).

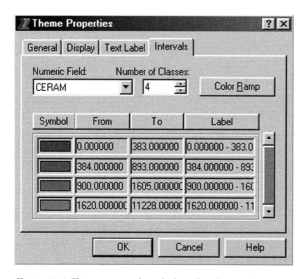

Figure 12.4 Theme properties window showing a colour ramp.

This shows the number of classes (4), the values included in each category, and the colours to be used to show them. Initially these colours were very distinct from one another (more suitable for indicating Unique Values), but this image shows the window after the **Color Ramp** button has been clicked, producing four shades of the same basic colour. The number of categories can be increased (up to 155) by typing a number in the **Number of Classes** field or using the scroll buttons at the end of this field. Each time this is done, the **Color Ramp** button has to be clicked in order to restore a suitable range of shades, and as more categories are chosen the ramp will change from one colour to two which blend into each other (from green to blue, for example). The colours used are decided by the software, but it is possible to force it to use your own. Having chosen the number of classes, double-click on the first colour to open the Theme Properties window.

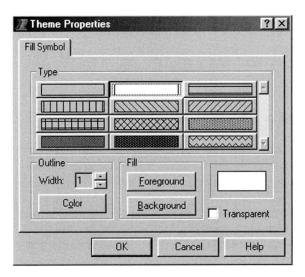

Figure 12.5 Theme properties window showing fill symbols.

This allows you to set the colour for the first class. For example, under **Outline** click **Color** and choose black, then under **Fill** click **Foreground** and choose white. The choices will be reflected in the preview sample at the lower right. Click OK. Now go to the last class in the list and do the same thing, this time choosing a black fill. This has established the colours for the two ends of the ramp, and clicking the **Color Ramp** button now will create a series of shades and/or colours between the specified points. In this example it will be a series of grey shades ranging from white to black (10 classes), and the displayed view would look like this:

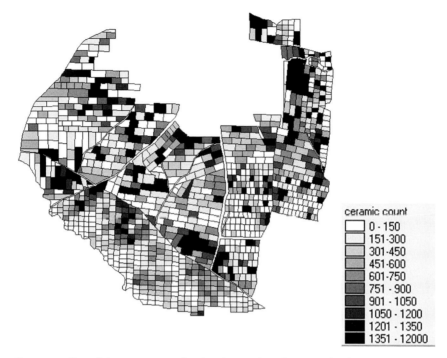

Figure 12.6 Map of the survey area showing the number of pottery sherds recorded in each transect by varying shades of grey.

In practice it will often be found that colour ramps don't differentiate well between classes because the colours created are *too* similar to each other and tend to blend rather too seamlessly. It's possible to choose exactly the colour and shade you want for each class, and in many cases this is what you will have to do. The numerical class boundaries may also need modification, as they are chosen simply by dividing the range of values by the number of classes, giving ranges such as 74–105, but in **Theme Properties** it is possible to set your own values of **From** and **To** (for the extremes of the class), and also of **Label**, which enables you to give a name to a class, rather than just accepting its numeric label. This has been done here, using class intervals of 150 (except for the last one).

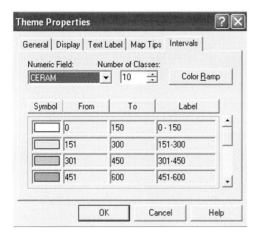

Figure 12.7 Theme properties window used to set specific class boundaries and shade colours.

Note that when entering new values in the From and To fields it's necessary to press the **enter** key after each one (rather than **tab**, as is common in table entries) or the value won't be changed, and that the Label field doesn't automatically update, it has to be done manually.

Having gone to the trouble of creating the legend you want it's important to remember to save it by right-clicking on the name of the theme in the legend area of the view and choosing

Legend | Save

to save the legend in a file from which it can be retrieved when needed.

Looking at the result, it can be seen that 'low', 'medium' and 'high' classes can be discerned, but there are a very large number of transects which appear to be more or less white, implying that there is little pottery there, when in fact there may be several hundred sherds present. This is a consequence of applying a scheme of equal class intervals over the whole data range when there are far more occurrences of some values than others. There are, for example, only 40 transects with ceramic counts over 2,700, while 561 (almost half) have values between 0 and 300 and 233 are between 300 and 600. It would be much better to try to create class intervals which reflect better the nature of the data set.

The intention here is not to interpret the data, nor to discuss the theory and methodology of this type of field survey, but rather to look at ways of displaying and manipulating the results. For the sake of clarity some simplification of the actual Boeotia survey analysis has been made in what follows; for more detail see Bintliff *et al.*, 1999. (There is a large literature on fieldwalking surveys, see for example Banning, 2002; Bintliff *et al.*, 2000; Haselgrove *et al.*, 1985; Schofield, 1991). It is immediately evident from this plot that there is clear clustering of ceramic density in certain parts of the area. The high counts around the concave area to the north are accounted for by proximity to the ancient city of Thespiae, which occupies the area immediately to the north, but there are other hot-spots which can't be explained in this way.

The ceramic counts contain a lot of information, but there are two things to consider about them. First, The transects are of different sizes, so to some extent a higher count in one transect compared with another may be caused simply by there being more area in which to count sherds. Second, the visibility of the ground surface varies from transect to transect, some having a bare soil, some a thin covering of crop, weeds or stubble, and some having a surface which is almost totally covered in vegetation; obviously this will also affect the number of sherds which can be seen. Clearly, it isn't possible to count the sherds which aren't visible, nor to make the transects all of the same size (though of course this could have been done at the start of the survey), but it is possible to do something to get a more complete picture of the actual density of pottery sherds on the surface throughout the survey area.

Taking the question of visibility first, an estimate was made in the field of the amount of ground visible in each transect, and this was recorded as whole-number values between 1 (little visible) and 10 (all visible, a fairly rare occurence); obviously if there was no visible ground the transect was not examined. The calculation of how many sherds might have been counted can be performed within a GIS, but it is rather more involved than might be expected, and it's probably better to do it in a spreadsheet and then add the results to the table of attributes of the theme, especially as a spreadsheet is probably the most convenient way of entering the information in the first place.

Suppose part of the spreadsheet looks like this:

	A	B	C	D
1	Transect	Count	Visibility	Vis. Corrected count
2	702	329	7	

Figure 12.8 Part of a spreadsheet showing transect number, sherd count and a visibility index.

Transect number 702 has a ceramic count of 329 and an estimated visibility of 7 (out of 10), equivalent to 70%. A column has been created to hold a figure of 'visibility-corrected count'. A formula to calculate the value of this new variable would be

```
=B2*(10/C2)
```

and the result would be 470. This formula could then be copied down the whole table to give a visibility-corrected figure for each transect. Most calculations would result in fractional numbers, which would be somewhat inconvenient (as well as suggesting an inappropriate degree of precision in what is an exercise in estimation). A better formula would be

```
=INT(B2*(10/C2))
```

INT is a spreadsheet function which turns the result of the calculation within the brackets into a whole number or integer.

This gives an estimate of the number of sherds which would have been counted if all the ground area had been visible, but it leaves the question of how to take account of the fact that the transects are of different sizes. Depending on how the transects were established in the field the area of each may already be available, but this won't always be the case. Calculating areas is laborious, but in a GIS the operation can be automated. Christine doesn't currently offer a built-in function, but the facility is available via a *script*, effectively a program which can be run within the software to perform the job. Most GIS packages allow scripts to be run, and they can be written by the individual user who has sufficient knowledge of how to do it. The script in this case is called **calculate_lengths_and_areas.cst**, and it's distributed with the software. The procedure to run it is as follows.

- Right-click on **Scripts** in the legend area, select **New Script** from the menu. A window will open in the drawing area, called **Script 1**, and this name will also appear in the legend area below the word **Scripts**. The window is currently empty.
- On the menu, choose **Script | Load Script**, and in the dialogue box navigate to the script file **calculate_lengths_and_areas.cst**; select it in the usual way.

    This file isn't 'the script' itself. It contains a text version of the instructions which make up the script, but these have to be processed before Christine can run them.

- The script text appears in the script window. Click on the menu command Run, and from the submenu choose **Check syntax** (the only command in this menu which is available at this point). Nothing appears to happen, but when you choose the **Run** command again, the submenu command **Run** is available. Click on this command and a dialogue box appears in which you can choose the View in which the script is to operate (press OK), then the Theme in that View (OK again). Once again, nothing appears to happen, but if you now right-click on the name of the Theme and choose the **Table** from the pull-down menu, two new fields will have been created in it (*assuming it to be a polygon theme*), called **Perimeter** and **Area**, and these will be filled with the appropriate values for each polygon.

This leaves the area values in the attribute table in Christine, and the information about pottery density in the spreadsheet. I have found it most satisfactory to transfer the area data to the spreadsheet and perform other calculations there, then finally copy it back to Christine.

First it's necessary to save the attribute table in its new form, with the area values (**Table | Save Table**) as a delimited text file. This is a plain text file in which a particular character is used to separate the values in individual columns (the user selects the character for delimiter, usually a comma). Open the table in the spreadsheet. The only information needed from this file is the area, and this can easily be copied and pasted into the file containing the visibility data.

	A	B	C	D	E	F
1	Transect	Count	Visibility	Vis. corrected count	Area	density(hec)
2	702	329	7	470	2975.16	

Figure 12.9 Spreadsheet showing additional information in the form of a visibility-corrected sherd count and the area of the transect.

The resulting spreadsheet might have a structure as shown here. Another field has been added (called **density(hec)**) which is going to contain the value of sherds per hectare (taking account of visibility as well). The formula to enter in this cell is:

$$= INT(D2*(10000/E2))$$

which gives a value of 1579. Again this is copied down the whole column.

To get this information back into Christine, I have found it best to save it not as a text file, but in the format called dbf ('dBase' – use the command **File** | **Save As** and choose the **dbf** option).

Right-click on **Tables**, choose **Open Tables**. In **Files of Type:** choose the **dBASE III (*.dbf)** option. Locate the file saved from the spreadsheet and open it. The file will appear in a new window, with the column names (which were originally pieces of text in spreadsheet cells) now formally identified.

With a table open the menu will contain commands appropriate to managing tables. Click on the command Tables and choose the option **Merge Tables:**

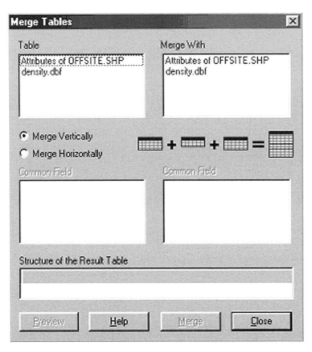

Figure 12.10 Dialogue box for merging tables in Christine GIS.

Under **Table** select the name of the table of attributes belonging to the shapefile (always called **'Attributes of. . .'** followed by the name of the shapefile. Under **Merge With** choose the name of the file which has just been added to the project, then click the button **Merge Horizontally** (the new table contains new columns to add to the attribute table, rather than new rows). A list of all the fields in each table will appear in the areas labelled **Common Field**, and here the name of the field common to the tables must be chosen. (In this case the common field would be the transect number, but it isn't essential for the fields to have the same name, though you have to make sure that they contain the same data type.) The **Preview** key can be used to see what the result of merging the tables will be (and once merged they can't be unmerged), before the **Merge** key is used to join the tables permanently.

With the new values now stored in the attribute table they can be used as the basis of a graphical scheme as described above:

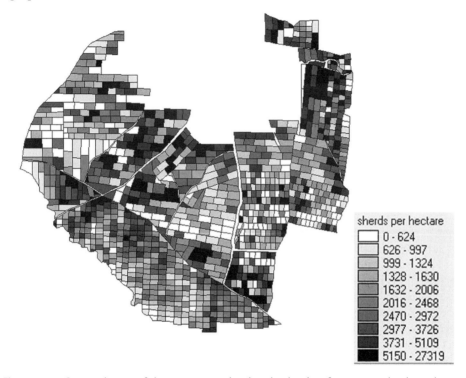

sherds per hectare

	0 - 624
	626 - 997
	999 - 1324
	1328 - 1630
	1632 - 2006
	2016 - 2468
	2470 - 2972
	2977 - 3726
	3731 - 5109
	5150 - 27319

Figure 12.11 Grey-scale map of the survey area showing the density of pottery as sherds per hectare.

This shows a grey-scale display indicating ten levels of ceramic density.

Chapter 13

A survey of an earthwork feature on Cockfield Fell, County Durham

The area of Cockfield Fell contains a number of earthworks which are scheduled monuments, but about which little is known, although they have been conjectured to be prehistoric in date by analogy with similar structures elsewhere. In addition to these, there are numerous relics of more recent industrial exploitation, mostly pits created in the process of mineral extraction, more extensive quarries, and spoil heaps. There are also the remains of railway lines which served the industries. The local vegetation type is rough grassland.

Some of the possibly prehistoric earthworks are covered in bracken growth and not easy to see, but one chosen for survey has a cover of rough grass with reeds growing in the ditch. The enclosure is roughly square in shape, although the northern side has been severely truncated by Haggerleases Quarry. Around most of the perimeter an outer bank is visible, with an inner ditch. There is little trace of an inner bank, and the outer bank is only faintly visible to the south-west. There may be an original break in the perimeter on the east side.

For the first survey the instruments used were a prismatic compass and a laser rangefinder, the latter having a claimed maximum range of 1000m (to a suitable target) and an accuracy of ±1m.

The area around the earthwork has evidence of the existence in the fairly recent past of a number of land divisions consisting of wire fences supported on wooden posts, with some of the latter surviving. Just a few metres to the south-west of the enclosure is a somewhat more substantial post, about 25cm square, standing to a height of about 1.4m. This was tall enough to be visible over the whole of the proposed survey area, which has only a gentle slope from north to south, and was chosen as an experimental target, to use as a reference point for the survey and so remove the need to carry anything larger to the site than the rangefinder and compass, both of which would fit in a reasonably large pocket.

The first task was to locate this reference point within the landscape. A compass resection would have been hindered by the fact that of the identifiable features which were present on the 1:50,000 scale Ordnance Survey maps, all of them were clustered to the west and north, with nothing suitable to the east or south. (The village of Cockfield is visible but the houses in it are not sufficiently differentiated on the map.) At a distance of approximately 1000m on the River Gaunless there are the remains of a viaduct which once carried the railway line, but while these are quite easily visible they are not easy to locate on the modern map. In view of this, a single compass bearing was taken to one of the most easily identified structures, the Stag's Head, a disused public house, and a distance measurement made with the rangefinder to a part of the building which was apparently present on the map. The bearing was 265° and the distance 439m. No attempt was made to correct the distance measurement for slope.

Since compass bearings take as their reference the direction of magnetic north, it is very easy to convert a bearing taken *to* an object into the 'back bearing', i.e. the bearing which would be observed at that object when looking in the direction from which the observation was actually made. This is done by adding 180° to the observed bearing, and if this comes to more than 360°, subtracting 360 from the answer. In this case the observed bearing was 265°; adding 180 gives 445, and subtracting 360 leaves 85. So the bearing of the survey reference point, taken from the Stag's Head, would have been 85°. This is of course a magnetic bearing, not a bearing measured from north as defined by the Ordnance Survey grid. Information on the map indicates that the current deviation of magnetic north from grid north is approximately 4° west, so 4° needs to be subtracted from the observed bearing, giving 81°. The position of the pub can be obtained from the map, and given a bearing and distance to the reference point, its co-ordinates can be worked out.

Using the 1:50,000 scale map, the location of the Stag's Head can be taken as NZ 111 252. The square NZ has its origin 400,000 metres east and 500,000 metres north of the false origin of the Ordnance Survey grid. To produce completely numeric co-ordinates for a point within NZ, we need to generate a pair of co-ordinates in which the easting is more than 400,000, and the northing more than 500,000 (i.e. 4 followed by 5 digits, and 5 followed by 5 digits). In this case if we add a figure 4 at the start of the easting, and a figure 5 at the start of the northing we get 4111, 5252. These numbers are too small by a factor of 100 (they each have only four digits, instead of six), so two zeroes need to be added at the end of each, giving 411100, 525200, the estimated distance in metres east and north of the grid origin.

The formula used to work out the *difference* in eastings and northings between two points is this:

Using E as the difference in eastings, N as the difference in northings, D as the distance between the points, and Bg as the bearing measured from one point to another,

$$E = D \times \sin Bg \quad \text{(distance} \times \text{the sine of the bearing)}$$
$$N = D \times \cos Bg \quad \text{(distance} \times \text{the cosine of the bearing)}$$

Since we must start from the known point (the Stag's Head), the bearing is 85°, and the distance was measured as 439m, so the equation becomes

$$E = 439 \times \sin(81)$$
$$N = 439 \times \cos(81)$$

Which is the same as

$$E = 439 \times 0.98769 = 433.59591$$
$$N = 439 \times 0.15643 = 68.67277$$

(The values of the sine and cosine have been given approximately; a calculator or a spreadsheet would give more figures, but the work here is of a relatively low order of precision. The co-ordinate differences should be given to the nearest metre.)

Adding the results to the estimated position of the Stag's Head gives

$$411100 + 434 = 411534$$
$$525200 + 69 \ = 525269$$

This is a very approximate figure, partly because the bearing is measured only to the nearest degree (it is possible to estimate to ½°, but in this case the figure was closer to the whole number), and partly because the distance measurement was measured to the nearest metre and not corrected for slope, but mainly because the grid reference to the Stag's Head is itself only very approximate. NZ 111 252 (a 'six figure' grid reference) defines a 100m square, and we only know that the point of interest is *somewhere* within it, which means that the location of the survey reference point is similarly limited in accuracy.

In order to obtain the best estimate of the survey reference point, OS digital data sets were used to obtain a location for the Stag's Head (or part of it) to the nearest metre. Using the 1:50,000 scale colour raster data a figure of 411226, 525267 was obtained (showing that the original estimated position was not very good anyway, even to six figures!). Adding the calculated differences to these figures gives an easting of 411660 and a northing of 525336, differing by 126m and 67m from the first estimate. Obtaining grid co-ordinates to the nearest metre isn't really feasible for most individual fieldworkers or small groups, unless their work is concentrated in small areas, as the cost of obtaining Ordnance Survey digital data (as noted elsewhere) is considerable, and the procedure fairly complex. The large-scale paper maps (1:10,000) are no longer available, and were themselves quite costly in any case. Probably the best solution is the use of small single-receiver GPS units, the sort which can be bought for £150 and upwards. Locations obtained using these instruments are accurate to within a few metres, and could satisfactorily be used to locate the survey reference point in a case such as this. A Garmin GPS12XL instrument was placed on the gatepost used in the survey, and gave co-ordinates of NZ 11668 25325, or 411668 525325. This differs from the estimate using the more precise location of the Stag's Head by 8m and 11m, which can be regarded as quite a good degree of agreement, though of course the GPS co-ordinates could have been generated with the same precision even in the absence of any identifiable mapped feature.

Once the co-ordinates of the reference point have been obtained, the same procedure of taking bearings and measuring distances can be used to fix the position of points on the earthwork enclosure. The advantage of using the rangefinder for measurement, and of taking the bearings *to* the reference point rather than from it is that a single worker can walk round the perimeter taking measurements at significant points (changes of direction, breaks, etc.) without needing anyone else to hold the end of a tape, and without having to mark the points of detail which are being measured. Obviously this would not be satisfactory for more precise work, but it offers a very rapid method of producing good-quality reconnaissance surveys.

Once it becomes necessary to carry out the calculations given above more than a small number of times, or in cases where confidence in using a calculator is lacking, it's worth employing the aid of a spreadsheet. The formulae given below are suitable for use in a Microsoft Excel® or OpenOffice worksheet.

Calculating co-ordinates from compass survey

This is the content of a spreadsheet file used to calculate co-ordinates from the compass bearings and rangefinder measurements made in the Cockfield Fell survey. In the first two columns are the field observations – the compass bearing as observed (i.e. *from* the observer *to* the post used as a reference object, and not corrected for magnetic variation from true north) and the distance measured with the rangefinder (not corrected for slope). These figures have of course just been typed in. The next columns are as follows:

Bearing from post is the magnetic bearing of the observer position *from* the post (obtained by adding 180° to the observed bearing).

Corrected bearing is the bearing from the post with a correction of –4° to account for magnetic variation (this is an approximate correction which is sufficient for the accuracy of this survey).

Bearing (radians) is the value of the corrected bearing converted into radians as required by the software (radians are discussed above, but one radian is equal to about 57.3°).

E diff from gatepost is the distance in metres of the observer from the gatepost measured along the easting (*x*) axis of the co-ordinate system.

N diff from gatepost is the distance along the northing (*y*) axis.

Easting and *Northing* are the complete numerical co-ordinates of the observer position (i.e. the distance in eastings and northings measured from the false origin of the co-ordinate system, a point in the Atlantic Ocean to the south-west of the Scilly Isles).

	C bearing to post degrees (mag.)	D distance to post m	E bearing from post (degrees)	F corrected bearing	G bearing (radians)	H E diff from gatepost	I N diff from gatepost	J Easting	K Northing
8	242	84	62	58	1.012291	71.23604	44.51322	411739.2	525369.5
9	238	81	58	54	0.942478	65.53038	47.61061	411733.5	525372.6
10	242	78	62	58	1.012291	66.14775	41.3337	411734.1	525366.3

Bearing to post	Field observation
Distance to post	Field observation
Bearing from post	=IF(C8 + 180>360,C8 + 180 − 360,C8 + 180) Calculates the bearing of the observer from the post: see below
Corrected bearing	=E8 − 4 Corrects the bearing by subtracting four (degrees) from the observed bearing, which is in cell E8
Bearing (radians)	=RADIANS(F8) Converts the bearing in degrees to radians
E diff from post	=D8*SIN(G8) Multiplies the distance by the sine of its bearing
N diff from post	=D8*COS(G8) Multiplies the distance by the cosine of its bearing
Easting	=411668 + H8 Adds the easting difference to the easting of the post
Northing	=525325 + I8 Adds the northing difference to the northing of the post

Calculating the bearing of the observer from the post

The formula for this simple calculation looks at first sight rather worrying:

=IF(C8 + 180>360,C8 + 180 − 360,C8 + 180)

It says above that the bearing *from* the observer is converted to the bearing *to* the observer (what a surveyor would call the 'back bearing') by adding 180° to the bearing observed in the field. This is true, but of course it can give rise to a bearing which is greater than 360°. On page 179 the solution to this is given: if adding 180° to the bearing gives a number greater than 360, then subtract 360 from it, and this is what the formula does.

It begins, as always, with the '=' sign, telling the software that what follows is a formula and not just a string of characters, and this is followed by the word 'IF', one of the many 'functions' of the spreadsheet; this indicates that the formula may have more than one outcome, depending on the result of a test of some sort. 'IF' is followed by an opening bracket (as always with a function), and immediately after this comes the test, followed by the two possible outcomes. In normal language the formula could be expressed as: 'If adding 180 to the number in cell C8 gives a result which is greater than 360 then subtract 360 from this result, otherwise display the result as it is.'

The small amount of effort needed to type these formulae into the appropriate cells will be amply rewarded. No matter how many measurements have been taken, the formulae only have to be typed once. As they are entered, the *result* of each calculation appears in the worksheet cell (though if the cell is highlighted, it is the formula, not the result, which is seen in the formula bar). Having completed the formulae for the first row (corresponding to the first distance and bearing measurement), the equivalent formulae may be copied into the subsequent rows very easily. Just click the mouse on the first cell containing a formula, and, holding down the left-hand button, drag the mouse along the row until the final cell is reached. This will cause a heavy outline to appear around the cells, with a small black square at the bottom right-hand corner of the cell at the right-hand end on the selected group. Release the mouse button, and place the cursor over this square. The cursor will change from its usual form of a thick cross with a white centre to a thin black one; now press and hold the left-hand button again, and drag the mouse down until every line corresponding to a pair of field measurements is highlighted. The correct formulae will be entered in all the cells, and their results displayed. Note that the formulae are not identical to each other, but are equivalent. In the first row the cell references will be to C8, D8, E8 etc., in the second to C9, D9, E9, and so on. It doesn't matter if you have 10 measurements, or 10,000, the formulae still only have to be entered once, and indeed they can be copied from this file to another, as often as required.

Plotting a survey with Terrain Tools

The problem with this is that most software of this kind, being aimed at the civil engineering market, is very expensive (typically several thousand pounds for a single installation) and therefore beyond the reach of most individual workers or groups on a small budget. Exceptions to this rule seem to be few, but one is a package called Terrain Tools, produced by a small company in Vancouver, British Columbia, Canada (Softree Technical Systems Inc., http://www.softree.com/index.htm). Softree do in fact produce sophisticated civil engineering software, costing several thousand dollars, but there is also a very useful freeware version, which can be downloaded from http://www.softree.com/products/ttools.htm.

When Terrain Tools is first started, this is what you will see, initially with the window called 'Plan:1' minimised:

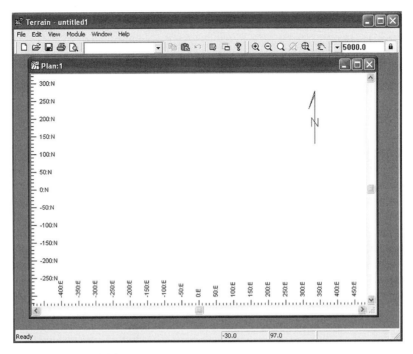

Figure 13.1 Terrain Tools initial screen.

The functions of the toolbar buttons are what would usually be expected of Windows® software. The box at the right-hand end of the toolbar, containing the figure 5000, indicates the scale of the current plan, which is of course empty at the moment. If you change this, which may be done either by using the scroll button and choosing an alternative, or by highlighting the figure 5000 with the mouse and then typing a new number (and then pressing the *return* key), nothing will happen to the size of the window, but the co-ordinates along the edges will change.

In order to get the information from our survey into a Terrain Tools plan, a little preparation is needed. At the moment the data exist as co-ordinates in a spreadsheet, but they need to be saved into a plain text file (often called an ASCII file) before they can be used. The most convenient way to do this is to copy the co-ordinate pairs for each feature type into a separate sheet of the workbook, and this can then be saved as a text file using the **File | Save As** command. In this survey there are three features (inner side of ditch, top of bank, and mound), so there will be three new sheets to create. Terrain Tools requires the data to be in the form of x,y,z, code, so the new sheets will need to contain information in this form:

411670.0   525382.0 ditch
411668.0   525369.0 ditch
411667.5   525356.0 ditch
411668.0   525349.0 ditch
411676.4   525337.0 ditch

```
411689.0   525331.4  ditch
411700.6   525330.2  ditch
411715.3   525333.3  ditch
411724.9   525336.1  ditch
411726.0   525352.0  ditch
411725.9   525362.6  ditch
411726.3   525368.9  ditch
411723.9   525380.9  ditch
```

(There are no z co-ordinates, but this will be dealt with during input of the file.)

The individual sheets need to be saved in the form of text files, which can be either 'tab-delimited' (where tab characters indicate the division between columns in the sheet), or 'comma-delimited'. The default filename extension for tab-delimited files is .txt, while for comma-delimited it's .csv ('comma-separated value'). When the sheet is saved in one of these forms you will see a number of warnings about possible loss of information, but these can be ignored. The plain text files may be opened with any word-processor or text editor, such as WordPad or Notepad; if you do this the file may look like this

```
411670.0      525382.0      ditch
411668.0      525369.0      ditch
411667.5      525356.0      ditch
```

if it's tab-delimited, or like this

```
411670.0,525382.0,ditch
411668.0,525369.0,ditch
411667.5,525356.0,ditch
```

if it's comma-delimited. Either type can be used by Terrain Tools. One problem which has been observed is that if there are blank lines at the end of the text file this may cause the generation of spurious points with zero co-ordinates, so a check should be made for these.

In the Terrain Tools window, click on

File | Insert File

and choose the name of the first feature type to plot. A window named 'Import Options' will open, and here some important information needs to be communicated to the software.

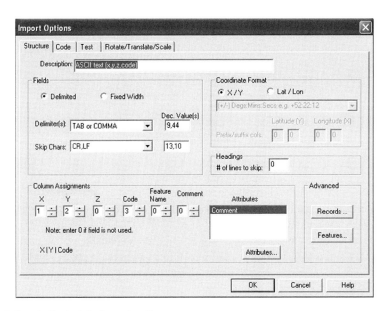

Figure 13.2 Terrain Tools data import options.

At the bottom of the window is an area labelled 'Column Assignments' which shows where x, y, z co-ordinates and other information are to be found in the file. In this case columns 1 and 2 are used for x and y, and 3 for the feature type, and these numbers must be correctly set here; since there is no z co-ordinate the z option must be set to zero (it actually tells you this on the screen). Other information may be given by clicking the 'Code' tab. Here, under 'Code Properties' Terrain Tools may be told how to treat the information in the file.

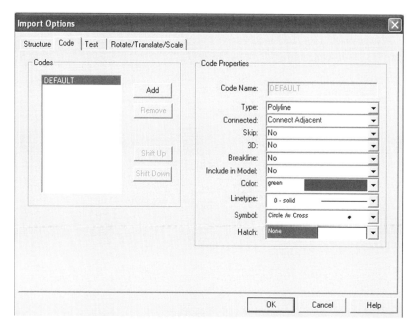

Figure 13.3 Terrain Tools data import options.

Type indicates what kind of feature we are dealing with. **Polyline** means what most people would call a 'line' feature – a series of points connected to each other (the prefix 'poly' means that there are, or may be, more than two points making up the line, so that it consists of a series of straight segments). All the features in the survey are polylines. The other type is **Point**, where each point represents an individual feature. Archaeological point features might be 'findspots' of artefacts, where the location has no real dimensions, or they could be features with real dimensions (round barrows, for example) which are treated as points because they will only be plotted at a scale at which their real size will be too small to see.

Connected This field determines whether the surveyed points will be connected to each other (in Polyline features) or not (Point features).

The next four fields (Skip, 3D, Breakline and Include in Model) can be ignored. Three of them relate in any case to functions of Terrain Tools which aren't present in the freeware version.

Colour allows you to choose the colour in which the feature will be plotted.

Symbol is the symbol used to represent the surveyed points. In the case of polyline features you may or may not want to be able to see the points themselves – if they are numerous they may just be a distraction – so one option in this field is **None**; alternatively you may select from quite a wide range.

Hatch is used when a polyline feature forms a closed figure and you want to fill in the space enclosed by the line. Over fifty different patterns of lines, dots, dashes and other symbols are available. Care needs to be taken in using this option. If a polyline does not form a closed figure (e.g. a stream or a track) but a hatch pattern is selected, the last point in the line will automatically be joined to the first with a straight line, and any closed areas formed by this operation will be filled with the selected pattern. This can produce some strange effects. For example, this line

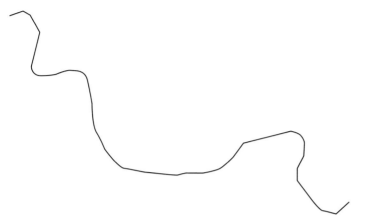

Figure 13.4 Line feature displayed correctly.

will look something like this

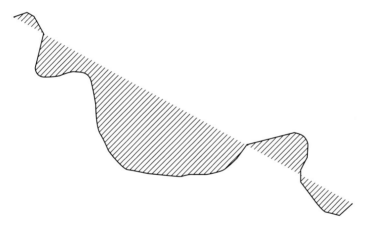

Figure 13.5 Line feature displayed with incorrect use of the hatch option.

if a hatch symbol is chosen. Related to this is another point to note. In the case of the 'mound' feature in this survey, just four points were measured. In order to create a closed figure with four sides it might be expected that it would be necessary to repeat the first point as a fifth, final point, like this:

411669.2	*525391.0*	*mound*
411678.0	525388.2	mound
411677.1	525382.3	mound
411668.0	525387.0	mound
411669.2	*525391.0*	*mound*

but in fact this file produces a figure like this one:

(though of course if a hatch symbol were chosen the space enclosed by the lines would be filled). If the fourth side of the figure is to be drawn, you actually have to repeat the first pair of co-ordinates *twice*, as in this example:

411669.2	*525391.0*	*mound*
411678.0	525388.2	mound
411677.1	525382.3	mound
411668.0	525387.0	mound
411669.2	*525391.0*	*mound*
411669.2	*525391.0*	*mound*

This may seem strange, but once the principle is understood it shouldn't cause any real trouble.

Having inserted all the files representing the surveyed features, the window containing the plan may look something like this, depending on the chosen options.

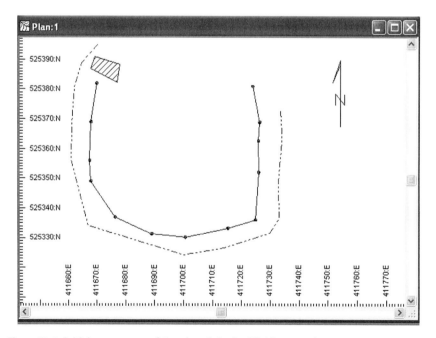

Figure 13.6 Initial appearance of the plot of the Cockfield survey data.

The inner side of the ditch has the individual points shown, while the top of the outer bank does not. The bottom of the ditch contained dense reeds (and water), and in addition an observer at the bottom of it would have been out of sight of the reference point most of the time. The south-west corner of the ditch appears cut off; this is because in reality it disappears altogether, though there is no clear indication of a break which could be considered original. The mound has been recorded as only four points, although its outline is not trapezoidal. At this stage the plan is 'warts and all'.

One feature of the drawing window which may be inconvenient is the North Arrow, which may become very large if you are zooming in. This can be removed from the drawing by using

> View | Active Window (Plan) Options

and unchecking the box labelled 'North arrow'. (This option will be used again later.)

The rendering of the site itself also needs some modification to make it more aesthetically pleasing and to add some more information content. The line of the inside of the ditch would probably look better without the individual points marked on it, and this can be achieved by left-clicking the mouse somewhere on the line to select it (the line will change colour to magenta, and the point nearest to the mouse position will be marked by a red cross) and then right-clicking and choosing from the pop-up menu the options

> Modify selected Features | Linetypes, Symbols

This gives access to the choices which were available when first creating the features, and the option of 'none' can be used to remove the points from the drawing.

The mound, as indicated, has only been recorded in a very basic way, just four points making a sub-rectangular shape. The field notes and sketch, however, indicate that it has a roughly elliptical form, so the current shape needs to be edited. Again, right-click on the feature in question (it's probably best to zoom in on it first) and choose

> Edit/Insert Points with Mouse

The cursor will change to look like a pencil. Left-click in a place where you would like to insert a new point, and the line will 'snap' on to the cursor, though at this stage no new point has been created, though as the cursor moves around the line will follow it and when the mouse is left-clicked again the point will actually be inserted.

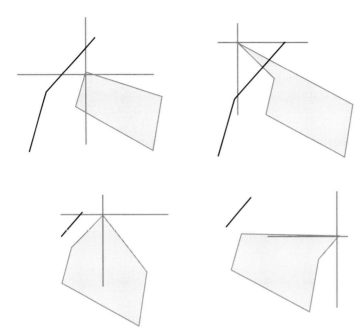

Figure 13.7 Editing a point.

In this way the outline can be re-drawn to be more realistic. During this process it's also possible to *move* points, as well as to insert them (this includes the original points and the inserted ones). As the cursor is moved about, when it's over an existing point it changes from the pencil shape to a small square, and a left-click at this moment will 'pick up' the point and drag it (another left-click will anchor it in a new position). The diagrams above show examples of the effect of picking up and moving different cor-ners of the original quadrangular shape. It would not, of course, be appropriate to move the points whose location was surveyed in the field, but it may well be necessary to move inserted ones in order to achieve an acceptable shape. To end the editing of the feature, right-click and select from the menu

   Edit | Tool Selection | Select with mouse

The feature will remain in the 'selected' colour until the mouse is left-clicked on another part of the drawing. After editing, the mound feature may look something like this:

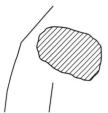

Figure 13.8 Edited appearance of mound.

As mentioned above, the bottom of the ditch was not surveyed for practical reasons. It may be desirable to show it, however, because it is a real feature which has been observed, and since other features have been surveyed it's quite possible to sketch in the ditch bottom, as long as it's made clear on the drawing or in associated documentation that this is what has been done. Using the commands

Edit | New feature

from the menu, or pressing **control-F** will bring up this dialogue:

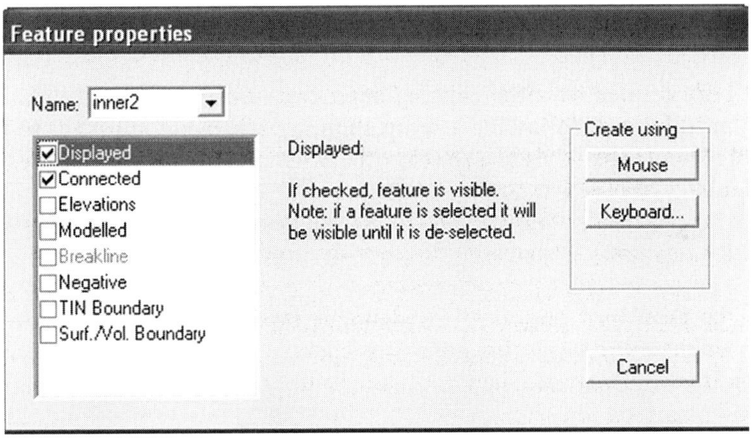

Figure 13.9 Terrain Tools Feature properties dialogue box.

A name may be given (the scrolling menu has only a very small selection, but any name may be typed into the **Name:** field). If the new feature is a line, make sure that **Connected** is checked, as well as **Displayed**, *un*check **Elevations** and **Modelled**, and click the **Create using Mouse** button. The same drawing tool will appear as was used to alter the mound feature, and a line representing the bottom of the ditch can be created midway between the two existing lines. These latter are themselves not entirely as they should be; they are rather more angular than field records and photographs show them to be, and they are connected up to make complete circuits, when in fact there is a substantial break in the south-west corner. In this case, rather than edit the lines, it may be better to use them as a guide to create new lines which are less angular and which show the observed nature of the features more accurately. In this picture

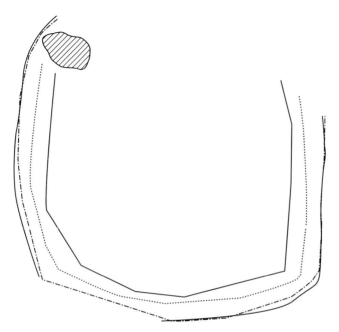

Figure 13.10 Editing the survey.

two lines have been created over the existing outer one, running through the actual survey points, but otherwise following a more curving path. We don't want to have both versions of the outer bank visible, so select the original line using the mouse, then right-click and use

Modify selected features | Properties

Then uncheck the **Displayed** option in the dialogue box. The selected feature will remain visible in magenta until the mouse is clicked elsewhere and it becomes unselected, then it will disappear (the line is still there, it just isn't being displayed). The drawing will now look like this:

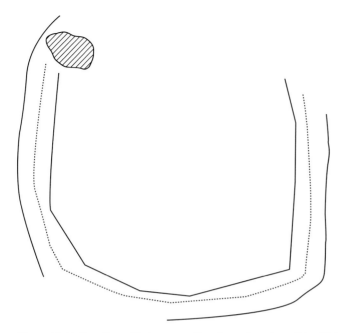

Figure 13.11 New line added representing the outer edge of the ditch.

Using the same procedure it's very straightforward to create a new line over the inner edge of the ditch. The north side of the enclosure is truncated by a deep, steep-sided quarry, and it will be as well to show this by putting a line feature to mark it (this will have to be estimated; the actual quarry-edge was too hazardous to approach closely enough to measure). Adding these lines will produce something like this:

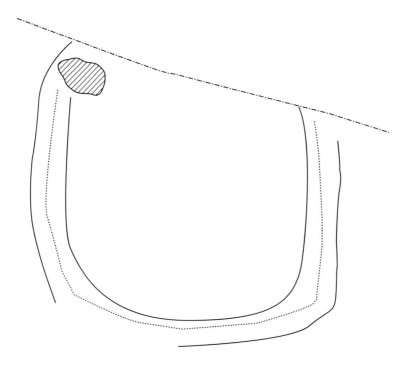

Figure 13.12 Addition of inner edge to ditch and the position of the quarry truncating the enclosure.

which is a considerable improvement over the original version (Figure 13.10), though it must be stressed that this new plan is based not only on the bearing and distance measurements, but also on the essential field notes and photographs which are as much a part of the survey.

The final thing to add is text, which will identify the different features to anyone looking at the plan. This can be done by labelling individual items, or by using a legend to match feature names to the symbols used to display them; the decision as to which is best depends partly on the complexity of the plan and partly on personal preference or a house-style. Using a legend is often the simplest way to convey the required information, but the freeware version of Terrain Tools doesn't include a tool to create legends, so it will have to be done manually.

Begin by right-clicking and selecting **Edit Labels with Mouse** from the menu. The pencil-cursor will appear again, but this time with the letters 'ABC' attached to it, to show that you are about to create text and not features. Click the mouse some-where near the quarry line (it doesn't matter exactly where) and this dialogue will appear:

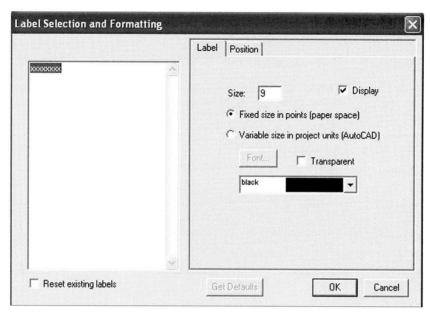

Figure 13.13 Dialogue box for creating labels.

The large area on the left is where you will type the label, and at first this contains 'xxxxxxxx', already highlighted, so that as soon as you type anything, it will be replaced. Type **approximate quarry edge** or something similar. On the right of the dialogue are the parameters for creating the label – **size** in page units (points) or project units (metres), **colour**, a **Display** check box, a **Font** button (disabled in the Freeware version) and a **Transparent** check box (this function relates to one under the Position tab).

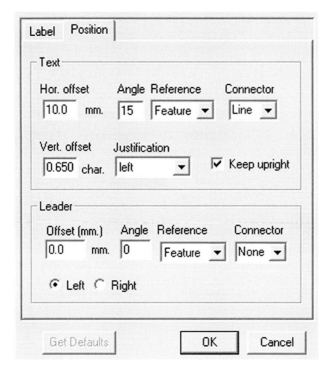

Figure 13.14 Dialogue box for positioning labels.

If the **Position** tab is clicked you will find a series of options for the positioning of the label with respect to the features, including offsets and angles. However, these can be changed interactively with the mouse, and this is probably the easiest way to do it. Under the **Text** heading, the **Connector** option permits the creation of a line underneath the text, or a circle or rectangular box around the text, and it is this circle or box whose transparency is controlled by the check box under the **Label** tab; if the **Transparent** box is checked this background is transparent, otherwise it will be opaque, and may obscure parts of the drawing, although it may also be useful to give prominence to the label. The **Keep upright** option is another useful one; if this is checked (the default) then rotated text will be kept as readable as possible (i.e. it won't appear upside down).

Using the **Keep upright** option would turn the text shown on the left above into the text shown on the right.

Under **Leader** there are options for creating lines and arrows connecting text to points on the plan, but ignore these for the moment. Clicking **OK** will cause the chosen text to appear on the screen, at first with a black line above it, this having small black squares at each end. If you place the cursor over the text it will change from the pencil form to a four-pointed arrow, indicating that the text can be moved by left-clicking and dragging to a new position; placing the cursor over the black square at the right-hand end of the line, however, changes it to a curved line with arrows at each end, this showing that the text can be rotated to a new angle, pivoting round the left-hand end of the line. If you double-click on the text the **Label Selection and Formatting** dialogue will open again, and changes can be made as detailed above. When the position and appearance of the text are as you wish, right-click and choose **Select with mouse** to end the text editing session.

If the **Leader** option has been chosen, one end of the line, or the point of the arrow, will initially be at the point where the mouse was clicked when label creation was initiated. The text will appear like this on the screen

Figure 13.15 Initial position of arrow and text label.

but by placing the cursor over the text, so that again it becomes a four-pointed arrow, the text can be moved relative to the end of the connecting line, or by putting the cursor over the right-hand end of the line *above* the text, the latter can be rotated relative to the arrow.

Figure 13.16 Text re-positioned with respect to arrow.

This procedure is rather tedious to describe, but in practice it's very easy to do. If at any time you wish to delete a label, just click the mouse on it, at which point a magenta box will appear round the text, and press the keyboard **delete** key. (A point to note: if you want to delete more than one label, hold down the *shift* key while clicking with the mouse, not the *ctrl* key.)

By using the label tools, the plan may now look like this:

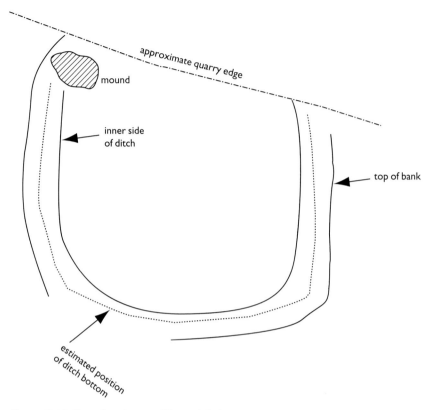

Figure 13.17 Plan of enclosure with text labels.

The arrow heads do look too big in relation to the size of the features they refer to, but on the printed page they will be a much more acceptable size relative to the archaeological features. Using the alternative of a legend (where the lines are created just as the new feature lines were, and the text consists of normal labels) will give a result like this:

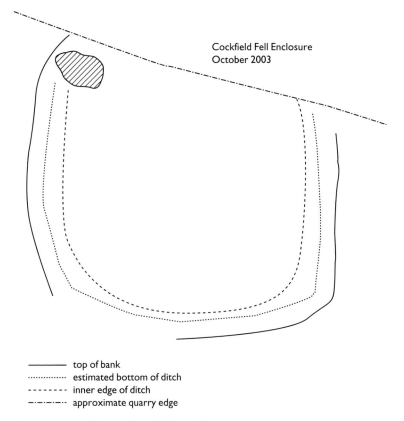

Cockfield Fell Enclosure
October 2003

———————— top of bank
·················· estimated bottom of ditch
- - - - - - - inner edge of ditch
—·—·—·—·· approximate quarry edge

Figure 13.18 Enclosure plan with legend.

In order to make the lines in the legend of equal length and to align them properly, as well as to draw the box round the whole legend, it's necessary to change the window options again, using

View | Active Window (Plan) Options

In the dialogue, under the **General** tab, check the **Snap to grid** box, and click the '+' symbol next to it. This allows the grid spacing to be set (5m was used in this case), and the **Show Grid** option to be checked. On clicking OK in each of the currently open dialogues the plan window will show a grid of small dots, separated by the specified distance, and when the **New Feature** command is used to draw a new line, wherever the mouse is clicked the point created will be attached ('snapped') to the nearest of these dots. This makes it easy to create a series of straight lines of exactly equal length, to align them precisely, and to draw a rectangular box. Note that the lines making up the 'legend' are, as far as the software is concerned, 'features', just like the lines which make up the archaeological site, while the text is of a specified point size (the size at which it will be printed). The consequence of this is that if you change the scale of the plan, the length of the legend lines and the size of the box will change, while the text will remain as it is, so the scale of reproduction of the plan must be decided before the legend is constructed. Snapping can be a very useful aid to drawing, but it must be turned off again before attempting the drawing of any real features.

So far everything has been viewed on the screen, but Terrain Tools make it quite easy to produce a neat, professional-looking page layout for printing, though there a few points to watch for. One is the question of *scale*. On the toolbar is a box telling you what the scale of the drawing is. In this box you can select from a range of predetermined scales, ranging from 1:1 to 1:5,000,000, or you can highlight the current figure and type a new one (followed by the **enter** key), if you wanted, for example, 1:750 or 1:2500, either to fit the page better or to match a preferred style. This is the scale *at which the plan will be printed*, not that at which it appears on the screen. You will notice that if you use the zooming tools the appearance of the plan on the screen will change, but the figure in the box will not. What does change, however, is the spacing of the co-ordinates along the left-hand and bottom edges of the screen, and this will be reflected on the printout unless the user takes control of the appearance of these figures (which are rather confusingly also referred to as a **grid**, though they are treated separately from the 'grid' of points used to control the drawing of features). The easiest thing to do is just to turn them off altogether, using the **Active window options** again, and just unchecking the **Grid** box; this will remove the figures from both the screen and the printout. Sometimes, however, it will be of use to have an indication of the co-ordinates, so rather than just removing the figures, they can be used purposefully. In the Active window options dialogue, next to the **Grid** check box is a '+' sign; clicking this will open the **Grid Options** dialogue

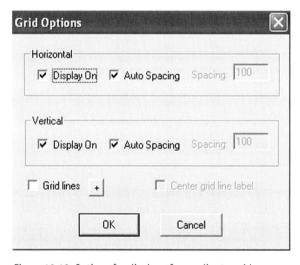

Figure 13.19 Options for display of co-ordinate grid.

and here the required changes can be made. Horizontal and vertical lines may be turned on and off independently, and their spacing may be set explicitly (the default produces a spacing of about 5m for a plan of this size, which can be rather intrusive; uncheck the **Auto Spacing** boxes and enter a figure of, say, 25m. If the **Grid lines** box is checked now, lines will be drawn across the whole plan, while if it is not, there will just be numbers at the edges. Yet another '+' next to this box will allow a line symbol and colour to be chosen for the grid lines. The use of these grid lines is again a matter of taste and practicality; sometimes they will be very helpful in describing and locating a site, but in other cases they may just obscure detail.

In this illustration

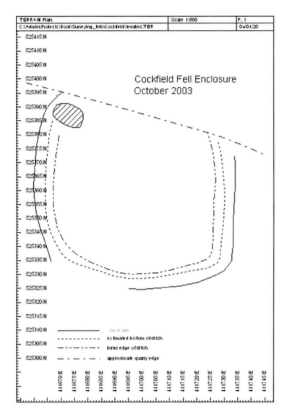

Figure 13.20 Enclosure plan with a 5m grid spacing.

the grid co-ordinates have been left at their default spacing of 5m, giving the edge of the page a cluttered appearance. (This image is taken from the **Print Preview** screen, which is accessed using the familiar ◱ symbol on the toolbar.) Altering the spacing to a more useful 50m (for this scale of drawing), enabling the drawing of gridlines, and changing their colour and symbol can produce something more like this,

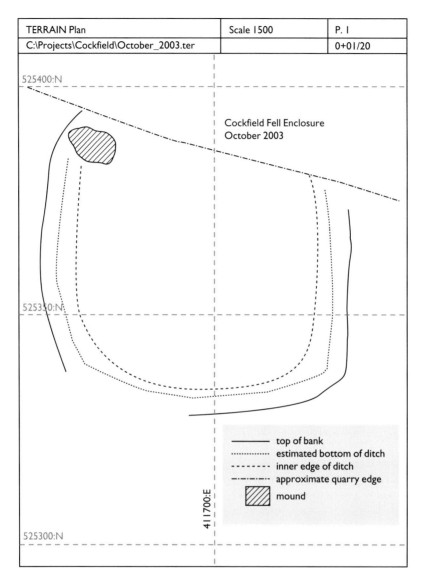

TERRAIN Plan	Scale 1500	P. 1
C:\Projects\Cockfield\October_2003.ter		0+01/20

Cockfield Fell Enclosure
October 2003

525400:N

525350:N

525300:N

411700:E

——————— top of bank
·················· estimated bottom of ditch
- - - - - - - - inner edge of ditch
—·—·—·— approximate quarry edge
mound

Figure 13.21 Enclosure plan with a 50m grid spacing.

in which the grid information has been retained, but without being intrusive. In this case, with no internal detail to be confused, it's useful to have the grid lines visible (it would be very easy for another user of the plan to give a grid reference of 525300 411700 to the site by using the crossing point of two lines). In this plan also, the legend has been given a background by drawing a new feature around it using the grid snap option to make a true rectangle, and giving the feature a 'hatch type' which is an opaque solid (this is an option in the hatch type list) coloured the same shade of grey as the grid lines.

TERRAIN Plan	Scale 1:500	P. 1
C:\Projects\Cockfield\October_2003.ter		04/01/20

Figure 13.22 Detail of text on the page layout border.

In addition to the features already mentioned, the page layout is given a default border (which can't be changed in the freeware version) which shows the name of the software used to create the plan, its scale, the date, and the file name and path. Since the latter cannot be changed, it's probably a good idea to keep the file path simple, or (as experience has shown) this text will overlap the box intended to contain it.

As a final addition to the plan, to give some more indications of features in the landscape which might enable another user to locate the site on the ground, a series of electricity pylons (in this case quite small structures made of wooden posts) were located by means of compass and rangefinder measurements made *from* the reference point at the gatepost, processed as above to generate a file of co-ordinates which was inserted into the plan in the same way as the archaeological features. (In this case it was obviously essential to give a symbol to the points, and disable the 'connected' option.) The archaeological site and the pylons cover too large an area to be seen on the screen all at the same time given the current scale of 1:500. Using the **zoom extents** button will show all the features on the screen (though the points representing the pylons look very small), but a page preview will show an almost blank page; another plotting scale has to be chosen, and by experiment 1:2500 was found to be suitable (this isn't one of the pre-defined scales, so it had to be typed into the scale box). When changing scales it may happen that the screen view of the features becomes very small, but the 'zoom extents' button will re-size them. The point symbols will now appear larger (the freeware version of the software doesn't allow point symbols to be re-sized).

There are many ways in which the appearance of the plan can be changed. It would be tedious to go through them all here, but the essentials of the controls have been described, and the user can experiment for themselves. This survey was carried out using easy to operate equipment which only requires one person (though of course for safety reasons it may be desirable for more than one to be present, depending on the conditions); the end result of plotting this simple survey using Terrain Tools is a professional-looking plan that no archaeologist should be ashamed to display in any context. In fact, given that the features have been enhanced by the use of non-measured data (field notes and photographs), their appearance may be considered 'too good', with the possibility of misleading another user into the idea that a more complex piece of fieldwork had been undertaken. As ever, the surveyor is required to use his or her integrity, and to make it perfectly clear how their result has been achieved.

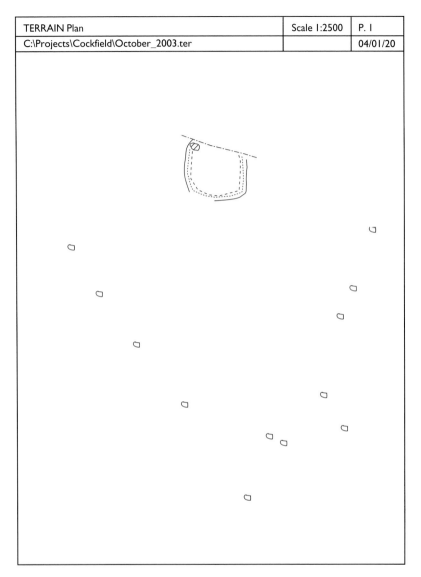

TERRAIN Plan		Scale 1:2500	P. 1
C:\Projects\Cockfield\October_2003.ter			04/01/20

Figure 13.23 Final Terrain Tools plan of the enclosure and other landscape features.

Plotting angle and distance in IntelliCAD

Creating the plan of the Cockfield enclosure using Terrain Tools was in many ways easy, because the software is designed to perform certain kinds of tasks in a way which is very straightforward for the user; a slight difficulty was that the survey information had to be presented in the form of co-ordinates, while the field measurements were in the form of bearings and distances. Effecting a transformation from the latter to the former was done fairly easily using a spreadsheet, but it is possible to plot the survey points directly through the medium of a CAD package, using this as a very accurate alternative to manual plotting with a protractor and ruler.

First, we need the co-ordinates of the gate post used as a reference point, given by the GPS unit as 411668 525325, and the field measurements:

Top of bank	Distance to post	Bearing to post	Distance to post	Bearing from post	Corrected bearing
	m	degrees (mag.)	m	(degrees)	
	84	242	84	62	58
	81	238	81	58	54
	78	242	78	62	58
	76	244.5	76	64.5	60.5
	69	254	69	74	70
	66	264	66	84	80
	62	268	62	88	84
	46	272	46	92	88
	32	275	32	95	91
	9.29	177	9.29	357	353
	32	171	32	351	347
	44	175	44	355	351
	56	178	56	358	354
	64	181	64	1	357
	70	186	70	6	2
Axes of mound	66	185	66	5	1
	58	193	58	13	9
	64	193	64	13	9
	62	184	62	4	0
Inner side of ditch	57	186	57	6	2
	44	184	44	4	0
	31	183	31	3	359
	24	184	24	4	0
	14.62	219	14.62	39	35
	22	257	22	77	73
	33	265	33	85	81
	48	264	48	84	80
	58	263	58	83	79
	64	249	64	69	65
	69	241	69	61	57
	73	237	73	57	53
	79	229	79	49	45

This is the complete set of observed and calculated distances and bearings, though of course it's the 'corrected bearing' (i.e. converted into a bearing *from* the post, corrected for magnetic variation from true north) which will be used.

To be able to plot the bearings, some preparation is needed. A feature of most CAD software (if not all) is that the direction defined by a bearing of zero isn't 'north' (i.e. the top of the screen, as a surveyor would normally expect), but 'east' (i.e. right), and angles increment anti-clockwise, not clockwise. This means that a line drawn from a point with a bearing of 180° (due south) won't appear as on the left, but as on the right.

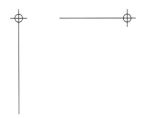

Figure 13.24 Difference between a field bearing and a bearing in CAD.

In order to put this right, you have to use the commands

Settings | Drawing Settings

and in the dialogue box click the **Drawing Units** tab.

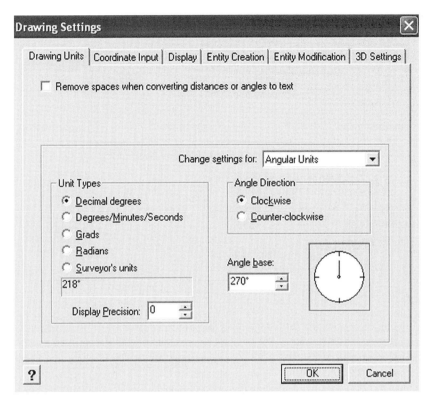

Figure 13.25 IntelliCAD drawing settings for angular units.

In the field **Change Settings for:** select **Angular Units**.

The 'clock' display shows the current setting, and changes need to be made to the **Angle Direction** and **Angle base**. Angle Direction is easily set to **counter-clockwise**, but entering the correct figure in the Angle base field isn't entirely intuitive. You might think the proper thing to do would be to click 'clockwise', and then enter '270' as the angle base, given that the starting point is to the 'east', but if you do this, then click **OK**, and then go back in to Drawing Settings to check the result, the Angle base number has actually changed to '90', and the indicator on the dial now points 'south'. What you have to do is to click 'clockwise', then enter –270 (minus 270). Instead of clicking OK, press the **tab** key, and you can see the setting take effect straight away. The display should then look like the illustration. Note that although –270 was entered, the figure showing is just '270'.

The reference point has to be plotted first, but the default point symbol is just a dot, of such a small size as to be almost invisible, and this will need to be changed if you are going to see what you are plotting. Use

Settings | Drawing Settings

again, and under the **Entity Creation** tab choose **Change Settings for: Points** to change the point symbol to something more visible.

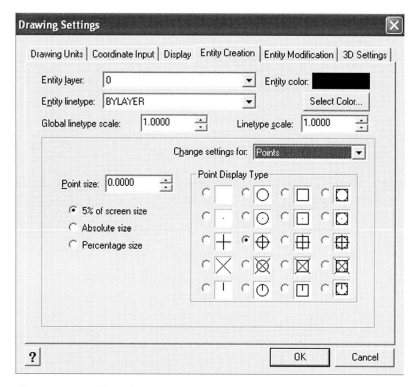

Figure 13.26 IntelliCAD drawing settings for point symbols.

To plot the point, use

Insert | Draw point

or click on the point drawing tool. The prompt will change to

Settings/Multiple/<Location of point>:

Which allows you to type the co-ordinates

411668,525325

(note that there is no space between the numbers). The point will be drawn, but it may not at first be visible on the screen. Clicking the **Zoom extents** button on the **View** toolbar will zoom in on the point, and it will for the moment fill the screen (it may also have a distorted shape, such as a circle appearing as an octagon). The default size for point symbols is 5% of the screen size, but zooming commands often ignore this. Typing the command **regen** (for 'regenerate') will restore the symbol to its proper size. (Note that using the **redraw** command or pressing the ✎ button won't have the same effect.)

The drawing should now be a large blank area with a single point in the centre. In order to plot distances accurately it will be necessary to use the **snapping** controls, to make sure that distances are measured from exactly on the point.

Double-click on **ESNAP** and set the snap entity to **Point**.

To create a new layer for drawing the lines to locate points (the lines won't themselves form part of the drawing, so they will have to be frozen) use

Tools | IntelliCAD Explorer

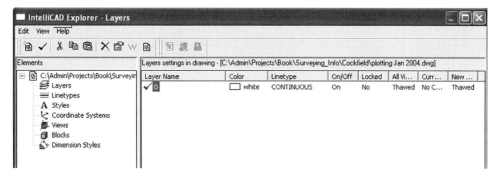

Figure 13.27 IntelliCAD Explorer control of layers.

The one current layer (0) is shown, with its colour as white, linetype as continuous. There is also a blue tick next to its name, to show that it's the layer on which drawing operations will take place. Choose

Edit | New | Layer

to add a new layer, which will appear on the right under layer 0. If you type a new name for it at this point, this will also appear in the right place, but you can re-name a layer at any time by right-clicking its name and choosing the **rename** option from the menu. Call this layer **lines**, and make it current, either by clicking the blue tick on the toolbar, or by double-clicking its name. It will also have the colour 'white'. Since the default screen background is black, white seems like a sensible colour to choose to draw in, though of course when the drawing is plotted, it will normally be onto white paper, and you might think objects drawn in white would be invisible. However, this is a strange kind of 'white', because while it appears white on the screen, when the drawing is to be plotted it automatically changes to black! Many people will prefer to have a white background on the screen as well, to give a better idea of what the plotted drawing will look like. This is achieved using

Tools | Options

and the **Display** tab, clicking the **Color** button, and selecting a new one. A large number of colours is on offer, with a row of nine popular ones at the top of the colour selection box (red, yellow, green, cyan, blue, magenta, white, dark grey, light grey). Just below this are a black rectangle (the default background colour), and a row of small blocks of grey and white. For a white background choose the white block at the right-hand end of this row (its number will appear as 255 in the 'current colour' box at the bottom of this window). Click OK in the Color and Options boxes, and the background will turn white, though any items already drawn in 'white' already will turn black, just as if they were being plotted on paper. This is a useful facility, but of course there may be times when you want to really use white, and not have it change to black. If so, use the other 'white' in the Color window (the one on the top row); this is colour number 7, rather than 255, and it will always appear white (but if you make the screen background this colour, any objects drawn in white will remain white, and effectively disappear).

Returning to the enclosure survey, it's now time to plot the positions of the survey points, but in IntelliCAD it will be most convenient to first of all draw lines of the correct length and bearing, and then use these to position the points.

Click on the line drawing tool, or type **Line**, to start drawing a line. The command line shows

> Enter to use last point/Follow/<Start of line>:

the cursor changes to look like a circle with a cross in the middle, and a pull-down menu appears showing options **Follow** and **Cancel**. Place the cursor on the reference point and left-click the mouse. The command line will show

> Angle/Length/<End point>:

as will the pull-down menu. Click on **Angle** in the menu or type **angle** (or just **a**) and press return. The command line shows

> Angle of line

Type the angle (in whatever units have been set; probably integers anyway for compass readings) and press return. (Note that it's better not to move the mouse during this operation; if it is moved in the drawing window, a series of lines at 90° to each other appears, centred on the original point, and these will remain in the display when the line has been drawn until the redraw command is used.)

The command line now shows

> Length of line:

Type this in. The command line shows

> Angle/Length/Follow/Undo/<End point>:

as again does the menu, although this has **Done** as the last option. Pressing **enter**, choosing **Done**, or right-clicking will end the drawing of the line. To start a new line, either use the line command again, or right-click (which will repeat the last command to be initiated, i.e. drawing a line).

Do this for each point, after which the drawing should look like this:

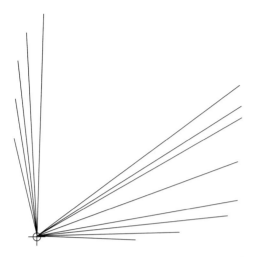

Figure 13.28 Angles and bearings to points on the enclosure plotted in IntelliCAD.

To plot the survey points, create a new layer, and call it **points**. You can open IntelliCAD Explorer either as before, or by double-clicking on the name of the current layer (lines) where it appears at the bottom of the screen. Make **points** the current layer. Before drawing the points, click on **ESNAP** again, and click on **Endpoint** under 'Entity Snap Modes'. (The endpoint of a line is regarded as a different kind of thing from a feature which consists only of a point.)

The **point** drawing tool can now be used to position a point at the end of each line. Take care that you plot as many points as you should; one of the lines is very short, and very similar in bearing to one of the others, so it isn't visible when the drawing is viewed to fill the screen, and you will have to zoom in to see it. This time, when the

Settings/Multiple/<Location of point>:

prompt appears, type **m** and press <enter> to enable multiple plotting of points without having to give the command again for each one; right-click to end drawing.

The drawing should now look as above, but with a point symbol at the end of each line. The problem of the almost invisible line is a weakness of this method. Indeed it may be the case that two points are on the same bearing, in which case the lines connecting them to the reference point would overlap completely, and the end of the shorter one would be hard to find. In such a case it might be necessary to plot one line and its associated point, and then delete the line before drawing the other one.

To remove the lines temporarily, rather than deleting them all, open IntelliCAD Explorer again. On the right-hand side part of the window looks like this:

Layer Name	Color	Linetype	On/Off	Locked	All Vi...	Curr...	New ...
✓ POINTS	☐ white	CONTINUOUS	On	No	Thawed	No C...	Thawed
LINES	☐ white	CONTINUOUS	On	No	Thawed	No C...	Thawed
0	☐ white	CONTINUOUS	On	No	Thawed	No C...	Thawed

Figure 13.29 IntelliCAD layer control.

One of the fields appears to be called **AllVi . . .**; this stands for All Viewports (the precise meaning of which isn't important at the moment). What is important is that in this column all the layers have the word **Thawed**, which means that they are visible in the drawing. If you click on 'Thawed' on the line which relates to the Lines layer, 'Thawed' will change to 'Frozen', and when the window is closed the lines will disappear and the drawing will look like this:

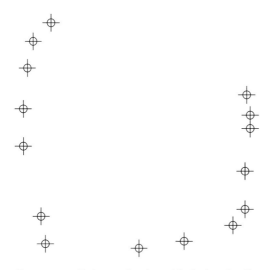

Figure 13.30 Enclosure drawing with the bearing lines frozen.

One of these points is of course the reference, and not a point on the enclosure. It might be a good idea to change its appearance, and perhaps put it on a layer of its own, so that it too can be turned on and off conveniently.

Open Explorer again, and make a new layer called, perhaps, **reference**; click on the name of its colour ('white') and when the colour selection box appears, choose another, contrasting colour, such as red. Close the Explorer window.

Click on the reference point to select it (the symbol will take on a dotted appearance) then right-click and choose **properties**. The Layer should be given as 0, and the colour as **BYLAYER**, meaning that this object will take on whatever colour is given to the layer. You could click the **color** button and choose a colour to apply permanently to the selected object, but on this occasion click instead on the **Layer** scrolling list, choosing **reference**. Click OK and the reference point should now appear in red, the colour of its new layer.

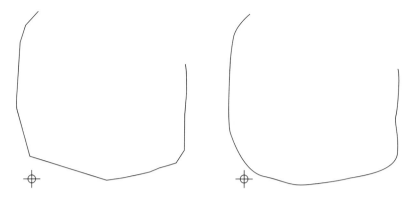

Figure 13.31 The enclosure drawn using a polyline (left) and a spline (right).

The other points can now be joined together to produce a line representing the top of the bank, and there are two options. One is to use a **polyline,** which will create straight segments, as on the left above, which is true to the information which has actually been observed, but doesn't give a very good impression of what the site actually looks like. Another possibility is to use a **spline,** a curved line which is mathematically fitted to a set of points (as on the right). This 'looks better', but, particularly where there are rather few data points, the curve may depart significantly from the real shape of the object. A spline is drawn in the same way as a polyline, again snapping the line to the points, but when the last point has been entered the operator is asked for two more pieces of information, the **starting tangent point,** and the **tangent for ending point.** This affects the way in which, particularly, the ends of the spline are drawn.

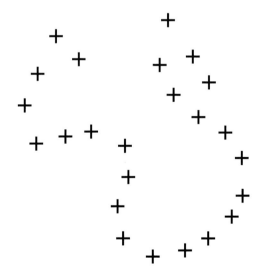

Figure 13.32 A set of points through which a spline is to be drawn.

In this example two splines are drawn through a series of points, differing only in the two tangent points which are given. The splines look like this (the tangent points are marked with small circles).

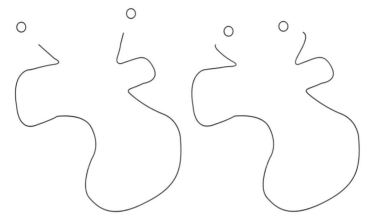

Figure 13.33 The effect on a spline of choosing different starting and ending tangent points.

The use of splines in surveying calls for great care. The best solution is always to take as many measurements as possible in the field, rather than to rely on smoothing out angularities, though there may be times when their use is justified, perhaps when delineating something which doesn't have a definite edge, such as a flint or pottery scatter.

The circuit of the bank top now being complete, the other features could be added in the same way, but plotting the bearings and distances like this is very laborious, and while it may sometimes be useful for filling-in odd details, it can't be recommended as a main technique, unless the process of calculating co-ordinates is completely unappealing, and even then, using a spreadsheet the labour only has to be performed once.

Advanced plotting in IntelliCAD

So far we have seen the results of plotting the survey with a sophisticated, if purposely limited, surveying software package, and with a rather laborious method in a general CAD package. This may have put the CAD software in a rather poor light, but it can be put to very effective use in ways which have now to be considered.

There are two things that put people off using heavyweight CAD software such as AutoCAD; one is undoubtedly the cost, which can be addressed by choosing an alternative (the only serious competitor currently being IntelliCAD), but the other is their supposed complexity. It's certainly true that you need to go through a learning process, and my own initial engagement with AutoCAD wasn't entirely pain free, but I was operating pretty well on my own, and finding what I needed wasn't easy. I hope that what follows will make it a smoother path for others, who will experience at an earlier stage than I did the great benefits of using CAD. You can use it to draw just about anything you can imagine – the trick is to know how to tell it what you want.

The basic operations of drawing have been covered elsewhere, and these will be used over and over again in any operation, but we don't have to restrict ourselves to manually (if that's the word) creating every point and line individually, which would take almost as long as producing a drawing using traditional methods. It will be necessary, though, to bite the bullet of reducing the survey measurements to co-ordinates.

The first method of speeding-up the transfer of field information into the drawing is a simple one, but one which is very poorly documented in CAD literature, even by the companies who produce it. It was discovered by Eiteljorg (2000) who has used it in three-dimensional modelling of architectural structures in Greece. To see how it works, let's look at the way in which a point is plotted using a pair of co-ordinates.

Give the command

point

or use the point tool on the **Draw 2D** toolbar. The prompt changes to

Settings/Multiple/<Location of point>:

and these same options appear in a pop-up menu. Clicking anywhere on the screen will create a point using the current point symbol, and the drawing operation will end. If instead you select the **settings** option, either by clicking on the menu or typing the letter **s** and pressing **enter**, a dialogue will open in which you can choose another point symbol, and when this has been done the prompt returns to what is shown above, allowing either the creation of the point, or the selection of the **multiple** option, which obviously will make it possible to create several points in one drawing operation. (Once multiple has been chosen, it disappears from the command prompt.) You can change the point symbol setting as often as you like during this process. When all the required points have been drawn, you can end the sequence by clicking **Done** on the pop-up menu, right-clicking the mouse, or pressing **enter**.

Apart from choosing a location with the mouse, we have already seen that a pair of co-ordinates can be typed instead, separated by a comma. When using Terrain Tools, data could also be transferred into the package using the comma-separated format, but in that case it was a whole file of information at a time (although the example used a fairly small number of points, the operation could be done with far more). IntelliCAD, like AutoCAD, won't just read a file of co-ordinates and use them as the basis of a drawing, but it is possible to acquire multiple data points from an external source. The points need to be in a file in this format

411733.5,525372.6
411734.1,525366.3
411734.1,525362.4

(no code information this time), and the file needs to be open (using any text editor or word-processor). Start the point drawing command as above, and choose the **multiple** option from the command line or menu. Don't do anything else in the IntelliCAD window, but switch immediately to the window in which the co-ordinates are to be found, and highlight them, then copy them in any of the usual Windows ways (right-click/copy, ctrl-c, edit/copy). Now switch back to IntelliCAD, and with the mouse pointer over the command line window right-click and select **paste** from the pop-up menu (if the mouse is over the drawing area when you click, the command will abort). The point command will be executed as many times as there are lines in the selected body of text, and each point will be plotted. As will be seen later, this simple operation can be used with many hundreds, or even thousands, of pairs of co-ordinates, and save an enormous amount of time. If the copied text ends at the last digit of the last number in the file, the drawing command will remain active, and have to be ended in one of the usual ways, but if an additional carriage-return has been included (i.e. the last line was blank, and has been copied along with the numbers) the command will be ended when it encounters the **return** character, just as if it had been typed at the keyboard.

The rest of the features may be added to the drawing in the same way, and it would be possible to change the point symbol so that different features had different kinds of point, but something of a disappointment is in store here. CAD software doesn't think very well of points, and in some ways provides rather primitive facilities for handling them. While changes of point symbol may appear to be effective, after any operation which involves re-drawing the screen (such as a zoom) *all* the points in the drawing will be rendered in the current point symbol. If all the features are to be plotted in the form of points, it may be as well to create the lines to join each set before the next one is plotted, so that confusion doesn't arise, but actually there is no need to plot the points *as* points, because this method of copying co-ordinates works just as well with polylines (and splines) as with point features.

In this diagram the site as it currently exists (Figure 13.34, upper) has been drawn using just four commands, one to create the bank line feature, one to create the lip of the ditch, one to plot the four points on the mound, and one to draw a spline, snapping to each of the four points in turn, then using the **close** option from the pop-up spline menu (also available by typing **c** on the command-line). In this case, at least, the spline makes a quite acceptable shape for what is essentially a rounded figure recorded by a small number of points.

This method is much more satisfactory than tediously plotting each point, and shows, in a small way so far, how much more desirable it is to work with rectangular co-ordinates rather than angles and distances.

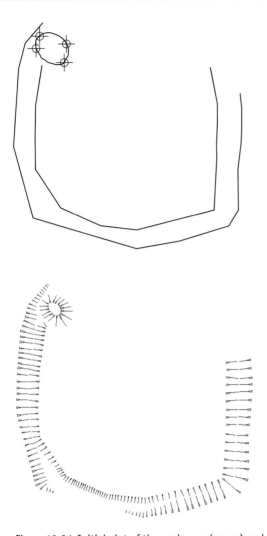

Figure 13.34 Initial plot of the enclosure (upper) and hachure plot (lower) created using IntelliCAD.

Of course, none of the plans so far produced looks terribly sophisticated compared with the sort of thing often encountered in publications, especially those produced by organisations such as the RCHM(E), excellent examples of which may be found in Bowden (1999). These survey plans, which many have regarded as classical examples of the art, are the product of great labour by skilled draughtspeople, particularly with regard to the production of the 'hachures' used in such great numbers. The hachure has been used for centuries to depict relief (as for example in the early editions of the Ordnance Survey maps of Britain), and consists of an object often described as 'tadpole-shaped', with a broad 'head' and a pointed 'tail', the head being placed at the top of a slope and the tail running downhill from it. Many variations on this general plan have been devised by individual workers, and some summarised by Taylor (1974) and Bowden (1999). In recent years, especially, the hachure has been criticised by many as being too much of a simplification, but it remains a favourite with many fieldworkers. Detractors mostly prefer to create more sophisticated models based on the collection of very large numbers of data points, and there are certainly arguments in favour of this, but the necessary time and resources are not always available to permit the collection of such data sets, and the hachure does make it possible to express very subtle changes in topography, some of which might be difficult to capture even with very complex technology. What is certain is that the production of a plan which includes large numbers of hachures makes great demands on the skill of the draughtsperson, as each one has to be drawn individually, and there are few uglier sights than a mass of badly drawn hachures. CAD obviously provides a potential way out of this, as it enables people whose artistic skills are less developed to produce very precise drawings of almost any shape, but the problem is then one of time again, and if they are not made the same shape they may well look as ugly as bad hand-drawn ones. The hachured plan in Figure 13.34 was created using the CAD script described in Chapter 9.

GPS survey

A rapid survey of the Cockfield Fell enclosure was carried out using GPS equipment supplied by Leica Geosystems. The aim was to produce a three-dimensional terrain model, and for this purpose a survey-grade instrument giving centimetre accuracy was required. (In an experiment with sub-metre GPS equipment it was found possible to produce a reasonable two-dimensional plan of the linear features, but the accuracy of the third dimension was insufficient to form a satisfactory model.) This grade equipment is invariably expensive; in the UK most manufacturers price it in the region of £30,000, depending on the precise configuration, and hire costs are about £800 per week, again depending on configuration. In the commercial field this level of expenditure, certainly of hiring, is often justified because of the extreme efficiency with which data may be collected, and even if a project extends over a long period it may be worthwhile using GPS to provide highly accurate control points which may then be used with lower-cost instruments such as total stations.

The equipment used was a Leica GPS1200 system, consisting of a reference instrument which remained stationary on a tripod, collecting information from the GPS satellites throughout the survey (data were logged every 15 seconds). This instrument communicates through a radio link with the roving instrument which records the location of detail points. By this means the position of the rover relative to the base station can be calculated with centimetre accuracy in real time, but the reference instrument can only calculate its own position to within about two metres. (It may seem odd that this more accurate system can't match the sub-metre accuracy of cheaper instruments, but it must be remembered that they are using reference information from other sources, such as the UK Coastguard beacons, while the GPS1200 reference station is working alone. It is still more accurate than the simple single receiver instruments sold for recreational purposes because it uses both the L1 and L2 wavelengths from the satellites, and comparing these – which are differentially affected by the atmosphere – makes calculation of a more accurate position possible.) To obtain centimetre accuracy for the whole survey it's necessary to post-process the data using an external source such as the UK Ordnance Survey's RINEX information.

The process of terrain modelling described here uses a software package called Global Mapper (www.globalmapper.com). This can be purchased online; the version described (5.10) cost approximately US$180.

Users of survey grade GPS equipment will usually have purchased software for data processing and display along with the instrument, and wouldn't need anything else, but this method can be used with data collected by other means (with total station, theodolite or level). All that is required is that each point is described by x, y, z co-ordinates in this form:

```
411668.5206 525382.9335 240.0472
411668.4903 525382.5713 240.0329
411668.3287 525381.6459 240.1065
411668.0075 525380.8967 239.7785
411667.9503 525379.7923 239.6602
411667.7983 525378.54   239.6675
```

The first two numbers are eastings and northings within the Ordnance Survey grid, but they could be arbitrary co-ordinates in a local system. The third number is elevation in metres. The data must be stored in a plain text file, and Global Mapper is unusually accommodating when it comes to filename extensions: *asc*, *csv*, *txt* and *dat* are all accepted. The file used in this case had a *txt* extension and used tab characters as a column separator.

The procedure is as follows. With Global Mapper running, use the commands

File | Open Generic ASCII text file(s)

After selecting the name of the file, this appears:

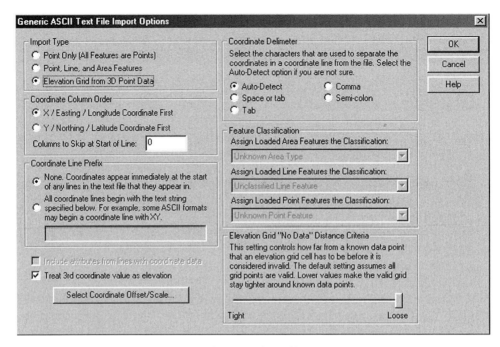

Figure 13.35 Global Mapper dialogue box for input of text files.

The appropriate options for this case are shown. **Import Type** has to be set to *Elevation Grid from 3D Point Data*, or the points will appear as just individual points and no surface will be created. **Coordinate Column Order** must indicate which co-ordinate comes first (and as can be seen, the software supports both plane and geographic co-ordinates). **Coordinate Delimiter** can be left on *Auto-Detect*. Global Mapper is very flexible in how it interprets the contents of the file; it can miss out whole columns of data, or skip over text at the start of each line, which can avoid a lot of manual editing in the case of some formats.

When **OK** is clicked the following appears:

Generic ASCII files do not contain projection information.
Please select the projection/datum for this file.
Check with your data supplier for this information if you do not have it.

Clicking **OK** again allows you to enter the appropriate settings:

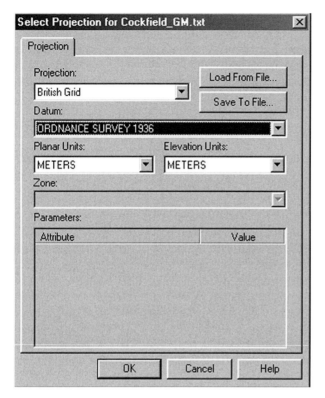

Figure 13.36 Selection of projection parameters in Global Mapper.

In this case the **Projection** is *British Grid*, and the **Datum** *ORDNANCE SURVEY 1936* (which is OSGB36). All units should of course be metres. Many different projections are supported, including Geographic (if co-ordinates are in the form of degrees of latitude and longitude), and UTM, but apart from the UK only a few specific national systems are available – France, Sweden, New Zealand, the Netherlands and the United States. The latter appears as *State Plane Coordinate System*, as obviously there can't be one projection for the whole of such a large area, and indeed most states have more than one (Alaska, for example, has 10 zones, California has seven, Texas has five, and many have two or three).

When the projection information has been entered, the image of the model appears:

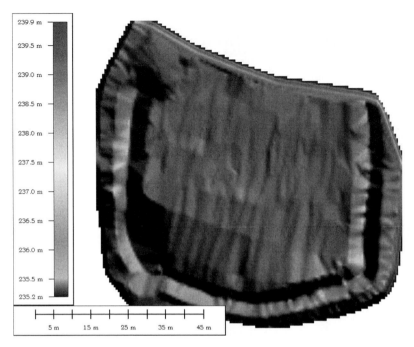

Figure 13.37 Global Mapper terrain model of the enclosure.

The default map uses a colour palette called the **Atlas Shader** (but shown here in monochrome), which assigns colours to elevation bands in the spectral order, while artificial illumination gives depth to the image. A legend shows how the colours are assigned, and there is a scale bar. The two last items can be toggled on and off using *shift-l* and *shift-s* respectively.

Figure 13.38 Global Mapper tool bar.

The type of shading may be changed by pulling down the menu at the right-hand end of the toolbar (see above), and modified further using

> Tools | Configure | Vertical Options

or

> Tools | Configure | Shader Options

This allows changing the **Light Direction** in Altitude and Azimuth, the **Ambient Lighting** from Dim to Bright, and the **Vertical Exaggeration** from Flat to High (making the surface look smoother or more rugged), and many more variations.

During the survey, points were taken at fairly regular intervals along the tops and bottoms of slopes, and these features have been captured fairly accurately. In the interior, however, where there are no discernable features, an automatic data-logging procedure was used, which generated co-ordinates at short time intervals as the instrument was moved in a zig-zag pattern over the site. This resulted in an unbalanced sampling as the lines along which the instrument travelled were much further apart than the interval between points on the lines, and this has led to the production of artefacts in the form of apparent long low ridges, which don't in fact exist.

If the image is satisfactory it can be printed as usual with

File | Print

(with various options including changing the background colour or printing at a chosen scale), or alternatively

File | Capture Screen Contents to Image

can be used to save the screen view in an image file. Available image formats are jpg, png, tif and bmp, and the size of the image (in terms of the number of pixels in width and height can be changed). Other options available are the production of a *world* or *projection* file. If the name given to the image file is, for example, *terrain.jpg*, a projection file would be *terrain.prj*, and it would contain information like this:

```
Projection    TRANSVERSE
Datum         OSGB_1936
Zunits        NO
Units         METERS
Xshift        0.000000
Yshift        0.000000
Parameters
0.999601 /* scale factor at central meridian
−2 0 0.00 /* central meridian
49 0 0.00 /* latitude of the origin
400000.000000 /* false easting (meters)
−100000.000000 /* false northing (meters)
```

Obviously this includes the projection type (the OS uses a transverse Mercator), the name of the datum, and the units in which locations are expressed. The *central meridian* is the line of longitude along which the projection surface touches the earth's surface (two degrees *west*, which is why it is negative) and the latitude of the projection origin is 49° north. The central meridian and latitude given are the true orgin of the projection, but for the convenience of having all co-ordinates positive a *false origin* has been declared just south-west of the Scilly Isles. The figures show that the false origin is 400 km west and 100 km north of the true origin (Ordnance Survey, 2000).

The *world file* gives a real-world location to the image so that it can be displayed along with other images or vetor data. The file looks like this:

```
0.12532153095965565
0.00000000000000000
0.00000000000000000
−0.12532153095962281
411632.02574590076000000
525404.78747439466000000
```

The first and fourth lines give the size of each pixel in real-world co-ordinates (this enables the image to be scaled). The second and third lines are parameters indicating the degree of rotation to be given to the image (none), and the fifth and sixth lines are the co-ordinates of the upper-left pixel.

The version of Global Mapper employed was incapable of producing three-dimensional images of surfaces (though later ones can), and so for a final type of display wire-frame and shaded surfaces were produced using the program **Contour**, which is fully described in the section on the survey of Lomello town centre.

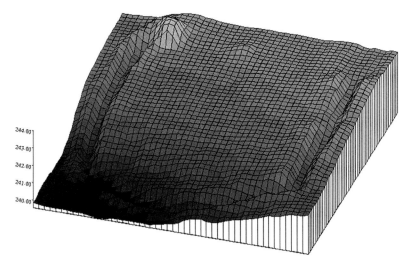

Figure 13.39 Shaded-surface terrain model produced using Contour software.

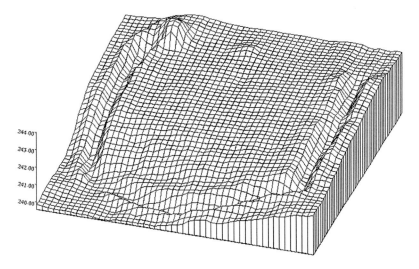

244.00
243.00
242.00
241.00
240.00

Figure 13.40 Wire-frame terrain model produced using Contour software.

Chapter 14

Durham City

The World Heritage Site in Durham City (within County Durham in the north-east of England), consisting of the medieval cathedral and castle, attracts visitors in very large numbers, at almost any time of the year. The construction of the castle was ordered in 1072, the cathedral founded in 1093. The castle, despite many later additions (including its conversion into the first college of the University of Durham in 1837) still has the characteristic shape of the motte and bailey plan. The historic centre of the city is very small, as the medieval buildings occupy most of the top of a steep-sided peninsula formed by a narrow loop in the River Wear. The strategic importance of this site is obvious, but as is often the case, despite this, the scale of the peninsula is such that in the national mapping scheme it doesn't look terribly impressive, and isn't particularly well defined. Given the commercial nature of the Ordnance Survey operation, there is also the problem of data copyright for anyone wishing to publish work involving a terrain model of this important site.

A terrain model could be produced by a competent archaeological surveyor in a number of ways. Given the resources, survey-grade GPS equipment would be an ideal choice, but for one thing. One of the charms of the centre of Durham City is that it is thickly wooded, and provides many shady walks along narrow paths on the river banks for both the tourist and those fortunate enough to work and study in Durham. For the surveyor, of course, the tree cover is a curse rather than a blessing, and renders GPS work virtually impossible over much of the area. The alternative would be a total station survey, which certainly is possible, but again the nature of the landscape presents difficulties. The steep sides of the gorge through which the river runs at this point, the tree cover and the winding paths, and on the top of the peninsula the narrow streets and terraces of buildings, all make long lines of sight impossible in most places, and a total station survey would require a very large number of stations to produce enough information to adequately describe the shape of the terrain. The presence of large numbers of pedestrian tourists also presents a problem, particularly on the narrow and steep riverbank paths.

Nevertheless, the work could be carried out, but it would require a considerable investment of time, and this would need to be justified in some way. It is possible to produce a terrain model using much simpler equipment, as shown in the survey of Lomello (see Chapter 15), where a simple automatic level was used. In that case, however, the work was being done in association with the local council, and the surveyors had access to the cadastral plan of the town, which showed building out-lines and land boundaries, and could form a satisfactory source of information for the location of the spot heights in terms of eastings and northings, although a co-ordinate system had to be devised for the purpose, as this was not marked on the map. It is possible to obtain large scale maps of the centre of Durham, as the Ordnance Survey mapping of urban areas such as this is at a scale of 1:1250, and includes very small details. The financial outlay involved in using this source of information isn't insignificant, however, and again there is the problem of copyright if a surveyor takes co-ordinates from an Ordnance Survey product.

So for the surveyor with limited financial resources, who wishes to avoid copyright problems, and who perhaps can't rely on having people to help all the time, what are the alternatives? What follows is a description of a survey carried out using a combination of hand-held devices, which generated enough spot heights of sufficient accuracy to enable the construction of a terrain model which can be used to describe the location of archaeological sites and structures in the central area of the city. It can't be regarded as a highly accurate survey, but it is fit for the purpose described. The instruments used were:

- a single-receiver GPS unit, of the kind used for recreational purposes, giving locations to within a few metres;
- a prismatic compass (another kind of sighting compass could have been used to the same effect);
- an Abney level (clinometer);
- a laser rangefinder giving distances to +/– one metre.

Two different modes of measurement were used. First, GPS points were taken at intervisible positions and the angle of slope between them was measured with the Abney level. Given the error associated with each GPS location these points had to be some tens of metres apart at least, to avoid confusion as to their relative positions. (It should be noted that many new GPS instruments of this type are able to use the facilities of Wide Area Augmentation Services, such as the European EGNOS, and should be able to determine their location more precisely, to within about three metres.) The other type of measurement was made from a GPS point and consisted of compass bearings to points of detail (on the bottom of walls of buildings, parts of bridge structures, paving slabs, tree trunks) accompanied by slope distance measurements made with the rangefinder and vertical angles from the Abney level. The compass bearings had to be corrected for magnetic variation (in fact the use of a sighting compass such as those made by Silva would have been useful here, as they allow this correction to be made on the compass itself, rather than having to do a calculation later, though this is a fairly trivial exercise). The equipment was not particularly expensive, apart from the rangefinder, which cost about £500 (though the compass and Abney level are available in more expensive forms); it must be said, however, that it can be troublesome to have so many different items to handle.

Calculations were carried out using a spreadsheet package; the formulae described here are suitable for use with Microsoft® Excel or the Open Office spreadsheet.

The first task was to prepare the GPS co-ordinates for further use. These had been stored in the GPS instrument as 'waypoints' (points to which the user of the instrument can navigate – in this case they were just being stored for convenience, rather than recording them in some other way). The data were downloaded to a computer in the form of a comma-separated text file using a cable connected to the serial port. This file was opened using the spreadsheet, and looked like this:

	A	B	C	D
1	point	date & time		
2	1	20/02/2003 09:09	NZ 27575 42311	
3	2	20/02/2003 09:12	NZ 27616 42388	
4	3	20/02/2003 09:13	NZ 27603 42421	
5	4	20/02/2003 09:14	NZ 27587 42428	
6	5	20/02/2003 09:17	NZ 27508 42428	

Figure 14.1 Spreadsheet showing GPS waypoints.

Each point is identified by a unique number, followed by the date and time of observation (in a single cell of the spreadsheet) and the co-ordinates of the point, in this case using the Ordnance Survey grid system (also in a single cell – although they appear to overlap into column D they are in fact in column C). Co-ordinates could have been in the form of latitude and longitude, but this would have made subsequent calculations very difficult. (If an exercise of this kind were being carried out in a part of the world for which a national plane co-ordinate system is not available it would be necessary to use the Universal Transverse Mercator system.)

The form in which the OS co-ordinates are given is that used conventionally when giving a reference to a hard-copy map, using a pair of letters to identify the 100km grid square in which the point lies, followed by numbers to indicate position within that square. For digital mapping purposes this needs to be converted into a completely numerical reference, and the easting and northing co-ordinates need to be separated from each other. Below is a section from the spreadsheet, showing the cells which contain the results of processing the downloaded data.

	A	B	C	D	E	F	G	H
1	point	date & time						
2	1	20/02/2003 09:09	NZ 27575 42311		27575	42311	427575	542311
3	2	20/02/2003 09:12	NZ 27616 42388		27616	42388	427616	542388
4	3	20/02/2003 09:13	NZ 27603 42421		27603	42421	427603	542421
5	4	20/02/2003 09:14	NZ 27587 42428		27587	42428	427587	542428
6	5	20/02/2003 09:17	NZ 27508 42428		27508	42428	427508	542428

Figure 14.2 Spreadsheet showing grid references converted into numerical co-ordinates.

The formulae in the cells on the first row are:

E2   =MID(C2,4,5)

All spreadsheet formulae begin with the '=' sign, to show that what follows is a formula and not just a string of characters. The command **MID** indicates that characters from the middle of the entry in cell C2 are to be copied into the current cell (i.e. E2); the figures following show that the copying should begin with the fourth character from the left (including the space between 'Z' and '2') and should include five characters. The result is that '27575' appears in cell E2. The characters are aligned to the left, which makes them look like text, but in fact they are treated as a number.

F2 =RIGHT(C2,5)

This uses a related function, which indicates that the five characters from the right in cell C2 should be copied into the current cell, so that '42311' appears in F2. These two operations have separated the easting and northing co-ordinates.

G2 =E2 + 400000

The OS 100km square NZ, within which Durham lies, has its south-west corner 400,000m east of the grid origin. As the GPS co-ordinates are given to the nearest metre (although they are not accurate to a metre) all that has to be done is to add 400,000 to the figure in cell E2, giving the number 427575. (Note that if we were using grid references from another source which were given to a lower precision, for example NZ 275 423, it would be necessary not only to put '4' at the front of the easting co-ordinate, but to add '00' at the end in order to get a number of the correct magnitude, 427500.)

H2 =F2 + 500000

In a similar way, since the south-west corner of NZ is 500,000m north of the grid origin this figure has to be added to the one in F2.

With the locations of the GPS points now in the correct form, the height differences can be calculated. It should be noted that the altitude figures which GPS units of this type generate are not suitable for use in a terrain model on this scale, as their inaccuracy is several times worse that the lateral inaccuracy, and strange results will be obtained.

Another spreadsheet was constructed on the following lines. The columns have been given headings to show what they contain.

	A	B	C	D	E	F	G	H	I	J	K
1	At	easting	northing	To	easting	northing	up/down	degrees	minutes	dd	slope rad
23	95	427420	541608	96	427365	541647	-1	2	10	-2.17	-0.04
24	96	427365	541647	97	427328	541658	-1	12	40	-12.67	-0.22
25	97	427328	541658	98	427309	541690	-1	14	40	-14.67	-0.26
26	98	427309	541690	99	427281	541704	-1	9	30	-9.50	-0.17
27	99	427281	541704	100	427218	541699	1	0	10	0.17	0.00

Figure 14.3 Spreadsheet showing slope in degrees and radians.

Columns A to F contain the point numbers and co-ordinates of the points from which and to which the slope measurements were made; on line 23, therefore, the observer was at point 95 and measuring the slope to point 96. If two workers had been involved in this survey it would have been possible for one of them to carry a simple target on a pole which showed by a mark the height of the observer's eye-level; the Abney level could have been sighted on this so that the measured slope was the same as the real one. Working alone, it was necessary for the observer to measure the slope to a point on the ground, and to calculate the correct slope afterwards (see below).

Column G contains the figure '1' or '−1', depending on whether the slope from the observer position is upwards (1) or downwards (−1). This was noted in the field.

Columns H and I contain the angle of slope in degrees and minutes, as read from the Abney level.

Column J contains a formula:

=(H23 + (I23/60))*G23

This adds the number of degrees of slope to the number of minutes divided by 60, to give the slope in degrees and decimals (hence the column heading 'dd'). This is then multiplied by the slope indicator in G23, so that a slope of 2.17° becomes −2.17° because it is downhill.

Column K converts the slope in degrees into a slope in radians, as required by the spreadsheet for use in further calculations; the formula is simply:

=RADIANS(J23)

The next section of the spreadsheet looks like this:

L	M	N	O	P	Q	R
e diff	n diff	distance	ht. diff.	obs grnd ht	ht diff + eye	trgt ht
55	39	67.42	-2.55089	41.947631	-0.8708873	41.07674
37	11	38.60	-8.67541	41.076744	-6.9954082	34.08134
19	32	37.22	-9.74019	34.081336	-8.060189	26.02115
28	14	31.30	-5.23865	26.021147	-3.5586523	22.46249
63	5	63.20	0.183836	22.462494	1.86383634	24.32633

Figure 14.4 Spreadsheet used to calculate three-dimensional co-ordinates

Columns L and M calculate the differences in eastings and northings of the observer and target points, the formulae being

Column L   =ABS(B23–E23)
Column M   =ABS(C23–F23)

These formulae subtract the easting and northing co-ordinates from each other; the ABS function returns the 'absolute' value of the calculation, i.e. ignoring any minus signs. In this case it doesn't matter which point is further north or east, only the magnitude of the difference, and in fact minus signs could cause problems so they need to be removed.

Column N now calculates the distance (the horizontal distance) between the two points, with   =SQRT(L23^2 + M23^2).

This uses the theorem of Pythagoras. The easting and northing differences represent the lengths of two sides of a right-angled triangle, while the direct distance between them is the other side. This formula takes the square root (the SQRT function) of the result of adding the square of the easting difference (L23) to the square of the northing difference (M23). The notation '^2' indicates 'to the power of 2', or squaring; it uses the character shift-6 on the keyboard.

Column O calculates the height difference between the observer (actually the observer's eye level) and the target point on the ground. The formula is =N23*TAN(K23), which multiplies the distance to the target by the tangent of the slope.

Column P contains the height of the ground point at which the observer stands. In this survey this is the same as the point which was previously the target, so the cell contains the formula =(R22), at the end of the preceding line.

Column Q adds the height of the observer's eye level (1.68m) to the height difference between the points: =O23 + 1.68. If the slope is downhill the calculated value may be small or negative. This represents the true difference in height between the two ground points.

Column R calculates the height of the target point by adding the true difference in height to the height of the observer ground point: =P23 + Q23.

This process calculates heights for all the GPS locations, but as noted above there are many places on the peninsula where GPS positioning is made impossible by tree cover or the presence of buildings close by. These areas were filled in where possible by occupying a GPS point and locating other visible points by taking compass bearings and measuring distances and angles of slope. These measurements may be converted into differences in eastings and northings from the observer position using the formulae in the following spreadsheet.

	A	B	C	D	E	F	G	H
1	Mag. Bg.	Bg rad	slope D	slope	slope rad.	horiz D	e diff.	n diff.
2	268	4.677482	47	-2.83	-0.04939	46.94268	-46.9141	-1.63828

Figure 14.5 Spreadsheet calculating co-ordinates from bearing and distance.

Column A contains the magnetic bearing; this must be converted to take account of magnetic variation.

Column B converts this to radians: =RADIANS(A2).

Column C is the measured slope distance (to the nearest metre, which is the accuracy of the laser rangefinder used).

Columns D and E show the measured slope (in degrees and decimals, converted from degrees and minutes as shown above) and the slope in radians.

Column F calculates the horizontal distance with the formula =COS(E2)*C2 (this is the cosine of the angle of slope multiplied by the slope distance).

Column G gives the easting difference with =SIN(B2)*F2 (the sine of the bearing multiplied by the horizontal distance).

Column H gives the northing difference with =COS(B2)*F2 (the cosine of the bearing multiplied by the horizontal distance).

The co-ordinate differences can be used to calculate complete co-ordinates by adding them to the co-ordinates of the observer position. In this example the measured point lies almost due west of the observer (a bearing of 268°), so the easting co-ordinate difference is negative, as is the northing (the point is slightly south). With complete co-ordinates and measurements of slope the heights can be calculated using the first spreadsheet shown above.

When all the calculations are complete the surveyor has a set of points located in three dimensions which can be used as the basis for the construction of a terrain model, as shown in the section concerning the survey of Lomello. As in the case of Lomello, the first step might be to use **Contour** to generate a terrain model:

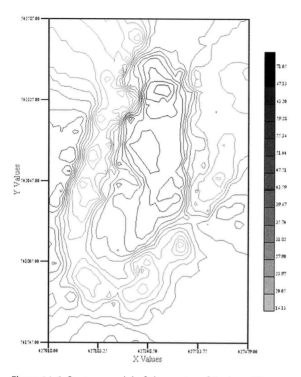

Figure 14.6 Contour model of the centre of Durham City.

In this contour map the co-ordinates along the margins are eastings and northings within the Ordnance Survey grid system, the units being metres. The steep sides of the river gorge are clearly visible on the west and south, and these are in general a good rendering of the real shape of the ground surface. At the north end of the peninsula the raised area of the castle motte is visible as concentric contours, although from the ground in a simple survey of this kind the motte is very difficult to reach. (Partly in order to test the survey methodology in a difficult situation, permission was not sought to carry out any work within the castle grounds, or in any other private areas, and measurements were made by compass and rangefinder from GPS points outside.) There are other places, however, where the contours form small sub-circles which don't represent real features, but rather reveal patchiness in the coverage of data points; this could of course be improved by adding new points and re-calculating the terrain model.

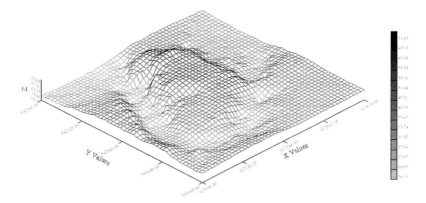

Figure 14.7 Wire-frame model of Durham City centre.

As might be expected, the 3D wire-frame and shaded models give a more complete picture of the terrain model, and show up the rather unrealistic 'bumps' in the low-lying areas close to the river. There is also an apparent (but not real) ramp joining the inner and outer sides of the peninsula on the east side. Again, this could be removed by the addition of more data points. When contemplating some of the deficiencies of this model, I was slightly surprised, and I suppose cheered, to find that in a model of the same area constructed using Ordnance Survey Profile contour data (digital contours at a scale of 1:10,000) there were obvious errors of a not dissimilar nature, with ramp-like features extending across what should be the river gorge. Terrain modelling is very demanding of its data sources, however these have been created.

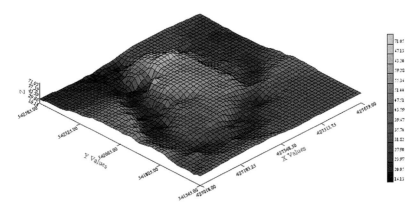

Figure 14.8 Shaded surface model of Durham City centre.

Finally, the data were exported from Contour, and used as the basis of a 3D surface mesh in IntelliCAD (as described in Chapter 15), which produced this, viewed from the north-east:

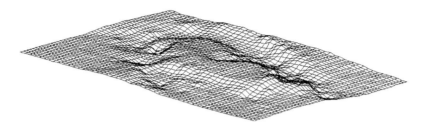

Figure 14.9 Wire-frame model of Durham City centre transferred to CAD.

The model has a number of flaws. The data on which it is based are of fairly low resolution, and it wasn't possible to cover the ground as completely as would have been desirable. Although the model doesn't show it, it has been explained that the peninsula is actually covered in trees and, very significantly, buildings. Apart from the cathedral and castle there is a cathedral school, the cathedral college, a number of university colleges, shops and offices and private houses. There are many places in which the surface has clearly been significantly modified, and others which are just completely inaccessible. It would be unwise to regard any particular part of the model as being 'accurate', but it does give an overall picture of the shape of the landscape, which was so significant in the choice of this place as the site for the cathedral, the castle, and the seat of a bishop who controlled a large part of northern England.

Chapter 15

Terrain model of Lomello

Lomello is a small town on the Po plain in north-west Italy, not far from Pavia. It lies within a flat plain (the Lomellina) formed during the last glaciation, which has been extensively modified by the levelling of fields for rice cultivation. The town itself, like others in the area, lies on a *dosso*, an eroded mound of earlier glacial formation, which protrudes from the extremely flat surroundings. It has long been important in the communication system of the area; in the Roman period it was a *mansio* on the road from Pavia to Turin, and its importance continued until the Middle Ages. There are surviving fragments of a Roman city wall, remains of a baptistery from the Lombard period (also commemorated in street names such as 'via Gundaberga'), and from the eleventh century the outstanding church of Santa Maria Maggiore, described as 'one of the most important edifces of the 11th century in Europe' (Porter, 1917). The survival of these monuments may have been helped by Lomello's reduction into a small agricultural town, preceded by the decline in the fortunes of the family of the palatine count. The only major modifications were reconstruction works undertaken in the 1940s (Blake, 1983).

The topographic survey referred to here was carried out in 1985 (Howard and Howard-Davis, 1986), at a time before electronic surveying instruments and digital methods of data capture and processing were available, at least to university archae-ologists. Existing usable survey information consisted of a cadastral map of the town showing building outlines, property boundaries and roads, but this had no graticule or indication of co-ordinates, nor of course did it have any contour information. A knowledge of the topography of the *dosso* was thought important for a better understanding of the archaeology of the town, and in addition to the absence of any large-scale contour plans, much of the elevated area was concealed from view by an abundant growth of trees and other vegetation in neglected or abandoned garden plots. An arbitrary bench mark was chosen on the threshold of the main door of the school which was used as the project headquarters (the work took place during the summer holiday), and most of the data collected was in the form of spot-heights determined at points identified on the cadastral map, measured using an automatic level. A grid system was then created on a transparent overlay to the map, and co-ordinates for the spot-heights read off from this. In some places steep slopes made standard levelling difficult, and in others (for example large private plots) there was little mapped detail; in these instances levels were determined by tacheometry, using a 20″ theodolite. It might have been better to carry out the whole survey by tacheom-etry, which would have been more flexible, but the time available for the work was limited. Short lines of sight imposed by narrow streets and buildings would have necessitated many set-ups of the theodolite, and the much greater time spent calculating co-ordinates and elevations made the approach (in what was effectively the pre-computer age as far as the fieldwork was concerned) unviable. Tacheometric calculations were in fact carried out using a pocket calculator, and initial visualisation of the data was in the form of contours plotted by hand on drawing film. On returning from the fieldwork, it was then possible to carry out computer processing of the survey results and produce contour plots and three-dimensional displays, but this involved the use of a multi-user minicomputer (a VAX-11) and a software suite called GINO. This was not an application package as we would now understand it, but a library of subroutines which had to be embedded in a FORTRAN program written by the user (and anyone who has written even very simple programs will know that it is impossible to get it right first time); the output from the program was sent to an off-line plotter which used liquid ink pens to draw the lines. The results were fairly satisfactory from an archaeological point of view, but had taken weeks, in total, to produce. There were also some inadequacies in the computer-generated contours, in particular lines which performed impossible loops, or in places crossed over each other.

Modern computer processing

Three-dimensional modelling and visualisation of land surfaces is often thought to be confined to expensive and sophisticated software packages, and to a large extent this is true, but there are some low-cost options, one of which is **Contour 2.4,** bundled with **CogoCAD 2.5** from CMT (www.cmtinc.com).

   This program will accept data in the form of what are sometimes referred to as 'triplets', tables in which each line represents a point which is defined by x, y and z co-ordinate values. The data from the Lomello survey had originally been written down on paper, of course, but were eventually transferred to a digital file in which each line consisted of the three co-ordinates separated by commas (the file was called **lomello.csv,** csv standing for 'comma-separated value'). Contour is quite happy with this format, but does require that the first line in the file is a 'header row', i.e. it doesn't contain any data, but rather the names which will be given to each column of data (it might be 'x, y, z', or 'easting, northing, elevation', or anything else).

   When Contour is running, the command

   File | Open

allows you to select the file type and navigate to its location. (Contour 2.4 will read directly from Microsoft Excel® version 4 worksheets, plain text files with .csv or .dat filename extensions, as well as its own .ftr files.)

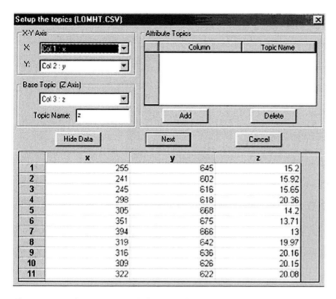

Figure 15.1 The Contour window in which the data are prepared to be read.

The data are read into a table and displayed. A field in the upper left of the dialogue box allows the selection of the appropriate columns for *x* and *y* data, if they aren't already named, and for the column which holds the *z* data, if there is more than one possibility. Click

Next

A dialogue allows the selection of a co-ordinate system; with my data the option 'unknown' was already selected, and I used this. (Contour can use geographic co-ordinates – degrees of latitude and longitude, called LLA here – UTM or US State Plane co-ordinates and a user defined format.) When

OK

is clicked an initial contour map appears, in the form of two-dimensional lines in default colours, with a colour scale and marginal figures indicating co-ordinate values.

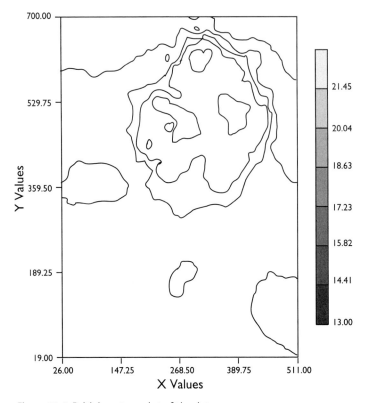

Figure 15.2 Initial contour plot of the data.

Clicking the

Setup

button on the toolbar produces a dialogue in which a range of parameters can be changed.

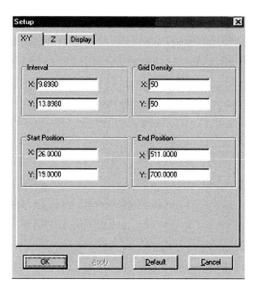

Figure 15.3 Dialogue box for changing the grid density of interpolated heights.

Although the original data were in the form of an irregular distribution of points, in order to produce this display a regular grid of cells has been generated, each of which contains a value of elevation which has been calculated from the nearest real points. Under the XY tab in the dialogue it can be seen that the number of cells is 50 in both *x* and *y*, despite the fact that the total area is rectangular. Changing the grid density from the default to the maximum of 100 produces smoother contours, while reducing the number makes them more angular. In the **Interval** fields (one for *x* and one for *y*) the size of the cells (in grid units) is shown, and this changes as the grid density is changed. Alternatively, the intervals themselves can be changed; in this case making both *x* and *y* intervals 10 (metres) produces a grid density of 50 in *x* and 70 in *y*.

Clicking the Z tab gives access to tools to change the number of contours, their value, and the symbols used to display them.

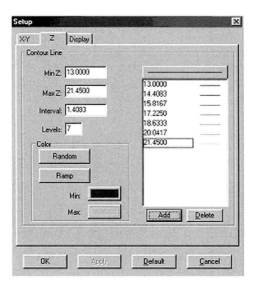

Figure 15.4 Changing the contour parameters.

An obvious thing to do is to set round values for maximum and minimum contours (in which case the interval may become an inconvenient fraction, such as 0.4118, which itself then needs to be changed), or to enter the number of levels. It's probably most convenient to set the contour interval and let Contour decide how many contours to plot. In all cases the **Apply** button has to be pressed in order to make the changes happen.

The default colour for the contour lines is green, in shades from dark to light. In the **Color** field the button labelled **Random** does what you would expect; it generates a random series of colours. This isn't often useful, as it removes the sense of changes in the magnitude of a variable, but **Ramp** does perform a useful function. The colours for minimum and maximum contours are shown as blocks, and clicking these in turn (after clicking Ramp) allows you to set the colours for each end of the scale (they can be different, such as red and blue), and then Apply creates a range of shades between the two extremes.

Double-clicking on a line colour in the ramp allows you to set its colour individually, and its symbol (solid, dotted, dashed).

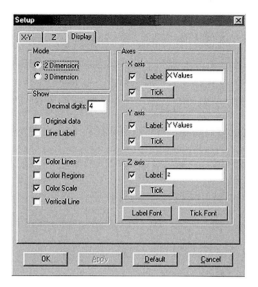

Figure 15.5 Changing other plotting parameters.

The default contour display is what Contour calls 'colour lines', but alternatives are available via the **Display** tab.

The **Line Label** check box allows labels to be added to the contour lines to show their elevation. These aren't always useful, but in many cases they are a helpful addition to the line colour. When this box is checked another, called **Freq**, appears. As its name suggests, this controls the frequency with which lines are labelled; the default of 1 labels each line. When the **Color Regions** box is checked the spaces between contours are filled with the colour of the lower contour bounding the region; if both **Color Regions** and **Color Lines** are checked the display will look like this (after Apply, of course):

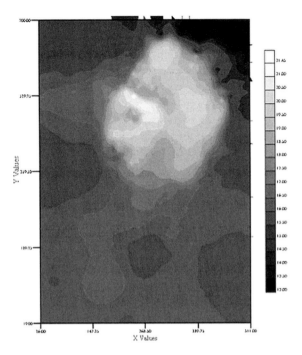

Figure 15.6 Grey-scale shaded plot.

(This makes more obvious the fact that some of the contours in the upper right corner overlap the edge of the model area; problems of this kind are not uncommon in contouring software, even expensive packages.) Perhaps rather counter-intuitively, if the **Color Lines** box is now unchecked, the display changes to:

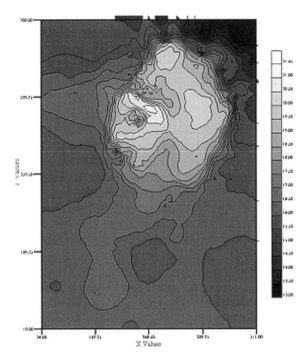

Figure 15.7 Shaded plot with black contour lines.

In fact, if both **Color Lines** and **Color Regions** are unchecked the display will show only black lines; it isn't an option to have no lines at all, but the coloured lines are visually absorbed into their neighbouring regions.

Along with the style of the contour display, there are options to show the original data points (which may indicate how reliable the different parts of the model are, as areas where data points are sparse can't be as close to the true shape of the ground as where the data points are close together), and to control the ticks along x and y axes, and the font and colour used to label the ticks. Most importantly, the **Mode** control allows you to switch between two- and three-dimensional displays. Just checking the **3 Dimension** option and clicking **Apply** will produce this:

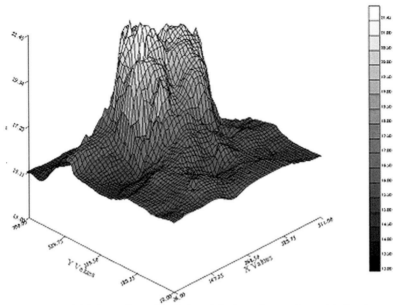

Figure 15.8 Initial three-dimensional plot of the Lomello terrain model showing vertical exaggeration.

(**Color Lines** are disabled, producing the grid of black lines; without this, against the white background the upper part of the model is almost invisible.)

Even without knowing the terrian, this seems unlikely to be an accurate representation of its shape, given that it is occupied by a town. In terrain modelling it is routine to exaggerate the vertical axis with respect to *x* and *y*, as slight but important variations may be difficult to see, but it can also produce an obviously unrealistic result. Going back to the **Setup** command, as soon as the **3 Dimension** option is selected another tab is added, called **3D View**:

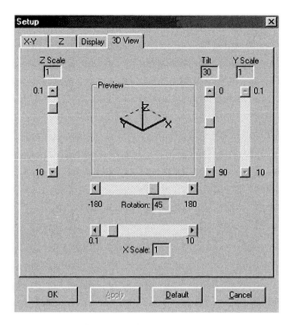

Figure 15.9 Dialogue box for changing 3D viewing parameters.

This controls the degree of tilt and rotation of the model with respect to the viewing position, and the scale of the x, y and z axes. These can be changed by entering numbers into the appropriate boxes, or more easily by using the slider controls (the small **Preview** model changes as you do this). Manipulating these controls can produce very different visualisations of the model:

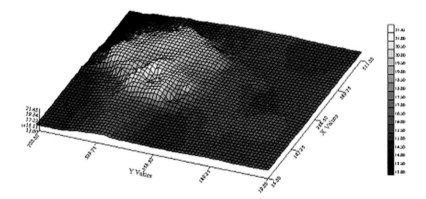

Figure 15.10 3D surface plot with modified vertical scale.

Contour 2.4 has the usual facilities for making hard copy of the results of its operations, under the **File** command there are **Print, Print Preview** and **Print Setup,** and these are so simple as to need no explanation.

This is about as far as things can be taken with Contour. It's a straightforward program which does a number of things well, producing useful visualisations of surfaces derived from irregularly distributed data points – the sort of data with which archaeologists most often have to deal. There is one additional function, however, which permits further development of the model, and this is the export of the gridded data which Contour has calculated. The command

File | Export

actually brings up a dialogue box called **Save As,** but this allows you to save the numerical values of the calculated grid in the form of x, y, z data files which can be sent elsewhere. These files can be in the form of text with spaces as separators (.dat) or commas (.csv), or they can be Microsoft Excel® format spreadsheets (.xls). The latter may be most convenient, as it allows for calculations to be performed (of course the text files could be read into spreadsheets).

Whatever format is chosen, the first lines of the file contain information about the grid and data source, before getting to the data, which in the example below are listed in columns called X, Y and MSL (the elvation values).

ASCII X,Y,MSL DATA by CMT

CONTOUR

COORD_SYS: UNK,255,(null),

Y: 19.0000000000,700.0000000000,70

MSL: 21.500000,13.500000,17

X	Y	MSL
26	19	16.11316
36	19	16.11316
46	19	16.11316
56	19	16.11316
66	19	16.11316

The next step in processing the Lomello data involves using the CAD software package IntelliCAD. This software has many facilities which Contour doesn't, but it isn't very suited to the production of a terrain model; it supports a data structure which can be used to express a terrain surface, but this needs as input a regular grid of data points, such as that which has been exported from Contour.

Assuming the exported data to be in the form of a spreadsheet file, this should be opened and the part of the file (most of it) which consists of the three columns of *xyz* data copied into a new worksheet. It isn't possible to take data directly from the spreadsheet into IntelliCAD, but for reasons explained below you may need to carry out calculations, and this is best done using the spreadsheet. When this has been done it will be necessary to save this worksheet again as a comma-separated file with **File | Save as** and choose the csv file type. This may seem unnecessarily cumbersome, but it's one of the penalties of using inexpensive software.

The csv file now has to be opened using a suitable text editor (so that it can be copied and pasted into IntelliCAD; Windows Notepad would work in principle, but this file is too big for it (and this will often be the case), so use Wordpad or a word processor.

In IntelliCAD, a new drawing is opened, a new layer made and set to be current. Experiment has shown that it's best not to use black as a colour for the layer, as the shaded views which will be produced don't look so good as in another colour (conventionally a shade of green or brown would probably be used, but this is a matter of taste).

Right-click in the toolbar area, choose **Draw 3D**, unless this is already showing. This toolbar contains the icons associated with drawing a range of three-dimensional surfaces; the whole bar looks like this:

The icon second from the right is the one for a **polyface mesh;** this isn't the one to use for a terrain surface, but if you click on it and hold down the left mouse button a *flyout* appears which has two other icons, one of which is for a **polygon mesh:**

This will replace the original one on the toolbar, and also start the command; the command prompt will change to

Number of vertices along primary mesh axis (between 2 and 256):

Enter the appropriate number (for Y axis), which in this case is 70 and press enter; the prompt becomes

Vertices along secondary mesh axis (between 2 and 256):

Enter 50 and press enter.

Command prompt: Vertex (1, 1):

This is an invitation to begin entering x, y, z values for each mesh point, which given the number of points ($50 \times 70 = 3500$) would be very tedious. The data already exist in digital form, though, in the csv file which is open in a text editor window, and can be copied from it into the command line. Go to the editor window, and highlight all the lines of data, then use **edit | copy** or click the copy button. Back in the IntelliCAD window, put the mouse pointer over the command area and right-click, choosing **paste** from the menu which appears.

For a few seconds nothing seems to happen, but then the command line will begin to scroll, showing

Vertex (1, 2): 26,19,263.473517
Vertex (1, 3): 35.89795918,19,263.5892331
Vertex (1, 4): 45.79591837,19,263.7368981

etc., as if the numbers were being entered from the keyboard. It will take some time for all the data to be read in. The grid should appear on screen, but it may be necessary to click the 'extents' button ⊕ . Since the view is 'plan' (looking straight down) there is no indication of height, but using

View | Look From | Aerial, Right Front (or one of the other options)

will show a 3D view. The result is likely to be disappointing at the first attempt, with hardly any visible variations in height to be seen. This is a very common problem with terrain modelling, and is a result of the unusual position from which we are viewing the surface. When we are standing on the ground, variations of a few metres seem quite significant, but when viewed from an aeroplane flying at a height of tens of thousands of feet even rugged hills look rather flat, and that is what is happening here. The terrain model is hundreds of metres wide and long, but the maximum change in the vertical dimension is only about 7.5m. It's routine in terrain modelling to enhance the z values with respect to x and y (this is what Contour does, for example), but IntelliCAD is using an x:y:z ratio of 1:1:1.

There isn't an easy way of changing the z values in IntelliCAD, so we have to do it elsewhere, and this is where the spreadsheet comes in. On the worksheet which holds the xyz values, enter a multiplication formula into a suitable cell; for example, if the data are in columns A–C, with the z values in C, in the first cell of column D put something like this (the multiplier will of course vary with the nature of the data):

=(C1*7.5)

then copy this down the whole of column D as far as the last row of data. We now need to delete the original column of z values, but there's a problem. These numbers are used in the formula which has just been created, and if they are deleted the cells in column D will all be filled with an alarming messasge

#REF!

The solution is to copy the whole of column D, then highlight another column, say E, **right**-click the mouse, and from the menu choose **Paste Special**. This will allow you to choose what to paste; choose **Values** (in Excel; in OpenOffice *un*check **Paste All** and **Formulas**), which will paste the current numerical values of the cells in column D, rather than the structure of the formula. Now you can highlight the whole of columns C and D (by clicking on the column names) and choose

Edit | Delete

This will leave three columns of data, containing x, y, and z multiplied by 7.5. Save this worksheet as a new csv file, and repeat the process of creating a polygon mesh in IntelliCAD.

The resulting model is much more 'three-dimensional' in its appearance.

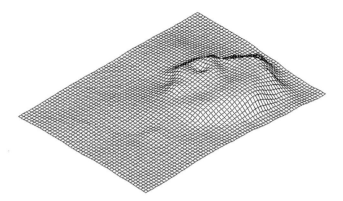

Figure 15.11 Lomello terrain model displayed in IntelliCAD as a wire frame.

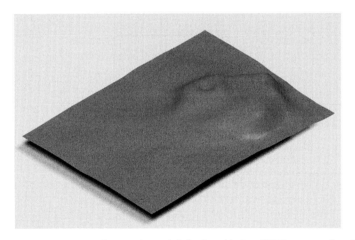

Figure 15.12 Lomello terrain model displayed in IntelliCAD as a rendered surface with artificial illumination.

Figure 15.13 The IntelliCAD render toolbar.

Rendering options can change the appearance of the surface. On the render toolbar, in order from the left are **wire frame, shade** (fills the cells with the colour of the mesh, while grid lines remain visible), **render** (solid surface with shading), and **full render** (a more sophisticated render, which takes more time but gives an improved appearance). After this is an option called **materials**, which allows you to change the apparent material of which the surface is composed, but in this version of IntelliCAD there are few to choose from, and they are not particularly useful for terrains (shiny plastic, glass, mirror, etc.). The next tool, **backgrounds**, is similarly limited in this version, but the next, **lighting**, can be used to considerable effect. There are a series of 'studio' options (spot light, side main light with filler, etc.), and also a 'sunlight', which can be changed (using the **customise** tab) in terms of its intensity, angle (i.e. azimuth – south, south-east and so on), and elevation. Changing these parameters can greatly alter the appearance of the surface, and used with care can bring out subtle features. It is of course possible to generate 'impossible' views, with sunlight coming from the north in the northern hemisphere, for example, or from impossibly high elevations for the latitude of the site. The image below has high-intensity light coming from the west at an elevation of about 40° (the slider controls only have angle figures at the ends, so angles can't be very precisely set).

Figure 15.14 Lomello terrain model rendered with low-elevation illumination from the west.

The render toolbar, like the others, can be found by right-clicking on the toolbar area and choosing it from the menu.

This may seem like a complex procedure compared with what is needed to produce a 3D visualisation in Contour, but intelliCAD is a far less specialised piece of software, and doesn't have built-in tools to do some of the things we need. The same is true of the much more expensive package AutoCAD in its basic form, though there are many versions which have been modified by the addition of specialised tools, including those for mapping.

However, if IntelliCAD is less specialised, it is much more flexible, as will now be seen.

Terrain models such as that shown here are commonly referred to as 'three-dimensional', but that isn't entirely correct. In surveying and GIS software it is usually the case that no two points can have the same x and y co-ordinates but different z co-ordinates. This means that while a surface can be plotted, vertical faces, such as normally encountered in buildings, can't be represented. This fact has led to the term 'two-and-a-half-dimensional' being applied to this type of modelling. In a situation such as that in Lomello we may be interested not only in the shape of the ground surface underlying the historic centre but in the standing buildings themselves, and for this purpose it becomes necessary to use a CAD environment. (Some GIS software does allow two-dimensional plans of buildings to be 'extruded' upwards, to give the appearance of built structures on the surface of a terrain model, but these are very simple and can't show complex shapes.)

This image contains part of the Lomello terrain model, with superimposed on it models of some of the historical built structures, the church of Santa Maria Maggiore, the baptistery, and part of the town wall, all of which exist in some form today, although the baptistery was heavily reconstructed in the twentieth century.

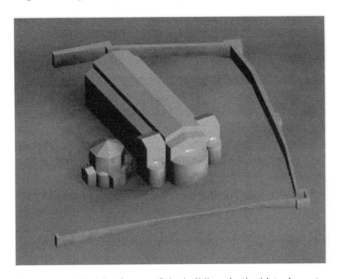

Figure 15.15 Models of some of the buildings in the historic centre.

At the time of the survey of the town, as described above, time or equipment to conduct a sophisticated building survey were not available, and what is seen here is modelled from ground plans, some field measurements of building heights, and photographs. Some parts of the wall have had to be inferred, as for example when only one surface was visible, the other being concealed within later buildings. Elevation data were available for many ground points around the buildings, and this has allowed them to be placed at their correct level within the model.

Many products exist to produce architectural models, and these are very sophisticated, allowing 'photorealistic' effects to be created, but they are also expensive. What is described here was produced using a version of IntelliCAD, which is capable of producing acceptable models with coloured and shaded surfaces, but not of the highest level of sophistication. (It should be noted that the cheapest IntelliCAD version, while it can generate the three-dimensional models, can't produce the rendered images with light and shade effects.)

It would be very time-consuming to describe every step involved in the production of the models seen above. They do, however, consist of a series of simpler shapes, the principles of which are describable.

Imagine the simplest building plan, a rectangle. A 3D image can be seen by using the commands

View | Look From | Aerial Right Front   (or an alternative direction)

Figure 15.16 Ground plan of a simple building.

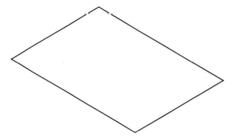

Figure 15.17 Three-dimension view of the ground plan.

This can be extended into a 3D object very simply. Attach a vertical line to one corner, of length equal to the height of the building. (Snap the first point to a corner, then give the second point as, e.g. @0,0,3, using relative co-ordinates in x, y and z.)

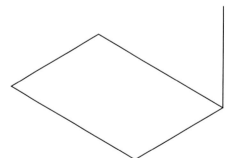

Figure 15.18 Ground plan with a vertical line added to enable the construction of a 3D surface.

Now use the **extruded surface** tool (on the Draw 3D toolbar, which needs to be enabled by right-clicking on an open toolbar and choosing it from the menu). The icon for this tool is 🔲 , and it's on a 'flyout' at the extreme right of its toolbar (it may not be visible until you click and hold the mouse over the right-hand icon, at which point a vertical line of icons will appear). The prompt line will show:

Select entity to extrude:

at which you click on the rectangle, then it changes to

Select line or open polylineline for extrusion path

which means clicking on the vertical line.
The 3D surface will be drawn:

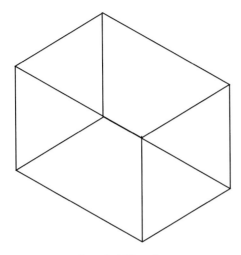

Figure 15.19 Extruded 3D surface.

It will be necessary to have the Render toolbar enabled as well, if it isn't already. Press the 🕳 button, or type the command

Hide

and the appearance of the structure will change:

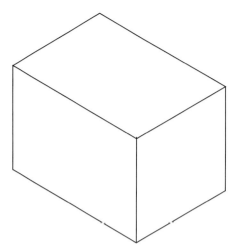

Figure 15.20 Extruded 3D surface viewed with the hide option.

this gives it the appearance of a solid, but it is actually a series of faces which can't be seen through. (More sophisticated CAD software is capable of producing models which are 'solid', and can be given attributes such as mass and centre of gravity, but this aspect of CAD work won't be referred to any further here as the software doesn't support it, although in some ways modelling solids can be easier than using surfaces.)

To give a sloping roof to the building, first add a vertical line to the middle of one upper edge (using the ESNAP **midpoint** setting for the first point).

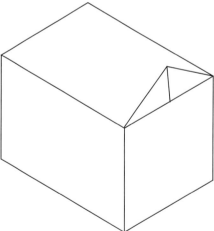

Figure 15.21 Construction lines added to the extruded surface to enable the creation of a roof.

Two other lines are now added from the top of this line to the upper corners. The vertical line can then be deleted, and the two sloping lines copied to the other end of the building. Three-dimensional faces (the 🖉 tool) are then created between the three points on each gable, and between the points on the gables and the upper corners of the wall on each side. Using **Hide** the appearance will now be

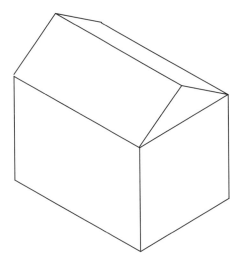

Figure 15.22 Simple building model with a roof.

Using the **Render** tool ( ) gives a more realistic version, with lighting effects and shadows:

Figure 15.23 Rendered building image with lighting effects.

note that the joins between the gable ends and the vertical walls have disappeared.

Using these procedures and simple variants on them it would be possible to create a range of buildings. Adding openings for doors and windows (described in the section on the survey of the Butter Market in Barnard Castle) is much more complex, and is one of the things which is easier to do with software which supports solid modelling.

Looking at the models of the Lomello buildings, it can be seen that to a large extent they can be broken down into simple rectangular components and sloping roof faces, but there are parts which have curved walls and roof sections, and these need a different approach. To go back to a simple example, think of a rectangular building to which a semicircular (apsidal) extension is to be added.

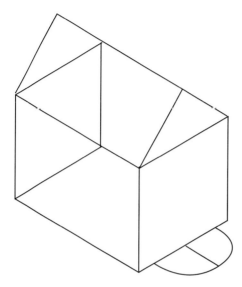

Figure 15.24 Wire-frame building with the ground plan of an apsidal end.

In the diagram a line has been added to the middle of one end, its length being the radius of the semicircle. (The building is 3 units wide, the semicircle radius 1 unit.) The semicircle itself is a polyline. To facilitate its creation a new co-ordinate system was added (using the **UCS** command and the option **3 Point**), making the corner of the building (the one nearest the viewer) the new origin, with the x axis being along the end of the building, and the y axis the longer side. This made it easy to specify the first point of the polyline as being 0.5,0 (0.5 units from the origin, and on the x axis). The prompt for the second point is

Arc/Distance/Follow/Halfwidth/width/<Next Point>:

at which you should type the letter 'a' (or choose **Draw Arcs** from a popup menu which also appears). The line on the screen changes to a curved one, and the prompt to

Angle/Center/Direction/Halfwidth/Line/Radius/Secondpt/Width/<End of arc>:

Type 's' for 'second point', and click on the end of the horizontal line which is furthest from the building. Next give the co-ordinates **2.5,0** and press enter (the last point on the arc is 2.5 units along the wall). Finally right-click to end the polyline, and it will look as it does above.

The semicircle and radial line now have to be copied to make the top of the curved wall. Select both by left-clicking, right-click the mouse, and select **Copy** from the popup menu. The prompt asks for a basepoint (click on any point on the selected objects, perhaps an end of a line), and a **displacement point**, at which type the amount by which the copied items need to be moved, e.g. **@0,0,3** if the wall is to be 3 units high. Remember that the @ symbol is vital as these are relative co-ordinates; if it is missed out the copies could appear anywhere.

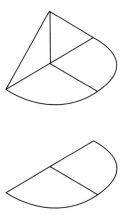

Figure 15.25 Upper edge added to the apsidal end.

Add a vertical line 1 unit high to the middle of the upper semicircle, and then another vertical line joining the bottom of this upper line to the middle of the straight side of the lower semicircle (so that it looks like the diagram below).

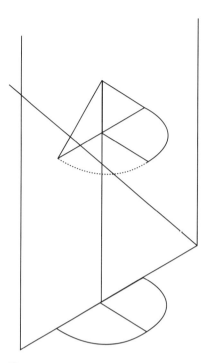

Figure 15.26 Vertical line added to the top and bottom of the apse.

The roof of this apse is going to have a fairly complex shape. It has two straight sloping edges, joining at its apex, and a curving lower edge. There are a range of surface tools available for making simpler shapes, such as a hemisphere, but this needs something else, called a 'Coons surface'. This is a surface defined by four edges enclosing an area, and it can be used in many situations to model something which is very irregular, such as the surface of a ruinous masonry wall, where the inner and outer edges have been measured (though care is needed, because the morphology of the surface is entirely mathematically based, and uses no real information apart from the shape of the edges). The crucial requirement here is to have four surrounding edges, and so far we only have three, the two sloping lines and the semicircle. The semicircle could have been created in two parts to begin with, but this would have made it more complicated. Instead, the procedure is to draw two new curved segments, based on the existing semicircle. Polylines can only be drawn in two dimensions, and this can make creating them in a 3D view rather complicated (it's easy to make a line which looks as if it's in the right place, only to find that it's ended up somewhere else). Careful use of the **ESNAP** control at the lower-right of the screen is vital. To change the settings of the snap tool right-click on it and choose **Settings**. To begin with, have just the **Endpoint** option enabled. Give the command to draw a polyline, and click on one end of the upper semicircle. Now, with the polyline command still active, right-click on ESNAP again, uncheck Endpoint and check **Nearest**, then click **OK**, which will take you back into the creation of the polyline. Give the command to draw arcs ('a'), then enter 's' (for second point) and click the mouse somewhere on the first half of the semicircle, near to the middle point of this first half (the yellow snapping symbol will appear when you are close enough to the line). This establishes the second point as being on the existing line. Now, still with the polyline open, go back to ESNAP and change the settings back to Endpoint, disabling Nearest, and finally complete the polyline by clicking on the end of the horizontal line which comes out at 90° from the wall of the building. Now if you click the mouse on this first half of the upper semicircle the selected portion should look as it does in the diagram above, i.e. a quarter of a circle. The method of creating this arc may seem very laborious, but it actually only takes seconds when you know what to do. There may be other ways to do it, but I have found this one to work reliably, while I have had many failures attempting to do it by other means. The business of changing the snapping settings seems to be particularly crucial, as if you have too many options engaged at one time there is a tendency for your line to snap to points you don't want.

The other half of the semicircle can be created in the same way, and this gives four surfaces surrounding the area to be filled with the Coons surface. The tool for this is on the flyout at the right-hand end of the Draw 3D toolbar, and it looks like this: ⊠ .

When you click on it you are asked to select the four edges (which should be done in turn around the perimeter, so that the second edge is one which joins the first), and then the surface will be drawn. As with other surfaces, this one may need an increase in the value of the variables **surftab1** and **surftab2** to make the surface look satisfactory (type the variable name, press enter, then type a number higher than the default of 6, perhaps 20). This roof may be connected to the ground by making an extruded surface from the lower semicircle, using the vertical line from the ground to the centre of the roof as the extrusion path. Using the **Hide** command the building now looks like this (with values of 20 for both surftab variables)

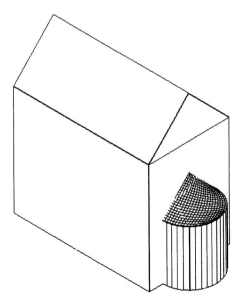

Figure 15.27 Building with completed apsidal end, viewed with the 'hide' option.

and like this in a rendered view.

Figure 15.28 Rendered version of completed building.

Although the buildings shown in the image of Lomello above are more complex than this, they have all been created using combinations of the same shapes that have just been described, although sometimes the thinking process took longer than actually making the elements of the model.

An aerial view of all the historic centre buildings, including the medieval *castello*,

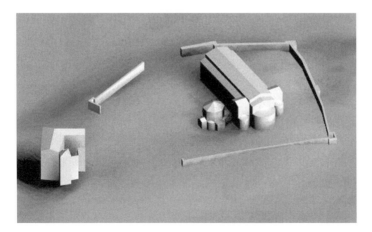

Figure 15.29 Models of the group of buildings in the historic centre.

gives a good idea of their relative scale, and a rendered view from ground level, with a selected background of clouds (originally blue and white)

Figure 15.30 Skyline view of the historic centre.

can go some way towards a realistic reconstruction of the visual impact of these buildings before they were surrounded by more recent ones (though the original height of the town wall is a matter for conjecture, and here it is shown at the maximum height which is known for certain).

Chapter 16

Sandoval County, New Mexico

For the information in this study I am grateful to Jack Young of the State of New Mexico Historic Preservation Division. The site in question is named LA 12147 located in the Bisti bad-lands, Sandoval county in Northwest/Central New Mexico. The site is on lands owned by the Department of Interior held in trust by the Bureau of Land Management. The legal co-ordinates for the site fall in the San Ysidro Quad (100 square mile area) Township15 north, Range 1east, Section 29 (mile square). This is a prehistoric Ancestral Puebloan (commonly called Anasazi) Room Block remnant. Based on observed surface ceramic types the date of the site would range from 650BP to 400BP. The primary features are buried masonry foundations for rectilinear domestic units. Some observed features are situated in 'mounds', indicating buried remains in situ: one is a refuse midden with buried artifacts and a grey staining to the soil and another is a dark carbon stain and scattered masonry. The site lies south and west of a large Jurassic sandstone outcropping, east of Canada de los Milpas Mesa and west of the same named drainage. It represents a Puebloan domestic site and habitations, where maze production in the flood plain would have been the primary pursuit. The soil type is a sandy loam and is eroded by intermittent sheet-washing. Vegetation on site is composed of range grass and Cholla (cacti). A pipeline bisects the site and has disturbed approximately 25 per cent of one feature. Very little of the structural remains projects above the ground, as may be seen in this site photograph.

Figure 16.1 Photograph of site LA 12147.

The site was surveyed by taking GPS points, and then producing a sketch map based on tacheometric measurements with a theodolite (transit). In this type of landscape GPS location is of the greatest importance, as few surface features are mapped and determining the position of the site by traditional surveying methods would be time-consuming. The information supplied to the author consisted of photographs of the site, a digital version of the sketch plan and the GPS co-ordinates (in WGS 1984 latitude and longitude).

While recording the location of sites such as this, which may at some future time need more intensive investigation and perhaps excavation, is clearly impotant, it may not be thought that as a surveying exercise (thanks to GPS) it presents many challenges, or that the resulting plan will be terribly exciting, consisting as it does of the outlines of the soil stains and slight masonry remains. This may be so, but as the site lies within the United States, for which many kinds of map data are freely available, this study presents an interesting opportunity to look at the ways in which archaeological sites may be considered as part of the wider landscape.

The production of map data for the USA is the business of the United States Geological Survey (USGS), many of whose products may be downloaded from web sites. One good source is the site belonging to ESRI (Environmental Sciences Research Institution), the producer of major GIS software applications such as ArcGIS and Arcview. From the site www.esri.com/data/download/index.html it is possible to download map data in a format known as TIGER (Topologically Integrated Geographic Encoding and Referencing). These data come in the form of *shapefiles*, a format devised by ESRI, and very widely used in the field of GIS and mapping. The format is useful, and data are readily located as they are listed by state and can be accessed via a clickable map. The names of some of the data sets are obvious (**urb** stands for urban areas, **wat** for water areas), while others are not: 'line features – Roads' are **lkA**; 'line features – Rails' are **lkB**. Others will be unfamiliar to those from outside the USA (**air**, for instance, refers to 'American Indian/Alaska Native Areas', and **aits** to 'American Indian Tribal Subdivisions'). A comprehensive list of data set names is available at the site.

The following sections describe the use of Christine GIS to produce a series of maps of the location of site LA 12147 based on TIGER data.

The first map is a small-scale one designed to show the location of the state of New Mexico (one of the TIGER files consists of the boundaries of all the states, though here it is shown without Alaska), and later ones are at larger scales and show various amounts of detail.

A new project is created, and the shapefiles of states added to it. For publication it was necessary to produce grey-scale maps, which means altering some of the colours which Christine would normally use.

- Add shapefile showing the coterminous states.
- Use **Project | Project Properties** and change **Selection Colour** to white.

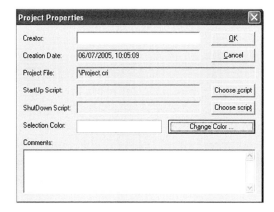

Figure 16.2 Christine GIS Project Properties dialogue box.

- Use **Theme | Properties** (right-click on theme name) and change colour to grey. (use the **Fill Symbol** tab).
- Use **Theme | Query**:

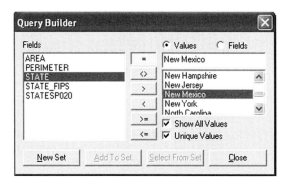

Figure 16.3 Christine GIS query builder.

In **Fields** click on **STATE**, press the '=' button in the central column (actually the default), check the boxes **Show All Values** and **Unique Values**, scroll down to **New Mexico** in the list of state names, then press **New Set**.
- The whole map now looks like this:

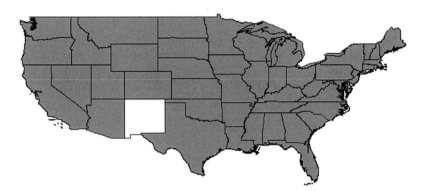

Figure 16.4 State boundaries of the USA, with New Mexico highlighted.

- Use **Theme | properties** again, this time clicking the **Text label** tab:

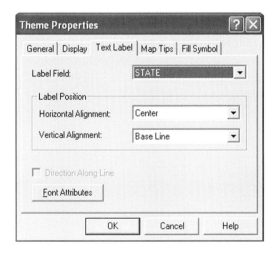

Figure 16.5 Christine GIS theme properties dialogue box, showing the text label tab.

In **Label Field** choose **STATE**; leave **Label Position** unchanged, and press **OK**.
- Using the label tool ⌖ allows you to put the name of the state onto the map by clicking the mouse; it will be necessary to zoom in somewhat to stop the name from overlapping the state boundary.

Figure 16.6 Map showing New Mexico state with text label.

- Add the boundary shapefile for Sandoval County, and label it in the same way:

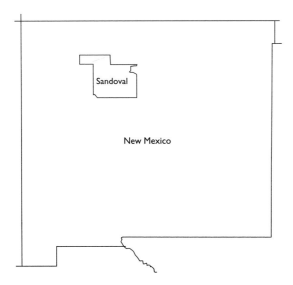

Figure 16.7 Position of Sandoval County within New Mexico.

- Deleting the shapefile of states and zooming in on Sandoval County:

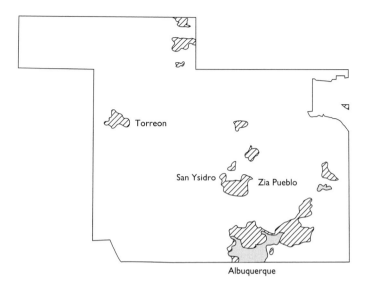

Figure 16.8 Named locations within Sandoval County.

- Two other shapefiles have been added, **urban areas** (grey) and **designated places** (hatched). In the current version of Christine GIS the placing of polygon labels can't be controlled fully, so those above have been added to an image file created in Christine using the **View | export** command.

- The **Tribal Subdivisions** data set was added next:

Figure 16.9 Sandoval County showing tribal subdivisions.

(Christine doesn't export the map legends, so again the legend shown above was captured from the screen using a graphics program.)

- Another data set which would be required would be **Roads**.

The amount of detail in the roads shapefile is considerable, down to the level of street names, as in this section of Albuquerque:

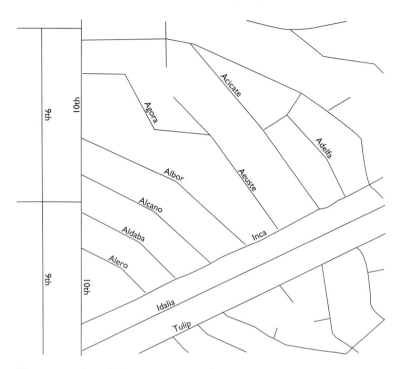

Figure 16.10 Part of Albuquerque street plan.

Below is an enlargement of the area of the archaeological site. The site has been added (along with another which was surveyed at the same time) as a shapefile made out of the co-ordinates of the GPS points (the method of doing this is described in Chapter 8).

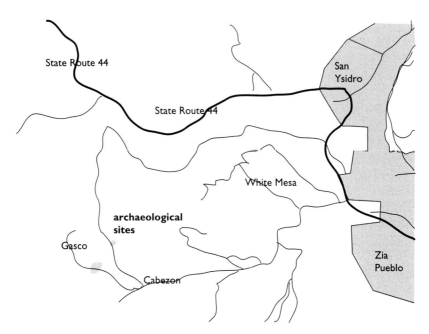

Figure 16.11 Mapped features in the vicinity of the archaeological site.

In the region of the archaeological sites many of the roads are of poor quality; in this map symbols have been varied to indicate the type of road in each case (the category of road comes as an attribute of each road segment in the shapefile). This is almost as far as the TIGER data can usefully go in terms of scale. Zooming in further to the location of site LA 12147 produces something like this:

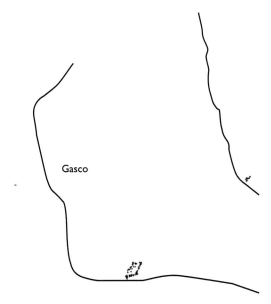

Figure 16.12 Large-scale view of the area of the archaeological site.

The map detail is skeletal at this scale. The site is visible as a series of points, which at even larger scale looks like this:

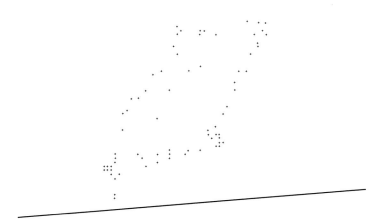

Figure 16.13 View of the archaeological site showing GPS points.

The TIGER data set, though, while extremely useful, is limited to vector data, i.e. objects which can be defined as points, lines and polygons, but other forms of data are available from US government sources. The USGS has a system called the **Seamless Data Distribution System** at http://seamless.usgs.gov which can supply not only the vector type data but others, including very usefully a mosaic of images from the Landsat satellite system (the Landsat Orthoimagery Mosaic product). A number of Landsat satellites have over recent years provided images of the earth's surface using a range of instruments, including one called the **Thematic Mapper** (known as TM) which records energy reflected from the surface in a series of wavelength-bands, including visible light and invisble infra-red. The Orthoimagery product consists of image data with geographic (latitude and longitude) co-ordinates using the North American Horizontal Datum of 1983 (NAD83). This means that they can be combined with other sets of data expressed in the same system. More than 700 Landsat 'scenes' have been resampled to a 1-arc-second (approximately 30-metre) sample interval, and three bands have been selected from the eight spectral bands available for each frame. These are bands 4 (near-infrared), 3 (red), and 2 (green), displayed not as you might expect but as red, green, and blue, respectively. The image is a 24-bit colour-infrared composite that simulates colour infrared film as a 'false color composite'. Band 4 is often used in combination with other bands as it contains more information than any other (in terms of the contrast in reflectivity from different kinds of surface), and false-colour composites, while obviously they don't give a realistic appearance, are very good at distinguishing different kinds of surface cover. (More complex processing of the images, usually involving calculations in which reflectivity in one band is compared with another, can produce very sophisticated information, such as determining the state of health of growing crops, when this is impossible in visible light alone.)

The Landsat data are downloadable from the web site, but there is a limit on the size of file which can be acquired in this way, and above this they have to be ordered on CD, which involves a payment. Browsing for data sets is quite easy via a map which can be zoomed in and out, though I have found that at some times of day it can be very slow, presumably because of the amount of traffic. The image comes in the form of a *tiff* file (Tagged Image File Format), a very commonly used format, but each tiff is accompanied by two other files which are small but crucial. If the image file is called *80598602.tif* (a typical name) the other two will be *80598602.prj* and *80598602.tfw*. The first contains information about the projection of the co-ordinate system, in this form:

```
Projection        GEOGRAPHIC
Datum             NAD83
Spheroid          GRS80
Units             DD
Zunits            NO
Parameters
```

The other is what is called a 'world' file, and it contains the co-ordinates of one corner of the image (the upper left) and the size of the pixels in the image, expressed in latitude and longitude. This enables software to position and scale the image correctly.

World files may accompany images in other formats, too, and the file extension is created by taking the first and last characters of the extension to the name of the parent image ('t' and 'f' in the case of a tiff file) and adding 'w' to give 'tfw'. A Windows bitmap file with a 'bmp' extension might be accompanied by a world file with the extension 'bpw', while a jpg format file ('jpeg') would produce 'jgw'. The contents of the world file to accompany one of these Landsat images would look like this:

0.00027776999999999999990
0.0
0.0
−0.000277770037000000010
−106.97080511500000
35.685374114981499

The first line gives the width of each pixel (in decimal fractions of a degree), and the fourth gives the height; these figures will be similar but not exactly the same. The height parameter is always negative, because while in an image file the position of a pixel is described in terms of its row and column position, counting from the top left, in the 'external' co-ordinate system the 'y' or 'northing' co-ordinates increment from the lower left. The two zeros on the second and third lines are 'rotation parameters', which describe how the image is to be rotated. Because these are orthoimages (horizontal and vertical in the image are true) they need no rotation, and so the value of these parameters is zero, but they must be present. The last two lines contain the longitude (negative because this image is in the western hemisphere) and latitude of the centre of the upper-left pixel in the image. When a suitable piece of software is asked to open the file *80598602.tif* it will first of all look for the projection and world files, and if these are present the information they contain will be used to locate and scale the image; if they aren't there (in the same folder as the tiff file) the image is displayed using just its own row and column co-ordinates. If a copy is made of the file, for example after processing to enhance its contrast, then new projection and world files must be made, using the name of the new copy (and of course if it isn't in tiff format the world file must be given whatever extension is appropriate).

It is possible to write your own world file to 'georeference' an image in this way, but you need to know the width and height of the image in real-world co-ordinates, and the number of pixels in the image, so that you can calculate the size of each pixel, and of course you also need to know the co-ordinates on the top left-hand corner. Some software packages will allow images to be georeferenced by clicking the mouse on points in the image and then typing co-ordinates for these points. The co-ordinates might be obtained from existing map data, or they might come from GPS information obtained in the field. A low-cost software package which will do this is referred to below (Global mapper).

A Landsat orthoimage of the landscape surrounding site LA 12147 is shown below. The original was in false colour. The image has been processed to enhance the contrast (using a package called Paint-Shop Pro, produced by Corel Corporation, www.corel.com), but any software for dealing with digital photographs could have been used.

Figure 16.14 Landsat orthoimage of the area of site LA 12147.

The image was opened using Christine GIS, and because the projection and world files are present it's possible to overlay other kinds of data onto the image, for example the GPS points which define the archaeological site and the TIGER shapefiles containing information about roads:

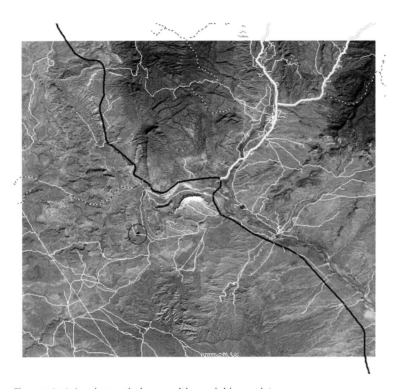

Figure 16.15 Landsat orthoimage with overlaid map data.

The site is shown here with a black circle surrounding it. Although beyond the scope of the present work, this ability to combine information of different kinds from various sources is very valuable to archaeologists and indeed anyone engaged in dealing with spatial data.

Although the image above can tell us a lot about the nature of the landscape, and although the patterns of light and shade reflect the shape of the ground surface, there isn't actually any formal information relating to elevation. Digital terrain models are available from the SDDS web site, but Christine GIS isn't able to use them (not in its current version at least), so another package has to be used.

The software chosen here is Global Mapper (www.globalmapper.com), mentioned briefly above. This is not freeware, but is very modestly priced compared with other packages of similar sophistication, currently costing $US279. (There is a freeware version, but the limitation on the number of different data layers makes it unsuitable for the current purpose.) This software is very suitable for use with USGS products, but it is generally a very flexible package, and is particularly well equipped with tools to both import and export a wide range of formats, including vector/raster conversion, and to change from one projection to another. These tools alone I have found so useful that they justify (to me at least) the cost of buying the software. Global Mapper is quite capable of handling the TIGER shapefiles which have been used so far, but it is equally able to deal with another USGS data type, the Digital Line Graph (DLG). This type was available from the USGS web site, but can no longer be obtained online, although it can be purchased on CD. These data sets have been used quite extensively, however, and may still be encountered in archaeological records. The information they contain is similar to what is found in TIGER, but the delivery format was one called SDTS (Spatial Data Transfer Standard), which caused problems in conversion for many software packages, even some of the major ones. Global Mapper was very capable with it, though.

This image shows a Global Mapper rendering of the roads close to site LA 12147, using DLG data. (The site is in the lower-left corner.) When using these data in Global Mapper different symbols and colours are automatically applied to roads of different classes, and road numbers are added, saving the user some time (unlike most GIS software, which require the user to define symbols and labelling).

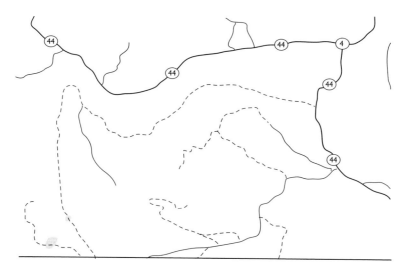

Figure 16.16 Digital line graph data displayed using Global Mapper.

In order to produce this monochrome image I have had to change these colours and some symbols (State Highway 44 was originally magenta, for example). Changing symbols in Global Mapper is done using the commands **Tools | Configure**, which gives access to the symbols used for points, lines and areas, and to tools for changing the current projection.

In addition to the sort of data which were available via TIGER, the SDTS format was also used to supply terrain models (called **DEM** – digital elevation models), which give a very vivid impression of what the landscape really looks like. The terrain models come at different scales, of which the most useful for the present purpose is 1:24000. The terrain model data are loaded in the same way as any other (the Global Mapper commands are rather familiar – **File | Load Data Files**, or click a folder symbol on the toolbar), and their presence dramatically changes the appearance of the screen:

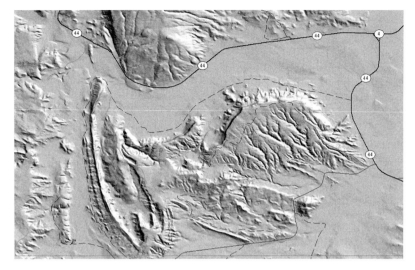

Figure 16.17 DLG map data overlaid on a digital elevation model.

Although this looks something like the Landsat image, it's based on digital informa-tion about the elevation of the land surface, rather than the reflectance of electro-magnetic radiation, and the light and shade are the product of artificial illumination; it's also much more detailed at this scale.

There is another very big difference, in terms of the structure of the data. It was shown above that the Landsat data come as a digital image file, accompanied by text files which describe the position of the image within a co-ordinate system. The DEM data don't exist as an image at all, but in the form of a data grid consisting of cells each containing a value of elevation; the image is generated by the software. The grid is of a form developed by ESRI, and its structure is a little complicated. For each grid there is a folder, the name of which is the name of the grid. In this case it was 34162405. The folder contains files called

dblbnd.adf
hdr.adf
sta.adf
w001001.adf
w001001x.adf

Another part of the grid, however, is a folder called INFO, which exists on the same level of the directory structure as 34162405; it contains files with the names

arc.dir
arc0000.dat
arc0000.nit

arc0001.dat
arc0001.nit

This complex structure makes it difficult to move or copy the data, and the best thing to do is not to try. They are downloaded in the form of a zip archive file, and in this form they can be moved from one folder to another and uncompressed there.

Global Mapper has a number of options for colouring the surface of a terrain model. Most involve multiple colours, but the one shown here (called Daylight Shader) is monochrome. The default colour is a rather odd shade of blue, and **Tools | Configure** has been used again to change this to white. (The grey shades come from the application of artificial illumination; if black is chosen as the surface colour the whole DTM will be rendered as black, with no variation visible.)

The amount of terrain detail visible at this scale is considerable, and even more can be seen by zooming in closer to the archaeological site.

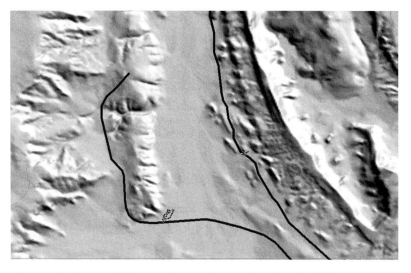

Figure 16.18 Detail of digital elevation model, showing site LA 12147.

The Jurassic sandstone outcrop to the east, and Canada de los Milpas Mesa to the west are clearly visible.

At this scale the road symbols have automatically changed; the line has become thicker, and as this has happened the dashed line has become a continuous one.

This displaying of archaeological information against the backdrop of a terrain model in this way can give the viewer a much better impression of what sort of relationship the site location has to the rest of the landscape, but it is possible to go much further in the way of analysing this relationship numerically. The field of Geographic Information Systems has had a considerable impact on archaeology in recent years (not always to the benefit of the subject, some might say). Discussions of GIS use in archaeology may be found in Wheatley and Gillings (2002), Lock (2000) and Gillings *et al.* (1999). Many kinds of analysis depend on the use of a terrain model in terms of elevation and variables derived from it, such as slope and aspect (the direction in which a particular cell in the model faces). These kinds of analysis are essentially beyond the scope of the present work, but one type of GIS procedure may be mentioned, that of visibility analysis. Archaeologists have often considered that the area visible from an archaeological site, or the area over which the site is visible, is likely to have been significant, perhaps from the point of view of defence, to keep migrating herds of animals in sight, to communicate with other groups of people using the landscape, or for religious reasons. The area visible from a particular place is frequently referred to as a 'viewshed', and many of the more sophisticated GIS software packages have tools for creating viewsheds. Global Mapper also has such a tool, although its purpose seems to be mainly the analysis of the likely coverage of radio signals broadcast from particular places. For this reason the tool is marked by a button with this symbol: 🜨 .

The effect is the same in any case, to generate an overlay on the map which shows the area within which an observer has a line of sight to a point on the ground (or a specified distance above ground, since the aim is to reach a radio antenna). Clicking the viewshed tool, then clicking the mouse on the point from which observations are to be made, produces this:

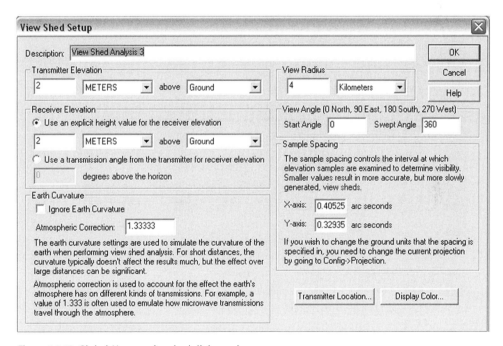

Figure 16.19 Global Mapper viewshed dialogue box.

Transmitter Elevation can be regarded as the same as 'observer location'; here it has been set to 2m, which is perhaps rather high for the average human eye level. **Receiver Elevation** could be set to zero, to give visibility of points on the ground, or it too could be set to some small value to allow for the possibility of seeing a person or an animal. The **View Radius** is the area within which the viewshed will be calculated. It isn't possible to give a maximum value for this, as certain objects may be significantly visible at great distances (a particular mountain peak, which might have religious or social importance, for example), while people or domestic animals might only be detectable over a few thousand metres. Here the value is set to 4000m. **Sample Spacing** governs the accuracy of the model by controlling the spacing between the points at which visibility is calculated; a smaller spacing gives a more accurate model, but at the cost of a slower processing time. The spacing units shown are in fractional seconds of arc, but the map projection can be changed to one based on metres if this value needs to be changed. Clicking **OK** shows the visible area:

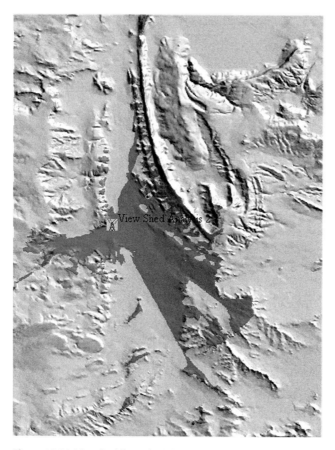

Figure 16.20 Viewshed from site LA 12147, overlaid on the terrain model.

The dark grey area is that which is theoretically visible from the site (marked by the antenna symbol). Generating a viewshed may often produce a surprising result, and perhaps change the way in which the site is regarded, but interpretation of viewsheds must be cautious. The viewshed is only as accurate as the terrain model, and that is a very unnatural model, with no light and shade, no dust, no mist or fog, no rain, and no vegetation. The viewshed is a statement of theoretical visibility, and of course we can't be sure that it would have been of any importance to the people who occupied the site, but it can be a starting point to a new phase of analysis, and comparing sites in terms of their visible area may be illuminating.

Related to the viewshed tool is the **Line of Sight** tool ⌇, which allows the user to draw a line between two points on the surface from which a profile and line of sight can be plotted. This is the result of plotting a line of sight between two points which are intervisible:

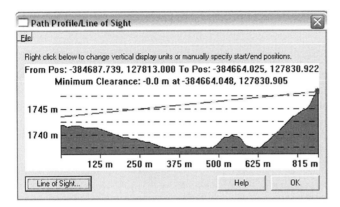

Figure 16.21 Global Mapper line-of-sight showing intervisible points.

and this is between two points which are not:

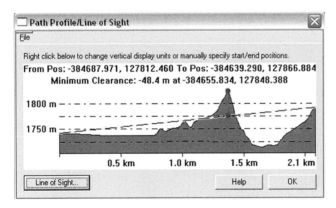

Figure 16.22 Global Mapper line-of-sight showing points which are not intervisible.

Global Mapper is a very capable software package, but there is one useful thing my version couldn't do, and that is to display a three-dimensional image of the ground. The software 3DEM, described elsewhere in connection with the SRTM terrain model data from the space shuttle, can create 3D displays, but it can't read ESRI grid format data. The extensive conversion facilities of Global Mapper are useful here, as they allow the grid data to be exported in the USGS DEM format which 3DEM can read, allowing the production of an informative display like this:

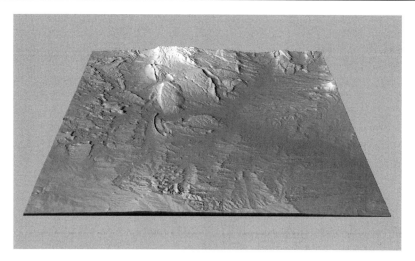

Figure 16.23 Three-dimensional display of terrain model.

Additional layers of information can be added as overlays on this surface. Vector data can't be overlaid directly, as a raster format is required, but Global mapper can export vector maps from its screen as image files, which allowed the production of this 3D surface overlaid with a map of local roads from a TIGER shapefile:

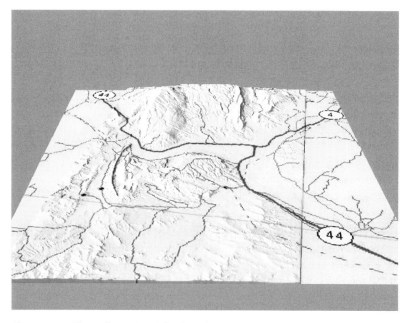

Figure 16.24 Three-dimensional display of terrain model with roads overlaid.

with the archaeological sites visible as tight groups of dots towards the centre left. Perhaps the most informative image of all was created by overlaying the Landsat orthoimage onto the surface, as this combines the measured elevation with information about the nature of the ground surface:

Figure 16.25 Three-dimensional display of terrain model with a Landsat orthoimage overlaid.

This view is from the west (unlike the others which are from the south). The main archaeological site is towards the front, circled. This view on its own gives a vivid impression of the site in its landscape, and it could form the basis of much more profound analysis.

Bibliography

Alcock, L. 1980, General Editor's Introduction, in Hogg, A. H. A. *Surveying for Archaeologists and Other Fieldworkers*, London, Croom Helm.

Allan, A. L., Hollwey, J. R. and Maynes, J. H. B. 1968, *Practical Field Surveying and Computations*, London, Heinemann.

Atkinson, K. B. 1995, Deville and Photographic Surveying, *Photgrammetric Record*, 15(86), 189–95.

Atkinson, R. J. C. 1946, *Field Archaeology*, London, Methuen.

Banning, E. B. 2002, *Archaeological Survey*, New York, Kluwer Academic/Plenum Publishers.

Bannister, A. and Baker, R. 1994, *Solving Problems in Surveying*, 2nd edition, Harlow, Longman.

Bannister, A., Raymond, S. and Baker, R. 1998, *Surveying*, 7th edition, Harlow, Longman.

Barnard, H. 2004, T16#178277: A Life of Travel and Tacheometry, The Reporter, 50, 28–9, Heerbrugg, Leica Geosystems.

Barrère, A. M. V. and Leland, C. G. 1889, *A Dictionary of Slang, Jargon and Cant*, London, Ballantyne Press.

Bettess, F. 1992, *Surveying for Archaeologists*, 2nd edition, Department of Archaeology, University of Durham.

Bintliff, J. 1997, Regional Survey, Demography and the Rise of Complex Societies in the Ancient Aegean: Core-Periphery, Neo-Malthusian and Other Interpretive Models, *Journal of Field Archaeology*, 24, 1–38.

Bintliff, J., Howard, P. and Snodgrass, A. 1999, The Hidden Landscape of Prehistoric Greece, *Journal of Mediterranean Archaeology*, 12.2, 139–68.

Bintliff, J., Kuna, M. and Venclová, N. 2000, *The Future of Surface Artefact Survey in Europe*, Sheffield, Sheffield Academic Press.

Bintliff, J. and Snodgrass, A. 1985, The Boeotia Survey, A Preliminary Report: The First Four Years, *Journal of Field Archaeology*, 12, 123–61.

Blake, H. 1983, Lomello, Lancaster in Italy: Archaeological Research Undertaken in Italy by the Department of Classics and Archaeology in 1982, University of Lancaster.

Bottrill, A., Peirson, G., Taylor, G., Parsley, S. and Thomas, P. 1998, New and Traditional Methods for Creating Three Dimensional Models of Structures, *Surveying World*, Vol. 6, issue 5, pp. 22–5.

Bowden, M. (ed.) 1999, *Unravelling the Landscape: An Inquisitive Approach to Archaeology*, Stroud, Tempus.

Coles, J. 1972, *Field Archaeology in Britain*, London, Methuen.

Condron, F., Richards, J., Robinson, D. and Wise, A. 1999, *Strategies for Digital Data*, York, Archaeology Data Service, also available from http://ads.ahds.ac.uk/project/strategies/.

CoolUtils.com, 2005, What is EXIF?, http://www.coolutils.com/Formats/EXIF.

Debenham, F. 1955, *Map Making*, London, Blackie.

Deville, E. 1895, *Photographic Surveying, Including the Elements of Descriptive Geometry and Perspective*, Ottawa, Government Printing Office.

Digges, L. 1571, *Pantometria*, London, Henrie Bynneman.

Digicaminfo, *c.* 2005, Digital Camera Lenses, 1. Basic Concepts. Focal Lengths, Fields of View and Depth of Field, http://www.digicaminfo.btinternet.co.uk/digitalcameralenses1.htm.

Eiteljorg, H. 2000, Using a Spreadsheet to Speed AutoCAD® Data Entry, Center for the Study of Architecture/Archaeology (CSA) Newsletter, XIII, 1, http://csanet.org/newsletter/spring00/nls0004.html.

Eiteljorg, H., Fernie, K., Huggett, J. and Robinson, D. 2002, *CAD: A Guide to Good Practice*, Arts and Humanities Data Service. Online http://ads.ahds.ac.uk/project/good guides/cad/.

English Heritage, 2002, *With Alidade and Tape: Graphical and Plane Table Survey of Archaeological Earthworks*, Swindon, English Heritage.

English Heritage, 2003, *Where on Earth are We?: The Global Positioning System (GPS) in Archaeology*, Swindon, English Heritage.

EOS Systems Inc., 2000, Determining Digital and Video Camera Format Size, PhotoModeler v4.0 Help File.

EOS Systems Inc., *c.* 2005, Support FAQ, http://www.photomodeler.com/cservfaqans.html.

Evans, S. E. 1968, The metric question, *The Times*, Monday, Jun 24, 1968; p. 25; Issue 57285.

Fletcher, M. and Spicer, R. 1992, The Display and Analysis of Ridge-and-Furrow from Topographically Surveyed Data, in Reilly, P. and Rahtz, S. (eds) *Archaeology and the Information Age*, London, Routledge.

Gillings, M., Mattingly, D. and van Dalen, J. 1999, *Geographical Information Systems and Landscape Archaeology*, Oxford, Oxbow Books.

Gillings, M. and Wise, A. 1998, GIS GUIDE to Good Practice, Archaeology Data Service, also available at http://ads.ahds.ac.uk/project/goodguides/gis/.

Gordon, K. I. 1993, *Fundamental Trigonometry and Geometry for Topographic Science: A Summary of Trigonometric Formulae and Proofs*, Glasgow, Department of Geography, Glasgow University.

Greed, C. 1991, *Surveying Sisters: Women in a Traditional Male Profession*, London, Routledge.

Greulich, F. E. 1999, The Barycentric Coordinates Solution to the Optimal Road Junction Problem, *Journal of Forest Engineering*, pp. 111–14.

Grose, F. 1785, *A Classical Dictionary of the Vulgar Tongue*.

Haselgrove, C., Millett, M. and Smith, I. 1985, Archaeology from the Ploughsoil, Department of Archaeology and Prehistory, University of Sheffield.

Hogg, A. H. A. 1980, *Surveying for Archaeologists and Other Fieldworkers*, London, Croom Helm.

Howard, P. and Howard-Davis, C., 1986, Survey in Lomello Town Centre, 1985, in Lancaster in Italy: archaeological research undertaken in Italy by the Department of Classics and Archaeology in 1985, University of Lancaster.

Huffman, J. 2000, Mils versus Mils versus Mils, http://www.boomershoot.org/general/mils.htm.

Lake, M. and Woodman, P. 2000, Viewshed Analysis of Site Location on Islay, in Mithen, S. (ed.), *Hunter-Gatherer Landscape Ecology: The Southern Hebrides Mesolithic Project 1988–98*, Cambridge, McDonald Institute for Archaeological Research.

Leica Geosystems, 2003, Training materials supplied on CD to purchasers of GPS equipment.

Lewis, M. J. T. 2001, *Surveying Instruments of Greece and Rome*, Cambridge, Cambridge University Press.

Lock, G. (ed.) 2000, Beyond the Map: Archaeology and Spatial Technologies, Proceedings of the NATO Advanced Research Workshop on 'Beyond the map: Archaeology and Spatial Technologies' held in Ravello, Italy, 1–2 October, 1999, NATO Advanced Science Institutes Series. Series A, Life Sciences, 321, Amsterdam, IOS Press.

Merrill, D. *c.* 2005, Digital Photography Essentials #001, 'Image Sensor Size and Field of View', Digital Outback Photo, http://www.outbackphoto.com/dp_essentials/dp_essentials_01/essay.html.

NASA, 2004, Shuttle Radar Topography Mission (SRTM), http://science.hq.nasa.gov/missions/satellite_5.htm.

NASA, 2005, Shuttle Radar Topography Mission: The Mission to Map the World, http://www2.jpl.nasa.gov/srtm/.

Olliver, J. G. and Clendinning, J. 1978, *Principles of Surveying*, 4th edition, London, Van Nostrand Reinhold.

Ordnance Survey, 2000, A guide to Coordinate Systems in Great Britain: 7 Transverse Mercator Map Projections, http://www.ordnancesurvey.co.uk/oswebsite/gps/information/coordinatessystemsinfo/guidecontents/index.html.

Parry, R. and Jenkins, W. R. *c.* 1946, *Land Surveying*, 5th edition, London, The Estates Gazette Ltd.

Partridge, E. and Beale, P. 1984, *A Dictionary of Slang and Unconventional English*, London, Routledge & Kegan Paul.

Peacham, H. 1634, *The Compleat Gentleman*, London, printed for Francis Constable (reprinted 1906, with an introduction by G. S. Gordon, Oxford, Clarendon Press).

Porter, A. K. 1917, *Lombard Architecture*, New Haven, Yale University Press.

Pugh, J. C. 1975, *Surveying for Field Scientists*, London, Methuen.

RCHME, 1999, *Recording Archaeological Field Monuments: A Descriptive Specification*, Swindon, Royal Commission on the Historical Monuments of England.

Ronan, C. A. 1991, *The Origins of the Reflecting Telescope*, London, British Astronomical Association.

Schofield, A. J. (ed.) 1991, *Interpreting Artefact Scatters: Contributions to Ploughzone Archaeology*, Oxford, Oxbow.

Smith, J. R. 1970, *The Times*, Tuesday, Jun 16, 1970; pg. X; Issue 57893.

Swallow, P., Dallas, R., Jackson, S. and Watt, D. 2004, *Measurement and Recording of Historic Buildings*, Shaftesbury, Donhead.

Taylor, C. 1974, *Fieldwork in Medieval Archaeology*, London, Batsford.

Usill, G. W. 1900, *Practical Surveying*, 6th edition, London, Crosby Lockwood.

Wheatley, D. 1995, Cumulative Viewshed Analysis: a GIS-based Method for Investigating Intervisibility, and its Archaeological Application, in Stancic, Z. and Lock, G., *Archaeology and Geographic Information Systems: a European Perspective*, London, Taylor & Francis.

Wheatley, D. and Gillings, M. 2002, *Spatial Technology and Archaeology: The Archaeological Applications of GIS*, London, Taylor & Francis.

Wright, J. 1982, *Ground and Air Survey for Field Scientists*, Oxford, Clarendon Press.

Wright, J. W. and Dahl, P. A., 1995, A Cheap, Quick and Safe Way of Surveying Glaciers, Photogrammetric Record, 15(85), 43–50.

Index

A9TECH 85
Abney level 23, 62–3, 229, 231–2
absolute accuracy 8
acceptable error 29
accessories 22
Adobe Photoshop 99
advanced plotting 216–20
Advanced tab 94
aerial photography 6, 97
aircraft 77
Alcock, L. 3
algebra 2, 32, 53, 55
algorithms 132
alidade 25–6
All Viewports 92
altitude 49, 146, 224, 231
American meridian 82–3
Anasazi 264
Angle base 209
angles 12–15, 17, 26–33, 35–7; CAD 87;
    control surveying 39–40, 43–4, 46–7,
    52–4; IntelliCAD 212, 216; intersection
    64, 66–7; measurement 20–3;
    photographic surveying 97–8, 102; slope
    62; telescopic theodolite 73; terrain
    modelling 252; triangulation 67;
    trilateration 68–9; Vernier scale 64
Angular Units 209
Animate Flyby 148
Antarctica 79
aperture 99
arc option 164
Arc/Info 109, 135
ArcExplorer 109
ArcGIS 109, 135, 265
archaeological societies 4
Archaeology Data Service 5–6, 8–9
Archimedes 1
archiving 5, 7–9
arctangent 55
Arcview 109, 135, 265

arithmetic 2–3
Arizona 83
artificial illumination 131, 134, 224, 279–80
artillery rangefinding 13
Ascension Island 74
ASCII files 185, 221, 248
aspect 280–1
astrology 1
astronomy 1, 12, 81
Atkinson, R.J.C. 25, 96–7
Atlantic Ocean 77, 181
Atlas Shader 224
atmospherics 75
atomic clocks 74
attach raster image 104
attribute tables 116–22, 169, 174–6
attributes 9, 120–1
Australia 79, 110
authorisation codes 22
AutoCAD 6, 85, 88, 101, 128, 155, 216–17,
    252
AutoLISP 128, 130
AVI format 148
azimuth 146, 224, 252

Babylonians 12
back bearing 36, 46, 179, 183
Balliol, B. 149
band 16–17
banks 10, 127, 178, 185, 191, 207, 215–16,
    218
Banning, E. 173
Bannister, A. 28–9, 38, 42
baptistery 237, 253
Barnard Castle Butter Market 98, 149–67,
    258
Barnard, H. 23
Barrère, A.M.V. 2
barrows 77–8, 108–9, 169, 188
Base Angle 105–6
base receivers 75–6